CONTENTS

Central Oregon Area Map

NOTE: MAP NOT TO SCALE

N

MILEAGE CHART TO OREGON CITIES

Bend to:	Miles	Bend to:	Miles
Albany	105	Lakeview	176
Black Butte Ranch	28	LaPine	30
Burns	131	Madras	45
Camp Sherman	35	Maupin	93
Chemult	65	Medford	178
Corvallis	116	Oakridge	115
Crescent	45	Portland	156
Crooked River Ranch	30	Prineville	35
Eugene	121	Redmond	16
Gilchrist	44	Roseburg	192
The Inn of the Seventh Mountain Resort	6	Salem	130
		Sisters	20
John Day	153	Springfield	124
Kah-Nee-Ta Resort	70	Sunriver	15
Klamath Falls	135	The Dalles	133

MILEAGE CHART TO AREA LAKES

Bend to:	Miles	Bend to:	Miles
Ana Reservoir	98	Lake Simtustus	53
Antelope Flat Reservoir	79	Lava Lake	41
Chickahominy Reservoir	102	Little Lava Lake	41
Crane Prairie Reservoir	45	Miller Lake	72
Crater Lake	119	Ochoco Reservoir	40
Crescent Lake	76	Odell Lake	79
Cultus Lake	48	Paulina Lake	33
Little Cultus Lake	54	Prineville Reservoir	50
Davis Lake	58	Sparks Lake	30
Delintment Lake	124	Suttle Lake	35
Devils Lake	31	Thompson Valley Reservoir	95
Diamond Lake	90	Three Creek Lake	130
East Lake	38	Todd Lake	27
Elk Lake	29	North Twin Lake	42
Green Lakes	33	South Twin Lake	44
Haystack Reservoir	32	Walton Lake	64
Hosmer Lake	39	Wickiup Reservoir	45
Lake Billy Chinook	40		

FISHING
Central Oregon
FOURTH EDITION

PERSONNEL

GEOFF HILL – Publisher/Editor/Advertising

VICKI HILL – Financial Manager

JAN SIEGRIST – Art Director/Production

KIM HOGUE – Administrative Assistant

PRINCIPAL WRITERS

GEOFF HILL, BROOKE SNAVELY, RAVEN WING

PRINCIPAL PHOTOGRAPHERS

GEOFF HILL, BRIAN O'KEEFE, BROOKE SNAVELY

Produced by

Sun Publishing

716 NE 4th Street
Bend, Oregon 97701

(541) 382-0127

www.sun-pub.com • sunpub@sun-pub.com

© Copyright 2001

ON THE COVER

This beautiful rainbow resides in Davis Lake

INSET:

Fall River holds some beautiful rainbows as well.

Photos by Brian O'Keefe

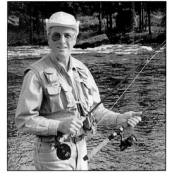

Geoff says "Let's go fishin'!"
Photo by Vicki Hill

Nearly seven years have passed since we published our first edition of *FISHING Central Oregon,* and since then, approximately 30,000 copies have been purchased. This book has proven very popular with local anglers as well as vacationers.

The emphasis has always been on quality, in the book's content as well as its presentation. Quality publications have been the standard at Sun Publishing for the past 29 years.

This, the fourth edition of *FISHING Central Oregon,* has been updated and includes over 200 full-color photos, plus many additional black and whites, detailed maps, and illustrations that help to complete the overall picture of Central Oregon's renowned waters.

Our coverage has actually gone well beyond what most people think of as "Central Oregon". Prior to working on our second edition, many anglers suggested that we include the McKenzie River and other waters outside of the Central Oregon region. We listened! We included the Western Cascades Drainages. Anglers and business owners asked if we could include additional popular waters, such as the trophy trout waters of South Central Oregon: the Williamson and Wood rivers, Agency and Upper Klamath lakes. They also asked if we would cover Mann Lake and the Donner und Blitzen River in the Steens Mountain area. We had requests for more information on the John Day River. Again, we listened!

All of the above are covered, with a special section for South Central Oregon beginning on page 118. The Western Cascades section begins on page 139.

Although Brooke Snavely and Raven Wing were not involved in this edition of *FISHING Central Oregon,* much of their work remains from the earlier editions.

See the "How-To" section to learn tips for all techniques of fishing, from trolling to jigging, from fly fishing to bait fishing, from spinners to crankbaits, and reading water and stalking. Information on float tubes is also included. The use of these portable crafts has become very popular on area lakes.

Many fishermen and fisherwomen opt to hire a guide when fishing the lakes and rivers of Central Oregon. So, we included information on how to hire a guide and what to expect on a guided trip.

Oregon's tremendous growth continues and that means a lot more fishing pressure on our lakes and streams. Therefore, we ask you all to do your part in preserving our fisheries. Please read the section on catch-and-release; it's the most important information in the book. We are not advocating that every fish caught be released, but rather the slogan, "Limit your kill, don't kill your limit". It would be difficult to release a record fish, for example, and many state records have been recorded by entries from Central Oregon — nine record fish to be exact (see pages 172 and 173).

In 2001, the Oregon Sport Fishing Regulations booklet

included major changes in our coverage areas. We make many references to this booklet in our text, using "OSFR" as the identifying abbreviation. Since this book will have a long life, and fishing regulations are always subject to change, we strongly recommend that anglers carry the current OSFR with them and always check it before fishing. Some of the changes included many additional waters that are open for year-round angling, reduced bait fishing areas, reduced catch limits, and many special closures.

Again, we have provided advertisers with an opportunity to tell of their products or services, such as resort/lodging accommodations, guided fishing trips, fishing equipment, and more (see the advertisers' index, page 176). We feel this is valuable information that would not otherwise be included. Advertising revenue also allows us to keep this high-quality book priced competitively.

Central Oregon and the Cascades offer some of the best trout fishing in the country. Read this book thoroughly and you'll be better prepared to be a successful angler.

Good Luck,

Geoff Hill
Editor/Publisher

1. Lisa Hawkins proudly displays a fat Deschutes rainbow.

2. Steve Kroll holds this near 10-pound Crescent Lake brown trout before releasing it.

3. This late fall brook trout was fooled by an artificial fly at Elk Lake.

4. A spin fisherman displays a powerful North Santiam steelhead.

5. Float tubing is popular on Davis Lake.

6. Fly fishers try their luck on the Deschutes headwaters.

7. Aerial view of Sparks Lake and South Sister.

8. A Rooster Tail spinner attracted this nice Deschutes brown trout.

9. Photo taken just before this Odell Lake bull trout (Dolly Varden) was released … as per OSFR booklet requirements.

10. McKenzie River drift boat fishing.

11. Approach and technique are important at Fall River.

12. Fall River holds some beauties.

13. The scenery as well as the fishing is spectacular at Crane Prairie Reservoir.

Photo 2 by Rick Arnold
Photo 7 by Geoff Hill
Photo 9 by Steve Kroll
All other photos by Brian O'Keefe

DESCHUTES RIVER

Size:	252 miles long
Depth:	flows vary with irrigation season & runoffs
Main Catch:	rainbow, brown & brook trout; kokanee; whitefish; steelhead
Best Methods:	depends on stretch of river
Season:	regulations complex; check OSFR

LITTLE LAVA LAKE TO WICKIUP RESERVOIR

From its origin as a murmuring brook exiting Little Lava Lake in the High Cascades, the Deschutes River flows 252 miles to its junction with the Columbia River and drops from an elevation of 4,739 feet above sea level to 186 feet. The uppermost 7 miles above Crane Prairie Reservoir is the only remaining free-flowing section of the river, offering outstanding spawning and rearing habitat for rainbow trout and kokanee. Excellent spawning gravel, healthy riparian zones, and natural flow and temperature regimes support stocked and wild rainbow trout, wild brook trout, native whitefish, spawning kokanee, and, below Crane Prairie Reservoir, brown trout.

In the 15-mile stretch from Little Lava Lake to Wickiup Reservoir, rainbow trout average 6 to 9 inches, with frequent catches of 12 to 18 inches in length. Brook trout average under 10 inches in length, even though the state record brook trout of 9 pounds, 6 ounces was caught in the headwaters in 1980. Brown trout, present between Crane Prairie and Wickiup Reservoirs, will average 12 to 14 inches, with some much larger. The native whitefish here are typically 6 to 8 inches and up to 15 inches. Packs of them can be seen resting on the bottom of deep holes.

From the headwaters down, the Deschutes River is a small stream meandering through mixed conifer and pine forest. More like a creek than a river, it can be waded across at

The very placid headwaters of the Deschutes River appear more like a creek than the origin of a mighty river.
Oregon Department of Transportation photo

many points. Many downed logs occupy the clear, cold water. The river has a large variety of water types including slow, deep slough-like pools near the headwaters and shallow, fast rocky riffles farther downstream. One of the prettiest stretches, full of meadows, flowers, pines, and views of Mount Bachelor, is upstream from the Route 40 bridge above Crane Prairie. At Browns Creek, 4 miles below Crane Prairie, the Deschutes becomes considerably larger. Some spots along the river are marshy, and mosquitoes can be bad, but mountain views, flora, and fauna are also abundant. Flows are lowest in the spring and highest in the fall.

Angling from the bank is possible in a few spots, but the best fishing is had by bushwhacking and wading. Fly angling with dry flies is the most productive method in the shallowest portions of the stream. Small Renegade, Adams, Elk Hair Caddis, ant imitations, and yellow Humpys are good choices

Deschutes River from Little Lava Lake to Wickiup Reservoir

▲ CAMPGROUND
- - - UNPAVED ROAD

N

for dries. Where conditions allow, fish nymphs, such as Pheasant Tail, Gold Ribbed Hare's Ear, and black APs. Close quarters with native vegetation doesn't leave a great deal of casting room, so bring extra flies. Along undercut banks and in deeper pools, some anglers work small spinners such as Colorados or Rooster Tails.

Anglers should be aware of varying seasons and catch limits for the Upper Deschutes River, always check the current Oregon Sport Fishing Regulations (OSFR) pamphlet before fishing. From Little Lava to Crane Prairie, the river is open the last Saturday in May to September 30, flies and lures only. There is a two trout per day limit, including brook trout, 8-inch minimum length with only one over 20 inches. Rainbow trout over 20 inches are defined as steelhead and must be released. From Wickiup to Crane Prairie, the river is open the last Saturday in May to August 31, flies and lures only, 2 trout per day.

This is a popular area for big game and waterfowl hunting, wildlife viewing, and bird watching. A favorite place for family outings, the Deschutes has many camping areas. Many other excellent fishing spots are nearby as well as opportunities to watch spawning fish, to boat, and to participate in other water sports. In the winter, this is a popular snowmobile and cross-country ski area.

Forest Service campgrounds on the river are located at Little Lava Lake, Mile Camp, Deschutes Bridge, Cow Meadow, and Sheep Bridge. Little Lava, Deschutes Bridge, and Sheep Bridge have drinking water. Only Mile Camp is no fee camping. All have outhouses and river frontage. Many opportunities for primitive camping are also available.

There is easy access to about 3 miles of the river along Route 46, beginning 2 miles south of Lava Lake and continuing downstream. Other road access is available at Mile Camp, Deschutes Bridge Campground, the Route 40 crossing, Cow Meadow, and below Crane Prairie at Brown's Crossing and Sheep Bridge Campground. These are the most heavily fished spots on the river. To observe the rest of the river requires a hike.

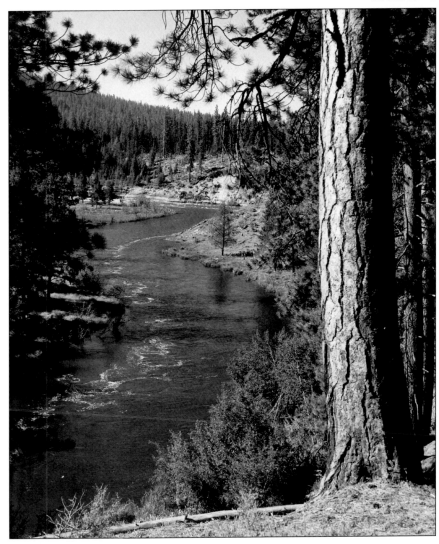

The Deschutes River near Pringle Falls. Oregon Tourism Commission photo

To reach this section of the Deschutes River follow directions to Lava Lake via Sunriver (page 80). Route 40 crosses the river 21 miles west of U.S. Highway 97 and meets Route 46 in another mile.

DESCHUTES RIVER: WICKIUP TO SUNRIVER

The best population of stream-inhabiting brown trout in the state lives in the Deschutes River below Wickiup Reservoir. Highly accessible and easy to drift, the river changes dramatically below Wickiup dam to become a slow, meandering, powerful body of water. This part of the river harbors brown and rainbow trout, the rare brook trout, whitefish, and transient fingerling coho and kokanee from Wickiup. Wild browns up to 15 pounds have been pulled out of this stretch, catches between 12 and 16 inches are common, and good numbers are available in the 20- to 24-inch range. A genetic mix of wild and stocked rainbow trout average 6 to 10 inches, with an occasional fish in the 12- to 14-inch range. Native whitefish are abundant and average 6 to 14 inches in length.

As of 2001, the OSFR from Wickiup Reservoir to Benham Falls allows 5 trout per day, which may include 2 non fin-clipped rainbow. Bait is allowed in this section. The season opens the Saturday of Memorial Day weekend and runs to October 31. Always check current OSFR before fishing.

The river runs in mainly one channel throughout this stretch, undercut banks are common, and shorelines lined with pine, bitterbrush, and willow are often highly eroded. Flows vary drastically with the irrigation season. The riverbed of fine sediment becomes sticky mud when exposed during low water. Woody debris in the river is scarce but is being added through habitat improvement projects. The river here is basically unwadable, often with steep shorelines and deep, powerful water. Bank fishing or drift fishing

Continued on page 10

ABOVE: A scenic bend in the river below Wickiup Dam.

RIGHT: The Deschutes twists and turns as shown in this aerial view looking south at Bull Bend Campground.
Photos by Geoff Hill

BELOW: A beautiful Deschutes brown trout.
Photo by Brian O'Keefe

For obvious reasons, the stretch of water near Lava Island Falls is not recommended for canoe travel! Photo by Doug Emerson

Canoe Safety on the Deschutes

Floating the famed Deschutes River in a canoe or boat can be a delightful, never-to-be-forgotten experience. In most respects, the Deschutes is a perfect river for drifting. While most of the river is quiet, rather placid water, *a few stretches are very dangerous and should not, under any circumstances, be attempted. Lives have been lost because people ignored the warning signs or underestimated the cascades.*

"All along the river, the Forest Service has posted warning signs of upcoming falls or rapids. If a boater or canoeist heeds these warning signs, they should have no problem. The time to pull in to shore is when you first see the warning sign. Inexperienced boaters or canoeists often underestimate the power of the river at the head of falls or rapids. Once you are caught in the fast water, consider yourself lucky if you get out alive.

"Just remember that the relative ease of floating the Deschutes can be misleading. Remember, too, that the river doesn't care.

"If boaters and canoeists observed just these three rules, there would be no deaths on the Deschutes. *First, a life preserver is a must. Second, know the river and the limitations of your craft. And, third, observe all the boating safety rules."*

The Boating Safety Rules recommended by the U.S. Coast Guard and the State Marine Board are printed herein.

The Deschutes National Forest has published a pamphlet on floating the Deschutes River. We recommend that you pick up a copy before you try the river. It could save your life.

Boating & Canoeing Safety Rules
(Recommended by the U.S. Coast Guard & State Marine Board)

1. Do not go out in rough water or threatening weather.

2. Never leave shore in a leaky or poorly constructed boat.

3. Equip boat properly with anchor, life preservers, oars or spare paddle, flashlight, and fire extinguisher (if motor boat).

4. Tell someone when and where you are going and when you plan to return (your chances of rescue are better).

5. Do not overload the boat (have plenty of freeboard).

6. Wear your life preserver. Have one for each person on board.

7. Instruct at least one of the passengers on how to operate the boat.

8. Keep clear of swimmers.

9. Familiarize yourself with the area.

10. Know how to swim.

11. Avoid excessive or sudden bursts of speed (you may be thrown overboard).

12. Reduce speed in narrow passages and congested areas.

13. Take the river brochure or a map in a sealed plastic bag.

14. Take drinking water and some extra food in case you have to stay out longer than expected.

15. Sheriff Search & Rescue – (541) 388-6502.

DESCHUTES
Continued from page 8

from a boat is the norm. Bordered mainly by Forest Service land above the LaPine State Recreation Area, the stretch below, through Sunriver is lined with homes.

All fishing methods can produce large browns through this reach of the river, but most anglers use whole crayfish or night-crawlers, particularly near Sunriver. One should fish close to the banks where the browns lurk. An especially effective technique is casting from a boat toward shore with spinning gear and a plug or lure such as a Rapala that imitates a baitfish. The best times of day are early and late when the sun is off the water. Fly fishers going for brown trout use streamers, such as brown Woolly Buggers, brown Matukas, and red and white bucktails. Good caddis and mayfly hatches make fly fishing for small rainbow and whitefish particularly productive, using dry flies such as Adams, Elk Hair Caddis, Comparaduns, and even Royal Wulffs. One may also want to try nymphing with orange Tied-down Caddis.

Often the mouths of the Little Deschutes and Fall River can be profitable areas to fish. Fall River joins the Deschutes just below the LaPine Recreation Area, and the Little Deschutes enters a mile above Sunriver. There is a boat speed limit of 5 mph.

Deschutes River Canoe Trip Guide: Wickiup Dam to Meadow Picnic Area

	Hours	Accumulative Elapsed Time	Approximate River Mileage
Wickiup Dam* to Wampus Butte Campground*	2:45	2:45	2.5
Wampus Butte Campground* to Bull Bend*	2:20	5:05	3.0
Bull Bend* to Wyeth Campground*	0:45	5:50	1.0
Wyeth Campground* to Pringle Falls*	0:30	6:20	0.5
PRINGLE FALLS – CANOE TRAVEL NOT RECOMMENDED – PORTAGE TIME 0:45			
Pringle Falls* to Tetherow Log Jam•	2:45	9:05	2.5
TETHEROW LOG JAM – CANOE TRAVEL NOT RECOMMENDED – PORTAGE TIME 0:10			
Tetherow Log Jam* to LaPine State Park	1:55	11:00	5.5
LaPine State Park to mouth of Fall River	2:20	13:20	3.0
Mouth of Fall River to Big River Campground*	2:40	16:00	5.0
Big River Campground* to Harper Bridge	4:10	20:10	7.0
Harper Bridge to Besson Camp*	1:00	21:10	1.5
Besson Camp* to Benham Falls*	5:10	26.20	8.5
BENHAM FALLS TO JUST SOUTH OF SLOUGH CAMP – TRAVEL NOT RECOMMENDED – ROUGH WATER			
Just south of Slough Camp• to Dillon Falls*	1:15	–	2.0
Dillon Falls* to Aspen Camp	1:00	–	1.5
ASPEN CAMP TO BIG EDDY – CANOE TRAVEL NOT RECOMMENDED – ROUGH WATER			
BIG EDDY TO LAVA ISLAND – CANOE TRAVEL NOT RECOMMENDED – ROUGH WATER			
LAVA ISLAND TO SOUTH OF MEADOW CAMP – CANOE TRAVEL NOT RECOMMENDED			
South of Meadow Camp to Meadow Picnic Area	0:15	–	0.5
MEADOW PICNIC AREA TO BEND NATIONAL FOREST BOUNDARY – CANOE TRAVEL NOT RECOMMENDED – ROUGH WATER			

*Boat Ramps to 18 feet

Just lazily drifting the river is a very popular pastime. However, the float from Wyeth Campground to Tetherow Log Jam should not be attempted in order to avoid Pringle Falls, a dangerous obstacle. A short distance below Sunriver, another stretch of life-threatening water begins at Benham Falls. *(See information on pages 9 through 11 for safe passage around these sections.)* The most popular drifts are the 7 miles from just below Wickiup Dam to above Pringle Falls, a 13.5-mile drift from Tetherow to Big River Campground, and the 7 miles from Big River to Sunriver. Five good boat ramps are available between Wickiup and Sunriver. Other amusements in the area include camping, hunting, bird watching, horseback riding, hiking, and wildlife viewing.

Beginning just below Wickiup Dam, Forest Service facilities include Bull Bend Campground and raft launch; Wyeth Campground and boat launch; Pringle Falls Campground and raft launch; Tetherow boat launch; and Big River Group Camp and boat launch. LaPine State Recreation Area, also with a crude boat launch, is situated between Tetherow and Big River. None of these sites has drinking water, except the state park. All charge a fee to camp. There are also many primitive sites available for camping, and there is a small boat ramp suitable for canoes at Harper Bridge on Route 40.

Several Forest Service roads parallel the river. The segment of the river from Wickiup Dam to Route 43 is paralleled by Forest Route 4370 on the west bank. Route 4370 can be reached either from Wickiup Reservoir (see directions to Wickiup Reservoir on page 45) or from County Route 43 off U.S. Highway 97, 3 miles north of LaPine. Forest Route 4360 runs west of the river from Route 43 to County Route 42. Below Route 42 and Big River Campground the only public access is along the west bank across from Sunriver which can be reached by taking the Sunriver turn (Route 40) from U.S. Highway 97, 15 miles south of Bend. Stay on Route 40 crossing the river at Harper Bridge. Small-boat access is available at the bridge. Continue another 2 miles to Forest Route 41 and turn right. Many spur roads lead down to the river from Route 41.

Deschutes River from Wickiup Reservoir to Sunriver

△ DAY USE AREA
▲ CAMPGROUND
◤ BOAT ACCESS
⌒ ⌒ UNPAVED ROAD

DESCHUTES RIVER: SUNRIVER TO BEND

The steepest gradient in the entire 252 miles of the Deschutes River begins 6 miles downstream from Sunriver at Benham Falls. From the falls to Bend, the river moves swiftly within a basalt channel, dodging a lava flow and breaking into a series of hurtling rapids and thundering falls. Upstream from Benham Falls, the river has the same placid character as between Wickiup and Sunriver. The brown trout fishing here is second only to the stretch above, with fish in the same size range. Some are monsters. Wild rainbow of 7 to 11 inches, occasionally to 14 inches in length, dominate the river from Benham Falls downstream. Whitefish are available all the way to Bend.

Below Sunriver, the vegetation changes to old growth ponderosa and aspen, and shorelines vary from marshy meadows to basalt bedrock. Flows fluctuate less because of tributaries, and the river features many deep pools, a more stable bank, and rocky instream structure. Spring River enters the Deschutes a mile downstream from Route 40. This mile-long "spring creek" holds few resident fish and is mainly spawning and rearing habitat for the rainbows, browns, and whitefish of the Deschutes. The lower half-mile of Spring River is accessible through Forest Service land.

Untamed whitewater and dangerous cataracts begin at Benham Falls and continue past Dillon Falls to Lava Island Falls 5 miles south of Bend. This section accurately reflects the river's name, Deschutes, "River of the Falls." The safest stretch for boaters is calm water between Benham and Dillon Falls. Popular whitewater run frequently by professional guides lies between Dillon and Lava Island Falls. Rafting trips can be booked with experienced companies in Bend and Sunriver.

Though much of the water is fast and dangerous between Sunriver and Bend there are still many good fishing spots along the banks. As with all of the upper Deschutes, the river travels mostly within one channel and water levels vary with the irrigation season. Few areas are wadable and most would be hazardous to attempt. From 1 mile below Meadow Picnic Area to Bend, the river is entirely flanked by private land. A short distance upstream from Bend, much of the river is siphoned off for irrigation from April to October, and, again, the character of the river changes as its volume drops.

Upstream of the falls, anglers should try bait or Rapalas early and late in the day for

The wild whitewater of Dillon Falls on the Upper Deschutes near Bend. Photo by Geoff Hill brown trout. From Benham Falls down, it is primarily a bank fishery and, at times, provides great fly fishing, although small lures are also used successfully. Small, flashy lures such as Thomas and Rooster Tails are productive. A fly box containing Adams, Elk Hair Caddis, Comparadun, and salmonfly patterns plus stonefly nymph imitations, Hare's Ears, and Pheasant Tails should be adequate. Whitefish are often caught while fly fishing for rainbow. Many anglers fish the tailouts of falls in October. Bait is no longer allowed from Benham Falls to Lake Billy Chinook, with the exception of Mirror Pond in Bend … especially for kids.

Below Benham Falls to Lake Billy Chinook, the river is open to angling year-round. The trout catch limit below Benham Falls is 2 per day, 8-inch minimum length, and no more than 1 over 20 inches. Rainbow trout over 20 inches are defined as steelhead and must be released. There is no limit on whitefish.

Boat launching is available at Harper Bridge, Besson Camp, Slough Camp, Dillon Falls, Aspen Camp, and Lava Island recreation sites. There is a boat speed limit of 5 mph.

Forest Service campgrounds exist at Besson Camp, Slough Camp, and Dillon Falls. None has drinking water or charges a fee to camp. Benham Falls, Besson Camp, Slough Camp, Dillon Falls, and Meadow also have picnic areas. All of these sites were converted to day-use only in 1997.

In addition to fishing, boating, and whitewater rafting, other options for entertainment include waterfowl hunting, photography, horseback riding, mountain biking, and hiking. Due to its proximity to Bend, many more people visit the river on a day-use basis than for overnight stays. Forest Service trails for mountain bikes, horses, and hikers begin at Meadow and continue to Benham Falls.

For access from Sunriver, follow directions in the Wickiup to Sunriver section (see page 11) to Route 41. To reach Besson Camp take spur road 200 off of Route 41 downstream from Sunriver. Back on 41 continue north, downstream, about 8 miles and turn on marked spur roads to Slough Camp. Dillon Falls is 2 miles north of Slough Camp, Aspen Camp another 2 miles, Lava Island another 2 miles. All are reached by spur roads from Route 41. About a mile north of Lava Island Route 41 intersects with Century Drive, Route 46. A right turn here will take you back to Bend in 7 miles. These directions can also be followed in reverse by taking Century Drive out of Bend toward Mount Bachelor and turning left in 7 miles onto Route 41 toward Deschutes River Recreation Sites.

Rod Malone proudly holds his big brown trout.
Photo by Dean Guernsey

Deschutes River from Sunriver to Bend

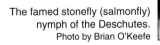
The famed stonefly (salmonfly) nymph of the Deschutes.
Photo by Brian O'Keefe

DESCHUTES RIVER:
BEND TO LAKE BILLY CHINOOK

The Deschutes River flows smack through the center of downtown Bend, attracting many visitors at Drake Park, Harmon Park, and Pioneer Park. At Drake Park, Mirror Pond offers a wonderful atmosphere for walks, relaxation, picnics, bird watching, floating, and fishing, especially for the kids. A little farther downstream, below the North Canal Dam all the way to Lake Billy Chinook, the river offers excellent winter fishing. In some spots, the river is wadable, in other areas, bank fishing is the rule. A preferred area for fly fishing, this section is not open to bait fishing; however, lures are popular. All fish in the river are wild, including rainbow trout up to 18 inches, averaging 7 to 14 inches. Brown trout can be found in all sizes, including a few monsters pushing 8 pounds. Bull trout are present below Steelhead Falls, and profuse numbers of whitefish are available throughout the river. Crayfish are common. Boating is not possible due to low flows and, because of frequent waterfalls farther downstream, is unsafe to attempt. The only navigable expanse is in the Deschutes Arm of Lake Billy Chinook.

From the north end of 1st Street in Bend down to the North Canal Dam, the river is accessible along the west bank, and fishing can be decent, especially when water levels are low in the summer. Deep pools and slow runs between rock-strewn stretches produce mostly small fish. In the winter, the river rushes over big boulders; during summer low flows, it swirls slowly past the same rocks. Water levels fluctuate greatly with the irrigation season. Fishing is best in between and around the boulders.

As the river leaves Bend, it passes the last man-made obstruction for 40 miles and becomes a wild, canyon river. More of the river banks are public land. Shorelines vary from flooded, marshy ground to blocky talus with some heavy vegetation of willow and alder. Around Lower Bridge, 25 miles below Bend, cattails and sedges dominate. Springs below Lower Bridge help to stabilize water levels, as does inflow from Squaw Creek. The uplands are covered with juniper trees and bitterbrush, and the basalt canyon is of varying depth. Outstanding wild rainbow and brown trout habitat exist from Lower Bridge downstream 10 miles to Lake Billy Chinook. The deepest part of the canyon, below Lower Bridge, has excellent slots and pools and the best potential for fishery on the river if flows could be stabilized. In-stream structure in the form of rocks, some woody debris, and occasional weedbeds is plentiful throughout the canyon. The area is rich in wildlife.

Access is limited by private land and steep canyon walls. The largest concentration of wild fish is from Big Falls about a mile below Lower Bridge to Lake Billy Chinook. Steelhead Falls is about 5 miles below Lower Bridge. At Lake Billy Chinook, the Deschutes joins the Crooked and Metolius rivers.

When fishing these rocky reaches, make sure your lure is near the

Deschutes River from Bend to Lake Billy Chinook

▲ CAMPGROUND
△ DAY USE AREA
■ RESORT

bottom. Small, flashy lures, such as Thomas and Rooster Tails, are productive. For fly fishers, a fly box containing winter stone fly, March brown, and salmonfly dry flies is a must when these hatches are in progress. Brown Woolly Buggers and beadhead nymphs are standard. Other productive patterns are Elk Hair Caddis, Comparadun, stonefly nymph imitations, Hare's Ear, and Pheasant Tail. Whitefish are often caught while fly fishing for rainbow.

Developed campgrounds are located at Tumalo State Park, Cline Falls State Park, and Lake Billy Chinook. No other official campgrounds are located on the river between Bend and Lake Billy Chinook, but, legally, you can camp anywhere on BLM land or the

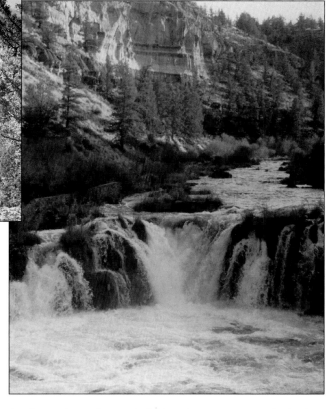

ABOVE: From Bend to Redmond, views of the Cascades appear around every bend in the river. Oregon Dept. of Transportation photo

RIGHT: Steelhead Falls, on the Deschutes, can be accessed through the Crooked River Ranch development. Photo by Geoff Hill

Crooked River National Grasslands not otherwise posted. Recreation options other than hiking and fishing are limited because of private land. Some hunting is possible. An abundance of raptors, fur-bearing mammals, and waterfowl make wildlife viewing rewarding.

Roads reach the river at Sawyer Park in Bend, Tumalo State Park north of Bend, Cline Falls State Park west of Redmond, Tetherow Crossing north of Cline Falls, and at Lower Bridge west of Terrebonne. Between Lower Bridge and Lake Billy Chinook, all access is by foot; nowhere can you drive right to the water. In only a few places can you get down to the river without ropes and pitons, and hiking within much of this steep canyon is strenuous.

Sawyer Park in Bend is reached by turning west onto O.B. Riley Road from U.S. Highway 97 across from Bend River Mall. The park is .5 mile down O.B. Riley. Continuing north on O.B. Riley Road will bring you to Tumalo State Park in another 4 miles. To reach Cline Falls State Park from Bend, take Highway 97 north then U.S. Highway 20 west toward Sisters. In 4 miles turn right toward the town of Tumalo and stay on this road (Cline Falls Road) for about 10 miles until it reaches the junction with State Highway 126. Cline Falls is just a stone's throw east on 126 and can also be reached from downtown Redmond, 4.5 miles farther east on 126. A primitive road follows the west bank of the river downstream from Highway 126 just west of Cline Falls through mostly private land. The BLM is currently negotiating a land exchange to add public land north of Highway 126 along the river. At Tetherow Crossing about 1.5 miles downstream from Cline Falls, there is a .75-mile stretch of BLM land. Another mile downstream is a brief .25-mile segment of public land above Odin Falls. The next chunk of BLM land is above Lower

Bridge and can be reached by numerous spur roads heading upstream off of Lower Bridge Market County Road. The Lower Bridge road heads west off Highway 97 just north of Terrebonne.

The most remote section of the river from Lower Bridge to Lake Billy Chinook has very limited access. Steelhead Falls and a primitive BLM road heading upstream from it offer the few access points reached through the Crooked River Ranch (CRR) development northwest of Terrebonne. *From Terrebonne, take the Lower Bridge road turning right into CRR in 2 miles. Stay on this main road (NW Chinook Drive) for 1.5 miles then turn left on Badger Road. Badger becomes Blacktail Drive and T's with Quail Road in about 1.5 miles. Turn right on Quail and in about a mile turn left on River Road which reaches the parking area for the trail to Steelhead Falls in about .75 mile.*

Steelhead Falls is about a half-mile hike downstream. From this point, the BLM road heads upstream with a few more trails down to the river coming off it before the road turns back toward the east, away from the river. From Steelhead Falls to Lake Billy Chinook, access is difficult to impossible except by hiking downstream from Steelhead Falls or upstream from Lake Billy Chinook.

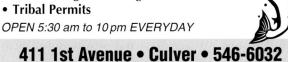

DESCHUTES RIVER:
PELTON DAM TO COLUMBIA RIVER

In the 100 miles of water from Pelton Dam to the Columbia River, the Deschutes River reveals itself as a big, broad-shouldered and powerful, desert-canyon river, decisively carving its course. Remarkable for its excellent flows year-round, world-class fishing for wild trout, a strong summer steelhead run, and spring and fall runs of chinook salmon, the lower Deschutes is nationally recognized and passionately appreciated. Add an atmosphere of cultural diversity created by the involvement of the Warm Springs Tribes in use and management and the river's designation as a National Wild and Scenic River, as well as a State Scenic Waterway, and you start to get the picture. Even though the Deschutes feeds into the Columbia only a 2-hour drive east of Portland, the majority of the river, accessible only by boat or long hikes, still maintains a feeling of wildness.

Rich in insect numbers and diversity, the Deschutes supports up to 1,500 wild rainbow trout over 8 inches per mile. Trout numbers gradually decrease downstream to the mouth. Fishing is great year-round. Lined with alder groves along some of its shorelines, talus slopes, and grass-covered banks scattered in between, the riverbed often has steep drop-offs or may grade into mucky eddies. Mainly, the river has a gradual slope covered with gravel and cobble. In places, weedbeds thrive in the river, and islands frequently split the river, but primarily it flows in one big channel. This is big water that cannot be waded across. Stream flow averages over a 69-year period show a range from 3,380 cubic feet per second (cfs) in July to 5,489 cfs in March. Thirteen major rapids and an impassible falls punctuate the waters between Pelton Dam and the Columbia. Main tributaries are the Warm Springs River and the White River.

One of the most important recreational areas in the state, the river attracts diverse users: anglers for trout, steelhead, salmon, and whitefish, whitewater enthusiasts, splash-and-giggle rafters, jet boaters, commercial guides, hunters, campers, and wildlife watchers. Land ownership is shared by the Bureau of Land Management (BLM), the Confederated Tribes of Warm Springs (CTWS), Oregon State Parks and Recreation Department, numerous private parties, and two railroads. Rules and regulations are continually changing. The Lower Deschutes River Management Plan Record of Decision II, adopted in 1993 and available from BLM, describes current and future management plans for the river. The river corridor has special regulations for boating, camping, firearms, fishing, and fires. As use continues to increase, it becomes more and more important to know the regulations and to be considerate of other users in order to maintain the rare quality of the Deschutes experience.

Please note that the 1996 flood caused major changes in the Deschutes from Pelton Dam to the Columbia River. One Class 4 rapids in particular, Whitehorse Rapids, suffered serious alteration.

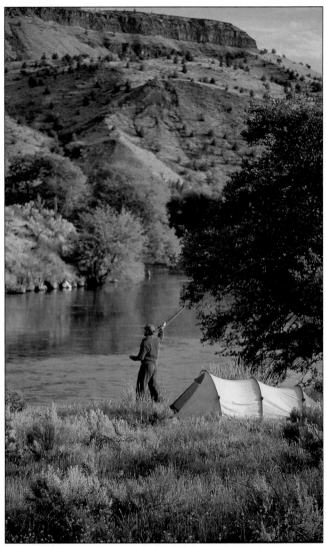

Fly fishing is the most popular technique for fishing on the Deschutes. Photo by Brian O'Keefe

Many other less dangerous changes also occurred in the river channel. Additionally, many boat-in and drive-in campsites were destroyed or permanently rearranged.

RULES AND REGULATIONS

Fishing Regualtions: An Oregon Angling License is required and all rules as described in "Oregon Sport Fishing Regulations" must be followed. Special "tags" are required for salmon and steelhead. Special permits are also required to fish the CTWS side of the river.

The regulations are complicated; check the rules before fishing.

Boating Regulations: A Boater's Pass is required of everyone in a floating device on the river and may be purchased for the day or season. Various restrictions concerning the use of motors are in effect. Measures were applied by the BLM in 1996 to reduce peak use of the river by commercial users. All boaters are asked to reduce their use on Fridays, Saturdays, and Sundays from mid-June through Labor Day.

BLM Camping Regulations: For all drive-in campgrounds and for BLM land between the locked gate upstream from Maupin to Macks Canyon, the stay limit is no more than 14 days out of any 28 days. At boat-in (undeveloped) sites, campers may stay no more than 4 days and must vacate a site for 3 days before reoccupying. The new site must not be less than .25 mile away. No more than 16 people are allowed in a group at boat-in sites, except between the locked gate and Sherars Falls where the limit is 24 people.

BLM charges $5.00 per night Sun.–Thurs. and $10.00 Fri.– Sat. for overnight use of drive-in campgrounds and $2.00 for each additional vehicle at that site. The maximum number of people per single site is 8. Some larger group sites are available for a charge of $15.00 per night Sun.–Thurs. and $30.00 Fri.– Sat. No fees are charged at undeveloped sites. Drinking water is available only at Maupin City Park and Macks Canyon BLM Recreation Site, and at Deschutes River State Park.

Many changes in BLM recreation sites started in 1997. Facilities may be different from those outlined in the following descriptions.

Private Property: Permission is required to camp on or use private property. The railroad tracks are private property. Walking along the tracks is technically trespassing and potentially dangerous, although warnings are rarely heeded, and laws are seldom enforced.

Warm Springs Reservation: Only 6 miles of river on the reservation side between Dry Creek and Trout Creek are open to the public for fishing, and a CTWS fishing permit ("Indian permit") is required. Along all other reservation land, you may not land a boat, fish, walk, or camp, including all islands and gravel bars west of mid-river.

Dangers: Be aware of the potential for incidents involving heat exhaustion, sunstroke, dehydration, sunburn, rattlesnakes, poison ivy, drowning, high winds, temperature extremes, fire, scorpions, and black widow spiders. Wading is dangerous; use a wading staff, studded felt soles, or cleats, if necessary.

Fire Regulations: From June 1 to October 15, rules are as follows:

No open fires, wood fires, or smoking outside of buildings, closed vehicles, or boats on the river.

During the remainder of the year, fires may be built only in fire pans (stoves are preferred). All ashes and charcoal must be packed out.

It is illegal to cut any firewood, dead or alive, in the river corridor.

Considerate use of the river includes disposing of cigarette butts in an ash tray or garbage can — not in the water or on the banks.

Litter: If you pack it in, pack it out! Never use toilets for garbage disposal. BLM is proposing that all human waste be packed out in the near future.

Firearms: No shooting from the third Saturday in May to August 31. No discharging of firearms in developed recreation sites.

Fish Species: All trout in the lower Deschutes are wild fish and native to the river. Stocking of trout was ended in 1979, whereas hatchery steelhead and spring chinook salmon are still stocked. Fall chinook are a wild run, but numbers are extremely low. Rainbow trout in the lower Deschutes are a unique group called "redsides" because of their broad, deep red stripes. The average catch is between 10 and 15 inches; 16- to 18-inch trout are not uncommon, and a few are even larger. These fish are strong and feisty and put up a great fight.

The stretch from Pelton Dam to Maupin holds the most trout, with

Lisa Hawkins shows off a Deschutes rainbow before releasing it back into the river. Photo by Brian O'Keefe

numbers gradually decreasing downstream to the mouth. During spawning season from April through mid-June, trout are especially vulnerable to exhaustion. Play the big ones gently at this time of year, revive carefully, and stay off the spawning beds.

Deschutes steelhead are a summer run of both wild and hatchery fish averaging 4 to 6 pounds, 24 to 26 inches in length. They usually show up at the mouth in July and are available near Pelton Dam through December. Steelhead "strays" from other rivers sometimes

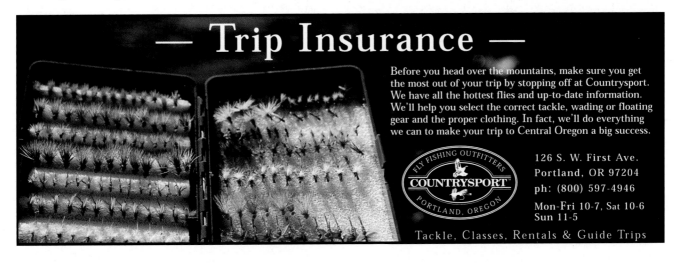

enter the Deschutes and stay for variable lengths of time. Some of these fish are as large as 20 pounds.

Two runs of chinook salmon enter the Deschutes: the spring run in April and fall chinook in June. The season for spring chinook in 2001 is April 7 to July 31. The fall chinook season had not been determined at this printing. The average spring chinook is 8 to 12 pounds with a few between 12 and 18 pounds. Fall chinook average 20 pounds. Some individuals may be as large as 40 pounds. Special regulations apply to the salmon seasons, so check before fishing.

Whitefish are native to the Deschutes and an indicator of excellent water quality. They are a member of the salmonid family along with trout, steelhead, and salmon. Usually easier to catch than the other species, they can be a lot of fun on light gear. They are good eating if cleaned "while still twitching" and kept cool, and they are superb smoked. Whitefish angling is especially good during the winter with small nymphs. Sometimes you'll catch them on big stonefly nymphs while trout fishing.

Bull trout are present mainly above Sherars Falls. These native fish are now on the threatened and endangered species list. While releasing them as the law requires, do so very carefully.

Coarse-scale suckers are often found in fast water where they hug the bottom, scraping algae off rocks. They will sometimes take a fly off the bottom and are also foul-hooked occasionally. A big sucker on the end of a line can give the angler the thrill of the day, at least until seeing what it is.

Northern pikeminnow are a native predator and are not very numerous in the cold water of the Deschutes, but become more common as the water warms downstream. They are part of the natural balance, feeding on juvenile salmonids. They will take dry flies, unfortunately.

Many other non-game species are present in the river, but they are seldom seen or caught.

FISHING TECHNIQUES

Trout and Whitefish: Ninety percent of anglers on the lower Deschutes are fly fishers. Catching trout on the Deschutes follows the usual scenario of attempting to find where the fish are and what they are eating. Whitefish are often caught while fishing for trout. The four most important groups of insects on the Deschutes are mayflies, caddisflies, stoneflies, and midges. Choose your fly patterns accordingly. Trout are most likely to be found near seams, drop-offs, small troughs, depressions in the bottom, back eddies, banks, in rock gardens and foam lines, and in the flats during a hatch.

Fly fishing techniques most often used are dry flies cast upstream, deep nymphing, emergers cast upstream, and the wet fly swing. Popular dry fly patterns are Blue Wing Olive, Pale Morning Dun, Sparkle Dun, Humpys, salmonfly patterns, Golden Stone, Griffiths Gnat, and Elk Hair Caddis. Emerger patterns should include a floating mayfly nymph, hatching midge, soft hackles, and caddis emerger. For wet flies, one should have soft hackles in all colors, Sparkle Pupa, Hare's Ear, Pheasant Tail, beadhead nymphs, flashback nymphs,

Prince Nymph or Zug Bug, Serendipity, October Caddis, and stonefly nymphs (Rubber Legs, Kaufmann's). Terrestrials such as hoppers and ant patterns should also be included in one's fly selection.

Spin fishers are successful during non-hatch times using small trout lures, such as Mepps, Rooster Tail, Panther Martin, and Flat-Fish, or flies with a casting bubble. Bright-colored lures can be used throughout the day since the Deschutes is always slightly off-color. Retrieve as slowly as possible, casting near rocks and into the flats.

Steelhead: Recognizing good steelhead water is even more difficult than finding trout lies. Usually the speed of the current, depth of the water, and bottom structure are the most important factors to consider. Prime lies are 2 to 6 feet deep and moving at the speed of a slow walk. The more difficult a run is to wade because of an assortment of boulder sizes, the more steelhead like it. Ledges and other drop-offs can be good, too. Fly fishers need heavier gear than for trout and at times sink tip lines. Fly patterns are much less important than finding the right water, but popular patterns are Green Butt Skunk, Articulated Leech, Macks Canyon, Purple Peril, Brad's Brat, Thor, Coal Car, Freight Train, and Silver Hilton. Some skaters or steelhead dries are used, too. All are presented with a 45 degree down and across technique. Deep nymphing with stonefly patterns will also catch steelhead. Persistence and being in the right place at the right time are the keys to catching steelhead.

Many anglers on the Deschutes fish successfully for steelhead with hardware and drift rods or heavier spinning rods. Spinners, spoons, and plugs can all be used effectively. Spinner and spoon selections can be bigger and brighter than knowledge would usually indicate because of the off-color water. Size 3, 4, or even 5 spinners in silver, nickel, brass, or black are popular choices. Mepps Aglia, Blue Fox Vibrax, Metric and Rapalas are all good choices. Stee-lee spoons are good producers as are plugs in silver, gold, purple, green, or blue. Some anglers use side-planers. Lures can be fished in the same areas as flies just as effectively and can be better than flies in deeper and rougher water. Spoons are usually better in deeper water than spinners, and plugs are definitely suited for deeper water. Retrieve lures as slowly as possible for best results.

Salmon: Open only occasionally, the Deschutes has been closed for salmon fishing in most years. However, the 2001 spring chinook run is strong, and the season is from April 7 to July 31. Fall chinook have a much longer run from mid-June to late October. The fish pool up below Sherars Falls, and most are caught within a mile (downstream) of the falls. Drift fishing tackle is used, usually with salmon eggs or commercially canned fish, a little yarn, a Spin n' Glo or Corkie in peach or green, and lead sinkers. Most anglers fish from the top of basalt cliffs below the falls by casting upstream and bouncing the bait along the bottom. Things can get crowded, often shoulder to shoulder. Bait can be used from the falls downstream 3 miles. Those shaky wood platforms at Sherars Falls are for Indian use only.

PELTON TO WHITEHORSE RAPIDS

Warm Springs to Trout Creek

The most heavily fished stretch of the whole river for trout, Warm Springs to Trout Creek is used by drift, walk-in, and bike-in anglers. The most intense fishing use is during the salmonfly hatch in late May. Excellent trout and steelhead fishing and non-technical boating along 9 miles of river give good reason for the popularity of this stretch. Warm Springs lies at river mile 97 (97 miles to the Columbia), 14 miles north of Madras, and about 3 miles below Pelton Dam. U.S. Highway 97 crosses the Deschutes River at Warm Springs. The boat ramp and parking area .25 mile south of the bridge has a double outhouse, garbage cans, lots of room to set up rafts and drift boats, and a gravel ramp. Camping is not allowed. Warm Springs has services and Indian permits, and Madras offers services, shuttles, and permits.

Deschutes River from Pelton Dam to Whitehorse Rapids

Map showing the Deschutes River from Pelton Dam to Whitehorse Rapids, including labels: WHITEHORSE RAPIDS Scouting Recommended, OAK CREEK, SKOOKUM CREEK, WARM SPRINGS RESERVATION No Trespassing, To Simnasho, WASCO COUNTY, WARM SPRINGS RIVER, Kaskela, SWAMP CR., Kah-Nee-Ta Resort, TROUT CREEK RAPIDS, South Junction, Dry Creek Special fishing permits required this side of river, DRY CREEK, To Portland, 26, Warm Springs, SHITIKE CREEK, Mecca, Warm Springs Access (State), Gateway Rec Site (BLM), TROUT CREEK, FROG SPRING CANYON, Gateway, PELTON DAM, 26, LAKE SIMTUSTUS, To Hwy 26, To Hwy 97, To Madras.

Legend: TOILET, DAY USE, CAMPGROUND, BOAT ACCESS, UNPAVED ROAD, RAILROAD

From the Warm Springs boat ramp, there is public access along the east bank about a mile upstream to private property. *To reach Mecca Flat, the next drive-in access, turn north onto a dirt road at the east end of the Warm Springs Bridge between the market and Deschutes Trailer Park. The road forks almost immediately; the first fork leads to the trailer park, the second is a private driveway, and the third is the road to Mecca Flat. It's about 2 miles to the parking area on a road which has deep holes, big rocks, and slides. High clearance vehicles will usually have no problem, but, after a hard rain, much of it turns to slime.*

The camping/parking area at Mecca has one outhouse only. Heavy use is obvious. About a mile of river can be fished upstream, but passing through the stile at the north end of the parking area leads to many miles of trail along the river that are suitable for hiking or mountain bikes. The trail runs all the way to Trout Creek Recreation Site 7.5 miles downstream.

A half-dozen latrines and boat-in campsites are situated along the trail between Mecca and Trout Creek. About a mile down from Mecca Flat, the property owners have kindly granted access to the river along their property. Across the river on the CTWS side lies Dry Creek Campground.

To drive to Dry Creek, take U.S. Highway 26 east from Portland or west from Madras. Just north of the bridge over the Deschutes at Warm Springs, turn onto a paved road toward Kah-Nee-Ta Resort. Stay on this road (Warm Springs Route 3) for 3 miles to the sign to Dry Creek. Turn right onto the gravel road and at the fork go right another .5 mile to the next fork. Take the left fork, and in .2 mile you will reach Dry Creek Campground. A Warm Springs permit is required to camp and fish here. There is an outhouse and garbage cans but no drinking water or boat launch. Camping is not allowed anywhere else along the river on the reservation side. There is a maximum stay of 10 consecutive days at Dry Creek. At the gate on the north end of the campground, a dirt road leads to the only stretch of river along the reservation from which the public is allowed to fish, with a permit. This 6-mile stretch ends across from Trout Creek Campground. You may walk or take a mountain bike on the road.

Trout Creek Campground is one of the more developed campgrounds and has the next boat ramp downstream from Warm Springs. This can be a very busy place during prime fishing season since it is the last boat ramp before Class 4 Whitehorse Rapids and for the next 30 miles. Trout Creek Campground has a good concrete boat ramp, level sites suitable for trailers and RVs, outhouses, garbage cans, a campground host, and no drinking water. Camping is $5.00 per night Sun.–Thurs. and $10.00 Fri.– Sat. nights.

To drive to Trout Creek, stay on U.S. Highway 97 north of its junction with Highway 26 at Madras. In 2.5 miles, turn left at the sign to Gateway and Trout Creek BLM. At the fork in 4 miles continue on straight to Gateway in another 4 miles. Turn right just after crossing the railroad tracks at the sign to Deschutes River and

Trout Creek. The road down to Trout Creek can be extremely rough and slow-going. It's about 3 miles to the campground.

Access downstream of the campground is cut off by private property, but the east bank can be fished for the entire 7.5 miles back upstream to Mecca Flat. It's a good trail, suitable for mountain bikes and hikers. The trail begins at the far south end of Trout Creek Campground. Horse access is allowed for the first 5.5 miles upstream.

Trout Creek to Whitehorse Rapids

Once below Trout Creek Campground, boaters are committed to running Whitehorse Rapids, a dangerous, lengthy Class 4 rapid, capable of capsizing any craft. Whitehorse Rapids is 12 miles downstream from Trout Creek Campground. The next boat ramp below Trout Creek is 30 miles downstream. The only drive-in site between Trout Creek and Whitehorse is at South Junction, but several boat-in campsites lie along the river between Trout Creek and South Junction.

To drive to South Junction, take the gravel road west, just north of the junction of U.S. Highway 97 with U.S. Highway 197, 33 miles north of Madras. There is a small sign to "South Junction" at the turn. The road is about 10 miles long, cut precariously into a steep sidehill for the last few miles. At the bottom of the hill take the right fork to reach the campground in another .5 mile. The road dead-ends at private property. The campground has two outhouses, picnic tables, a few juniper trees, and charges $5.00 per night Sun.–Thurs. and $10.00 Fri.– Sat. Campsites are quite a distance above the river and on the "wrong" side of the tracks. There is about 1.5 miles of river access blocked above and below by private property. Some anglers walk the railroad tracks to reach more public land, technically trespassing but seldom enforced. At South Junction, poison ivy grows profusely and persists all the way to the Columbia. The next drive-in recreation site is 25 miles downstream from South Junction at Nena day-use area.

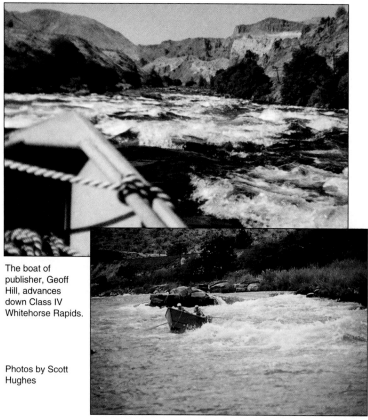

The boat of publisher, Geoff Hill, advances down Class IV Whitehorse Rapids.

Photos by Scott Hughes

Hill mulls his plight after striking a boulder and heading down backwards. A quick spin move gets the bow in front and safe passage is made.

WHITEHORSE RAPIDS TO LOCKED GATE

From Whitehorse Rapids at river mile 76 to the locked gate at river mile 59, all sites are boat-in or hike-in only. At river mile 69, the Warm Springs Reservation ends, and fishing and camping are again allowed on BLM land along the west bank. This point is also the powerboat deadline and a boundary for changes in fishing regulations. Regulations upstream from the boundary are regular season with an extended steelhead season along the east bank only. Below the boundary the river is open year-round on both banks.

Many anglers walk up from the locked gate to fish. The road goes in 13 miles all the way to North Junction (Davidson) at river mile 73 but passes through mostly private land. Access to the river is limited from these points. Bicycles are not allowed on the road. In the first 9 miles, private and BLM land alternate with "Deschutes Club" property, so be careful to stay on the road when it is paralleled by private land. The 4 miles farthest upstream is all private property. The gatekeepers house, a few miles above the locked gate, has a register outside near the front door where one must sign in and out.

LOCKED GATE TO SHERARS FALLS

Locked Gate to Maupin

From the locked gate, the river is accessible by road all the way downstream to Macks Canyon, a total of 35 river miles. Eight miles of rough road parallel the river between the locked gate and Maupin. Whitewater between the locked gate and Maupin includes one Class 3 and one Class 4 rapids plus many other minor chutes.

Numerous BLM campgrounds lie along this part of the river, but none has drinking water. All charge $5.00 per night Sun.–Thurs. and $10.00 Fri.– Sat. to camp and have at least one outhouse, garbage cans, and a few tables. There is no campground at the locked gate. Nena Recreation Site is .8 mile below the gate, Devil's Canyon 2 miles below the gate, Long Bend 2.5 miles, Harpham Flat (CTWS) 3.5 miles, and Wapinitia is 4 miles from the gate and 3 miles from Highway 197. Most have launching areas. Wapinitia is popular with rafters putting in for the drift to Maupin or Sherars Falls. Harpham Flat is the major take-out point for commercial drifters coming from Warm Springs or Trout Creek and has five group sites.

Maupin is located on U.S. Highway 197 at its crossing of the Deschutes. From Portland, take U.S. Highway 26 and turn east on State Highway 216 between mileposts 71 and 72. Travel east 27 miles to the junction with Highway 197, turn right, and Maupin is 3 miles south. To get to the locked gate, continue through Maupin to the southern edge of town just south of The Oasis Resort and take a paved road to the right before going up the hill to leave town.

From Madras, take U.S. Highway 97 for 33 miles to the junction with Highway 197, continuing on Highway 197 another 22 miles to Maupin.

To get to Maupin from I-84 east of The Dalles, take U.S. Highway

Scouting is recommended before tackling Oak Springs Rapids.
Photo by Geoff Hill

Deschutes River below Locked Gate to Sherars Falls

N

To Hwy 197 (1.5 miles)

Oak Springs Hatchery

OAK SPRINGS CREEK

WASCO COUNTY

SPRING CREEK

To Portland

197 Maupin

BOXCAR RAPIDS (Scouting Recommended)

WAPINITIA RAPIDS

WAPINITIA CREEK

CHICKEN SPRING CANYON

STAG CANYON

197

To Madras

Maupin City Park

BAKEOVEN CREEK

To Shaniko

WINTER WATER CREEK

216 Sherars Bridge

WHITE RIVER

SHERARS FALLS
WARNING! DO NOT ATTEMPT TO BOAT FALLS!

LAST TAKEOUT BEFORE FALLS!

OAK SPRINGS RAPIDS (Scouting Recommended)

BOAT ACCESS
△ DAY USE
TOILET
- - - UNPAVED ROAD
RAILROAD

197 south through Dufur (small community, some services) past the turn to Tygh Valley, reaching Maupin in 40 miles.

Maupin to Sherars Falls

The most popular whitewater section on the river is between Long Bend Recreation Site, 2.5 miles below the locked gate, to Sandy Beach (CTWS) above Sherars Falls. Trout and steelhead fishing is good between Maupin and Sherars Falls. The Falls is the best place to fish for chinook salmon. Maupin is a small town of 400 souls who cater to fishing and whitewater enthusiasts. Activity revolves around river recreation, and the town really hops during summer vacation. Maupin has gas, lodging, restaurants, guide services, groceries, taverns, a fly shop, shuttle service, and boat rentals. The only RV hookups on the entire lower river are at Maupin City Park for a cost of $16.00 a night on weekends, $14.00 weekdays. Tent camping is $10.00 a night for up to two tents and two vehicles, with additional charges for extra vehicles and people. The Park also has group sites for $50.00 a night, drinking water, and a new dock.

Downstream from Maupin, a paved road follows the river for 8 miles to Sherars Falls. From the south end of the bridge over the Deschutes in Maupin, take a paved road (Bakeoven Road) that runs along the east bank of the river to "Deschutes River Rec Area." In about .5 mile, past Maupin City Park, there is a left turn onto the Deschutes River Access Road which continues along the east bank to Sherars Falls. Sherars Falls and Bridge may also be reached from Grass Valley on Highway 97 by taking State Route 216 for 21 miles to the west, or from Tygh Valley on Highway 197 by driving State Route 216 east for 8 miles.

Oak Springs Hatchery, an access point on the west river bank, is reached by turning off Highway 197 about 3 miles north of the junction of 197 with State Route 216 west. It's about 3 miles to the hatchery, of which the first 2 miles are paved. Continue past the hatchery and park near the railroad tracks. Footpaths run both up and downstream.

Among the many campgrounds and day-use sites between Maupin and Sherars Falls, Maupin City Park is the only site with full facilities. One mile downstream from the beginning of the access road, Oasis Recreation Site offers camping, outhouses, and garbage cans and charges a fee. There is no drinking water.

Grey Eagle, at 1.5 miles from the access road, is a small area for day-use only. Blue Hole, 3 miles below the beginning of the access road, provides camping and is set up specifically for handicapped access, with a ramp and platform from which the wheelchair-bound can fish. The outhouse and picnic areas are wheelchair accessible, as well. Handicapped anglers have priority.

Oak Springs Recreation Site and Oak Springs Rapid, a Class 4, is next at 3.5 miles. Some rafts take-out at Oak Springs Campground above the rapids.

CTWS-owned White River, at 5 miles, has a toilet, no water, tables, shade, or boat launch but has campsites. CTWS-owned Sandy Beach, at 6 miles, is a heavily used take-out point above Sherars Falls and has no overnight camping. There is a nice beach here and lots of room for rafts. Sherars Falls take-out (CTWS-owned), located .5 mile above Sherars Falls on the west bank, is now closed to the public.

Overnight parking for RV's and trailers is available at Sherars Bridge, but it's too rocky for tent camping. This site is also owned by CTWS and may be closed in a few years. Currently, no fee is charged to camp, and there are no tables or drinking water. Below Sherars Falls, the access road continues down the east bank to Macks Canyon.

Deschutes River below Sherars Falls to Macks Canyon

▲ CAMPGROUND
◢ BOAT ACCESS
▸ TOILET
〰 RAILROAD
--- UNPAVED ROAD

N

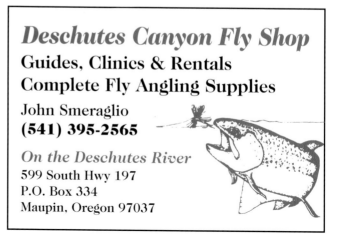

SHERARS FALLS TO MACKS CANYON

The primary use of the Sherars Falls area and the heaviest fishing pressure anywhere on the lower Deschutes occur during the chinook salmon runs. Some folks walk the railroad tracks to reach more river for other types of fishing. Otherwise, there is little use by anglers in this area. Less than a mile east of the falls on State Highway 216, a very rough gravel road, the Deschutes River Access Road, parallels the river for 18 miles to dead-end at Macks Canyon Recreation Site. From Sherars to the mouth, most anglers are after steelhead. Trout fishing is only fair. Prime time for steelhead is August to mid-October. At other times of the year, this stretch enjoys peace and quiet with anglers few and far between. The access road is notorious for eating tires; be prepared! Macks Canyon is a major destination for drift boats coming from Twin Springs and for jet boats coming from the mouth.

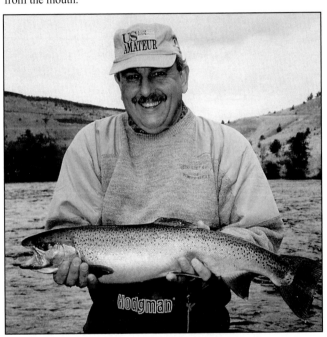

A nice Deschutes steelhead is proudly displayed by Mike Maier,
Deschutes Country administrator, golfer, and fisherman.
Photo courtesy of Sunriver Guides & Outfitters

There are two developed campgrounds in the 18 miles along the access road: Beavertail and Macks Canyon, but there are many other primitive campgrounds available. Buckhollow is located .5 mile from the junction with State Route 216 and this is the first boat put-in below Sherars Falls. There are not any signs, no camping, and no facilities except a rough boat launch.

Pine Tree is next, 3 miles below the junction, and was a popular boat launch before the 1996 flood. Twin Springs, 4 miles from the junction, is the first campground and was developed in 1997 as a boat launch to replace Pine Tree. Oak Brook, 6.5 miles down, has camping and no ramp. Jones Canyon, at 8 miles, has camping but no boat ramp, although some rafters use the bank at the far north end. Gert Canyon is at 8.5 miles, has camping and no ramp. Beavertail Recreation Site, 9.5 miles down the road, is a large campground with hand pumps for drinking water, a good gravel boat launch, and a sandy area for rafts. Rattlesnake Recreation Site has two sections separated by a gulch, 10.5 miles down the access road. Both parts offer camping but no boat ramp. Macks Canyon is at the end of the 18 miles of motor vehicle torture. It is the largest of the campgrounds, has a pressurized water system, wheelchair-accessible toilets, a day-use area, good gravel boat ramp, and lots of parking. All of the campgrounds mentioned previously have outhouses, garbage cans, and tables. The BLM has plans for many changes in these sites in the near future.

MACKS CANYON TO KLOAN

Macks Canyon to the Columbia has the lowest concentration of trout but is a very popular steelhead fishing area, especially for jet boaters. The heaviest fishing pressure is from July through October during the steelhead run. All boaters in this section, drifters and motorized, alike, need to be experienced. The next take-out is at the mouth 24 miles downstream from Macks Canyon, and several nasty rapids are in between. The only drive-in access is at Macks Canyon and 16 miles below at Kloan.

It is possible to continue below Macks along an abandoned railroad grade on foot or mountain bike all the way to the Columbia, but rockslides and gullies in the first 4 miles make the going tough. After 4 miles, the going is easy all the way to the mouth.

To get down to the river at Kloan, for the last 1.5 miles, it is recommended that you have a high-clearance vehicle with 4-wheel low and a surplus of intestinal fortitude. Don't even think about attempting it after a good rain; it turns to slime. The simplest way in to Kloan is off Highway 197, east of The Dalles (services available at The Dalles). Get onto Fifteenmile Road heading east and paralleling I-84, following a sign for "Petersburg School" and passing The Inn at The Dalles. Three miles from the Highway 197 junction, the road forks; bear left. In 3.5 miles you pass through the town of Petersburg School, after nearly 9 miles, Fairbanks. At 12.5 miles, turn left onto graveled Fulton Road which forks in 1.5 miles, take the right fork. In another 2 miles, you arrive at the canyon rim. You may want to stop here and contemplate an imminent demise as you squint at the river nearly 1,000 feet below. The road reaches the river in a little over 1 mile, and at that point you may drive either upstream or down and park near the railroad tracks. Then it's a short hike to the river. Several footpaths head upstream and downstream. You can camp here, but there are no facilities.

KLOAN TO COLUMBIA RIVER

It is 7 river miles from Kloan to the mouth of the Deschutes. The only drive in access points are at Kloan, Heritage Landing, and Deschutes River State Park at the mouth. All other campsites are boat-, hike-, or bike-in from either the mouth or Macks Canyon. Trout fishing is only fair due to a smaller population, but the fish are more willing since they have much less pressure from anglers. From just above Kloan down to the Columbia River, the Deschutes falls through a series of serious rapids beginning with Class 4 Washout Rapids just above Kloan and continuing 2 miles below Kloan with Class 2+ Gordon Ridge Rapids. Colorado Rapids, a Class 3, is a mile below Gordon; Class 4 Rattlesnake Rapids comes up in another mile; and 2 miles farther is Moody Rapids, a Class 2. Then you're in The Dalles Pool.

At the mouth of the river there are two developed sites, one on each bank of the river. Both are managed by the Oregon State Parks and Recreation Department. The State Park is on the east bank, Heritage Landing, on the west bank. To reach these locations, drive to Biggs either from I-84 exit 97, or from Highway 97, following signs to Deschutes State Park. Biggs is a small town with some services. It can be very busy at the mouth during steelhead and salmon season.

The state park is a verdant campground with drinking water, toilets, garbage cans, grass and shade trees, and picnic areas. There is no boat ramp here; one should use Heritage Landing. The state park can accommodate motor homes up to 30 feet in length but has no hookups. Deschutes River State Park is open from mid-March to early November and can be continually full from July through October, depending on fishing success. The park is open for day use the rest of the year. There are 35 primitive campsites, stays are limited to 10 out of 14 days, and the fee to camp is $10.00 a night. Access to the river upstream from the State Park is excellent for 20 miles. Access via hiking, mountain biking, and limited horseback riding is allowed.

Heritage Landing is the take-out for drifters and the put-in for jet boats. There is a 5 mph boat speed limit in this area. The ramp can be extremely busy, so courtesy is a must. Rafters should use the adjacent beach and not the concrete ramp. There is a 15-minute maximum allowed for loading and unloading. The Landing has garbage disposal, flush toilets, and parking for trailers and day-use. Camping is not allowed. There is a poorly maintained trail upstream from the day-use parking lot. Many anglers walk up the railroad tracks to their favorite spots.

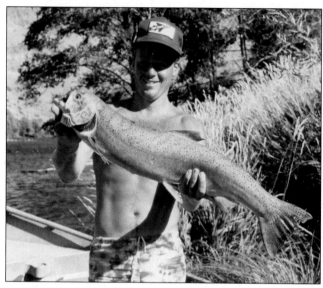

ABOVE: Scott Hughes, the publisher's nephew, proudly displays his dandy, "contest winning," Deschutes steelhead!
Photo by Geoff Hill

BELOW: The publisher, Geoff Hill, displays his "runner-up" steelie. Photo by Scott Hughes

The Rewards of the Lower Deschutes

The Lower Deschutes twists and turns as it passes through deep canyons on its final miles to the Columbia. Along the way anglers encounter a variety of water in which to try their luck.

CLOCKWISE:
Tying the "right" one on makes all the difference.

The Deschutes changes faces around every bend.

Angler Jeff Rose and his companion pose with their nice steelhead.

Using flies which imitate the tiny mayfly often brings success to anglers on the Deschutes. Photos by Brian O'Keefe

The Lower Deschutes River reflects a spectacular high desert sunset. Photo by Geoff Hill

METOLIUS RIVER

Size:	20 miles in length
Depth:	varies; maintains constant flow
Main Catch:	rainbow & bull trout; kokanee; whitefish
Best Methods:	fly fishing
Season:	entire year; check OSFR
Best Time:	late April through early July
Tips:	catch-and-release of all fish

The Metolius River basin is an exceptional collection of lush meadows, gushing springs, robust riparian zones, giant ponderosa pines, raging rapids, basalt canyons, transparent, turquoise-colored water, and huge, native bull trout. Spring-fed, the Metolius maintains constant temperatures, flow, and superb water quality in a stable channel. It supports a tremendous variety of insects. One of the most beautiful areas in Central Oregon, the Metolius is mainly a fly fisher's stream. Fishing is good year-round. This river takes time to learn but offers substantial rewards. Catch-and-release of all wild fish is required throughout the length of the river. Few, if any, clipped rainbow remain.

The Metolius supports remnant planted and wild rainbow trout, wild bull trout, a few brook and brown trout, whitefish, and kokanee. All age classes of rainbow trout are present. Wild rainbow average 8 to 16 inches, with many as big as 3 to 5 pounds and a few even larger. Bull trout range up to 15 pounds, averaging 5 to 6 pounds. Brook trout are rare, very small, and mainly in the uppermost 5 miles of the river. Native whitefish are fairly abundant throughout the river. A spawning run of kokanee enters the river in September from Lake Billy Chinook.

Heavy stocking of rainbow trout in the Metolius River ended in 1996. The river is now managed entirely for wild fish. Small native rainbow are common in the easily wadable section from Lake Creek to Camp Sherman. Elsewhere, look around bridges, under bank cover, and near in-stream structure. Some of the most productive patterns are Comparadun, Clarks Stone, Elk Hair Caddis, Green Drake, Flying Ant, Blue Dun, Renegade, beadhead nymphs, Olive Hare's Ear, Zug Bug, Golden Stone, October Caddis, Serendipity, Sparkle Pupa, and Woolly Bugger. Try streamers for the larger fish, quarter downstream and retrieve slowly with occasional twitches. Keep streamers on the bottom with a fast sink tip line. Zonkers, Matukas, Stovepipes, white or black Deceivers, and variations on Muddlers are all good streamer choices.

The larger, wild rainbow trout prefer the deeper spots in the river, like Popcorn Hole below the Camp Sherman bridge, the deep pool where Canyon Creek enters, and the Idiot Hole 150 yards upstream from Wizard Falls Bridge on the east bank. Bank cover and bank structure are very important habitat for all fish in the Metolius, particularly since there is little cover mid-stream. Bridges also offer an agreeable environment. No fishing is allowed within 100 feet of the Camp Sherman Bridge.

Bull trout are known to lurk beneath underwater ledges and logs and under heavy bank cover, waiting to ambush rainbow and whitefish. These piscivorous char will take a 10-inch streamer and, it is assumed, the same size natural. The bull trout tend to be in the lower sections of the river, and fishing for them is best at the Dolly Hole, Canyon Creek inflow, and Allingham Bridge. Articulated flies, sculpins, and big streamers of all kinds, size 2/0 to 6, are most commonly used.

Brown trout populations are low in the Metolius, and these trout are seldom fished for specifically. They are found mainly in tributaries to the Metolius, most of which are closed to angling. Only occasionally are brown trout caught in the river, itself.

Brook trout numbers are very small as are the fish, most no larger than 8 inches in length. They can be caught on dries and nymphs.

Native whitefish are found throughout the river and are usually taken on small weighted nymphs. Winter angling for whitefish can be excellent.

Fishing for aggressive male kokanee in the fall can be a lot of fun with bright flies as the fly fisher's best bet.

The Metolius emerges as a small wadable river from springs at the base of Black Butte and flows about 20 miles to Lake Billy Chinook. Shorelines are primarily composed of brushy banks with forest behind. There are some weeds in the river and a few small islands. The river follows mainly one

Bull trout (Dolly Vardens) are a common catch in the Metolius.
Photo courtesy of Sunriver Fly Shop

WARM SPRINGS
INDIAN
RESERVATION

Road 1499

Road 64

Monty

METOLIUS RIVER

METOLIUS
RIVER

N

LAKE BILLY
CHINOOK

Candle Creek

Lower Bridge

Bridge 99

Pioneer Ford

Wizard Falls
Fish Hatchery

Allen Springs

Canyon Creek

Gorge
Pine Rest
Smiling River
Allingham
Camp Sherman

Camp Sherman

DAVIS CREEK

LAKE CREEK

Riverside
Metolius
Headwaters

Road 14

20

▲ CAMPGROUND

△ DAY USE AREA

PAVED ROAD

UNPAVED ROAD

TRAIL

certain closures.

A wide variety of hatches occur on the Metolius. Midges hatch year-round, and there are Blue Winged Olives and hatches of small caddis in the middle of winter. Other mayfly and caddis species emerge in warmer months, and stoneflies in late spring and early summer. Popular hatches include a size 14 to 16 March Brown from February through April, and Green Drakes in sizes 6 to 10 from late April through early July. Golden Stones and Salmonflies in sizes 6 and 8 produce explosive surface takes mid-summer. Little Summer Stones and Yellow Sallys, sizes 14 to 16, hatch from August to the first week in October. Don't forget ants and hoppers during the warm summer months. Up-to-date hatch information is available from The Fly Fisher's Place in Sisters and the Camp Sherman Store and Fly Shop in Camp Sherman.

For the sake of explanation, the river is often divided into three sections, one from Lake Creek to Canyon Creek, the second from Canyon Creek to Bridge 99, and the last from Bridge 99 to Lake Billy Chinook, but even within these sections there is a great variety of water types. The most popular section of the river is the 10-mile stretch from Lake Creek to Bridge 99.

Lake Creek to Canyon Creek: This stretch is the easiest to wade. Some very large, wild fish hang out between Lake Creek and Camp Sherman. No angling is allowed within 100 feet of the Camp Sherman Bridge. There is some private property along the west bank in the Camp Sherman area. Camp Sherman to Allingham is heavily fished, and, downstream, Allingham Bridge is a popular and very productive spot. Below Gorge Campground, the river is bordered by private land on both banks for .5 mile, but then Forest Service land continues from Lower Canyon Creek Campground on downstream. Allingham Bridge is mid-way between Lake Creek and Canyon Creek.

Canyon Creek to Bridge 99: "The canyon" is the most isolated area in this length of the river. Accessible only by trail, the canyon starts at Lower Canyon Creek Campground and ends just above Wizard Falls Hatchery. It is accessible from trails on both banks, most easily from downstream. There is good fishing for 10- to 13-inch wild fish in this stretch. The river gains size, depth, and strength from Canyon Creek, and wading becomes difficult to impossible. A .75-mile stretch above Pioneer Ford Campground is bordered by private property.

Bridge 99 to Lake Billy Chinook: Heavy water predominates from Bridge 99 to the mouth. Angling is difficult, but there are some nice fish. Good lies are few and far between, and 4-wheel drive and bush-whacking skills may be required. At Bridge 99, Forest Route 1499 begins where the pavement ends and runs downstream on the east side of the river for about 11 miles to its end at a trailhead. The trail continues for 2 miles along the river to connect with County Route 64, 6 miles from Monty Campground and Lake Billy Chinook. Candle Creek Campground is located on the west side of the river and is accessed by crossing Bridge 99 and following the unpaved

channel. There are many good spots to fish from shore, and in many stretches, bank-fishing is the only option. Where possible, wade into the river to escape grabby vegetation and cast toward the opposite shore.

Regulations require that all fish must be released unharmed. No fishing is allowed from a floating device. Special seasons apply to specific sections on the Metolius. The river above Allingham Bridge is open the Saturday of Memorial Day weekend through October 31, fly angling only with barbless hooks and catch-and-release for all fish. Below Allingham Bridge the river is open the entire year. The same fly angling only requirement to Bridge 99. Below Bridge 99, flies and lures are allowed and still catch-and-release for all fish. Anglers should always check the current OSFR before fishing as there are additional special regulations for the Metolius regarding road. Just north of the campground, the Warm Springs Indian Reservation occupies most of the west bank, and access is denied.

Artificial flies and lures are legal in this stretch, and, in this fast-moving section of the river, compact, heavy lures work best. Try FlatFish, Wobble Rites, Mepps, Super Dupers, and maybe even Rapalas.

Excellent camping facilities in old growth ponderosa pines exist along much of the river. Heading downstream from the headwaters, the Forest Service campgrounds are Riverside, Camp Sherman, Allingham, Smiling River, Pine Rest, Gorge, Canyon Creek, Allen Springs, Pioneer Ford, Lower Bridge, Candle Creek and finally, Monty Campground, about a mile upstream from Lake Billy Chinook. All pay campgrounds have drinking water. Canyon Creek, Candle Creek, and Monty charge no fee. A store, gasoline, and fly shop are available in Camp Sherman, and several motels, resorts, and RV parks are situated nearby.

The Metolius is an excellent family recreation area. Non-fishing options include visiting The Head of the Metolius, a gorgeous area, or the Wizard Falls Hatchery to view brook trout, brown trout, rainbow trout, cutthroat, kokanee, large Atlantic Salmon, and huge brood trout. The Metolius basin is also a beautiful area for camping, hiking, and mountain biking.

To reach the Metolius River from Bend take U.S. Highway 20 west through Sisters. Ten miles west of Sisters turn right onto County Route 14 following signs to Camp Sherman and the Metolius River.

From the Willamette Valley take U.S. Highway 20 east over Santiam Pass. The turn to Camp Sherman is about 12 miles east of Hoodoo Ski Area. Once on County Route 14 it's about 4 miles to the turn to the headwaters, 5 miles to the Camp Sherman Bridge, 10 miles downstream to Wizard Falls Hatchery, and 14 miles downstream to Bridge 99.

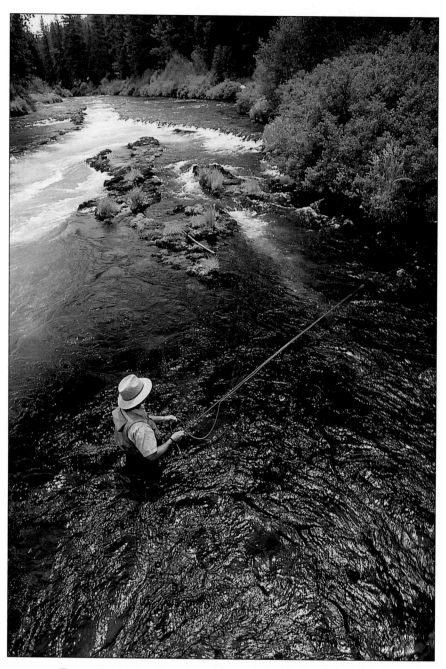

The scenic Metolius River can often be a real challenge for fly anglers, but offers substantial rewards. Photo by Brian O'Keefe

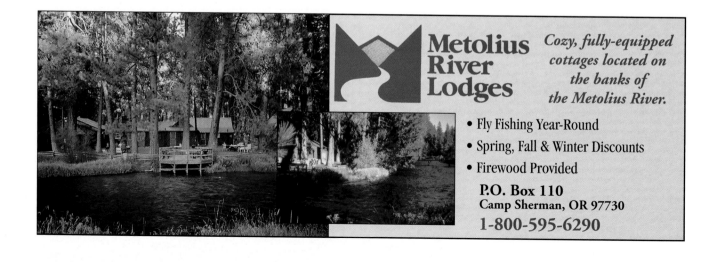

CROOKED RIVER

Size:	main stem over 100 miles in length
Depth:	levels fluctuate
Main Catch:	Inland redband trout; whitefish
Best Methods:	fly fishing; spinners; bait-plunking & drifting (check bait limitations)
Season:	entire year; check OSFR
Best Time:	when water temp. 40°F
Tips:	fishing best between mileposts (MP) 12 & 19 on State Hwy 27

The Crooked River experience is one of rugged, dramatic canyons, enthusiastic fish, Wild and Scenic tracts, bald eagles and king-fishers, and cool, spring-fed headwaters. The river maintains a wild feeling, even in the most popular sections. Well-known locally for dependable fishing and routine rattlesnake sightings, this comparatively small river pro-duces and supports excellent populations of trout and whitefish. In 1984, the Crooked River yielded the runner-up state record inland redband trout of 4 pounds, 9 ounces.

The main stem, formed by the South Fork and North Fork, flows over 100 miles north-west to Lake Billy Chinook and is a major tributary to the Deschutes River. In general, you will find a variety of deep pools, shal-low riffles, rocky shorelines, and channels full of boulders and cobbles throughout the length of the Crooked River. A few meadow portions are the only exceptions. Water lev-els fluctuate with spring runoff and the irri-gation season.

The North Fork of the Crooked River originates in the Ochoco Mountains 75 miles east of Prineville. Angling is fair for wild rainbow trout. The South Fork of the Crooked River begins about 60 miles east of Bend. It has been stocked annually since 1981 with Deschutes redsides and also con-tains a few smallmouth bass and brown bull-heads. The South Fork is open only to angling with artificial flies and lures and has a 2 trout per day catch limit for trout, open to angling the Saturday of Memorial Day weekend through October 31. Check the reg-ulations for details. The North and South Fork meet along the Post-Paulina Highway about 25 miles east of Prineville. From this point downstream to Prineville Reservoir, the river is severely affected by overgrazing and irrigation withdrawals and support only skimpy numbers of smallmouth bass and brown bullheads. Access is limited, as the

TOP: The silt-colored water does not affect the fishing, however, the spectacular scenery can be a distraction to anglers.
Photo by Geoff Hill

BOTTOM: This angler enjoys a pleasant winter day fishing on the Crooked River.
Photo by Brian O'Keefe

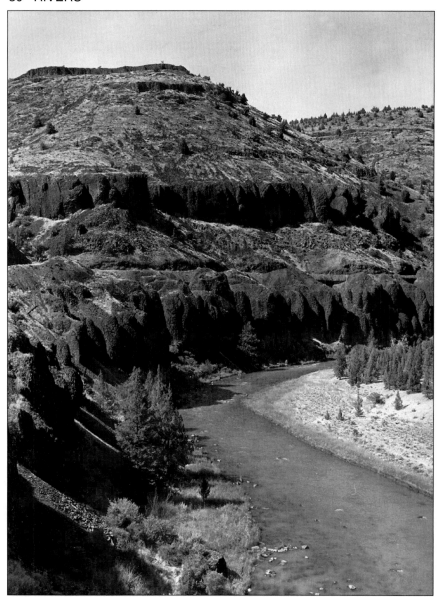

river is almost entirely bordered by private land.

Without a doubt, the best fishing on the river is in the 8 miles below Bowman Dam and Prineville Reservoir. Here, the Crooked River is a rich, thriving, tailrace fishery and a designated Wild and Scenic River. Don't be discouraged by the off-color water caused by fine sediment from the reservoir; it doesn't slow the fishing down. Rainbow trout are the dominant species here, combined with whitefish and occasional bass and bullhead fugitives from the reservoir. All are wild fish except for escapees through the dam. The average trout caught is 8 to 11 inches, with many from 12 to 14 inches and a few up to 19 inches. There is a nice variety of riffles, runs, pocket water, and deep pools in this stretch. The grassy, rocky shoreline generally supplies sufficient casting room. Wading is tough, slippery, with many sneaky "tripper" rocks. Weed beds and algae can frustrate the angler at times.

Paved State Highway 27 parallels the river for the 19 miles from Prineville south to

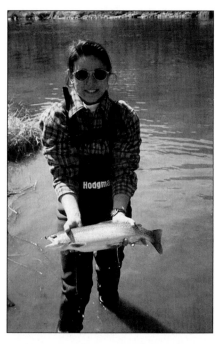

ABOVE: Oregon's aptly named Crooked River slices through a narrow canyon. This stretch of the scenic stream is just below the Prineville Reservoir.
Oregon Dept. of Transportation photo.

RIGHT: Rainbow trout are the dominant species here. All are wild except a few escapees from Prineville Reservoir.
Photo courtesy Sunriver Fly Shop

Bowman Dam. The area from Milepost 12 to the dam above Milepost 19 is the most popular fishing stretch on the Crooked River, and it is all BLM land. Water levels are lowest in the winter while Prineville Reservoir is filled and highest from mid-April to mid-October during the irrigation season. Another chunk of public land lies around MP 8.

Open year-round, the river has sections that may be frozen in winter. From the Saturday of Memorial Day weekend through October 31, the catch limit is 2 trout per day with a 8-inch minimum length and no more than 1 over 20 inches. Bait may be used during this period. During the rest of the year, the river is open only to fishing for trout with artificial flies and lures; no bait is allowed during this time. Angling is closed for 150 feet downstream from Bowman Dam.

Angling is usually excellent whenever water temperatures are above 40°F. Still-fishing and drifting bait through slower sections of the river are the most popular methods during the regular season, but fly fishing is coming up fast and is virtually the only method used during the catch-and-release season. Bait anglers commonly use Power Bait, cheese, or single eggs on size 14 hooks. Bait is most successful during turbid, high water. Spinners can be particularly productive in late summer, casting into deep pools. Fly fishers have good luck with scud imitations, bead-head nymphs, and attractor dry flies through most of the year. Midge hatches occur all winter, and there are some excellent caddis and mayfly hatches during the warmer months.

The stretch of river from Prineville west to U.S. Highway 97 is entirely private land. From Highway 97 to Lake Billy Chinook, there are plentiful public grasslands and BLM land, but the river lies at the bottom of a very deep, steep canyon. Access is limited by this terrain and a lack of roads. The water holds mainly rainbow and an abundance of whitefish in the same size range as in the river below Bowman Dam. Around Smith Rock State Park, there are a lot of rough fish

but a little farther downstream, springs kick in to cool the water and support a good trout population again. Below Opal Springs, the river begins to pick up species from Lake Billy Chinook.

Most campsites along the Crooked River are primitive, except for the profusion of BLM campgrounds below Bowman Dam. Only one of these has drinking water. All have outhouses and garbage cans, and all charge a fee to camp.

The Crooked River is most easily reached from Highway 27 south of Prineville and along the Post-Paulina Highway east of Prineville. With maps, time for exploration, and 4-wheel drive, you can find your way to the North and South Forks and to the canyon section between Highway 97 and Lake Billy Chinook through the Crooked River Ranch development north of Terrebonne. To reach Prineville see directions to Prineville Reservoir (page 55).

The Crooked River is a great place for a family fishing trip.
Photo courtesy of Fly and Field Outfitters

FALL RIVER

Size:	8 miles long; 25'–50' wide
Depth:	water levels fluctuate
Main Catch:	rainbow, brook, & brown trout; whitefish
Best Methods:	fly fishing only with barbless hooks
Season:	entire year above falls; check OSFR
Best Time:	evenings; June, July, August
Tips:	access easiest in the 2 miles above and below hatchery

Fall River is a crystal clear spring-creek — its banks lined by meadows and lodge-pole pine, and its water punctuated by a wonderful waterfall. The river is open to fly fishing with barbless hooks. Fall River is an outstanding contributor of brown trout to the Deschutes River and provides excellent winter habitat for numerous species. Its pristine water supports a productive hatchery and contributes invaluable water quality to the Deschutes system. Legal size rainbow trout are stocked several times a year and merge with the naturally reproducing brook, brown, and rainbow trout. Native whitefish inhabit the river below the falls.

Fall River is located in the Deschutes National Forest close to Bend and is a very popular fly fishing stream. Emerging full-size from rushing springs, it flows east 8 miles through rolling pine forest and empties into the Deschutes River between Sunriver and LaPine. The water is very clear and cold year-round, with steady flows and temperatures. The river has a variety of depth and structure and averages 25 to 50 feet across. Some willows line the banks. The streambed is mainly of fine pumice, easy to wade, but it can be very soft in

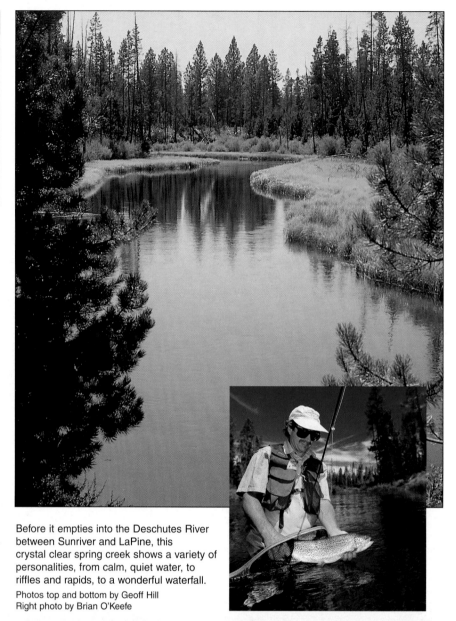

Before it empties into the Deschutes River between Sunriver and LaPine, this crystal clear spring creek shows a variety of personalities, from calm, quiet water, to riffles and rapids, to a wonderful waterfall.

Photos top and bottom by Geoff Hill
Right photo by Brian O'Keefe

places. Many downed logs in the river provide cover for the trout, and weedbeds provide insect habitat. Half of Fall River's 8 miles are bordered by private property and the remainder by National Forest land. Most of the private land is along the lower 4 miles of the stream. Watch carefully for "No Trespassing" signs and be prepared for ravenous mosquitoes.

Wild brook trout in Fall River average less than 8 inches in length. Brown trout to 8 pounds have been pulled out of Fall River, although the average catch will run up to 10 inches, and anglers will probably catch many in the 6- to 8-inch range. Rainbow trout average 8 to 12 inches, with an occasional hold-over to 20 inches. Rainbows over 20 inches are defined as steelhead in streams and must be released. Whitefish are typically 6 to 12 inches.

Evening is usually the best time to fish, and June, July, and August are the most popular months. Catch limits are 2 trout per day with an 8-inch minimum length and no more than one over 20 inches. As of 1997, Fall River, above the falls, is open to angling year-round. Downstream from the falls, the river is only open from the Saturday of Memorial Day weekend to September 30. There is no limit on size or number of brook trout or whitefish. Always check the current OSFR before fishing.

Successful dry-fly patterns for Fall River include Adams, Renegade, Comparadun, and Elk Hair Caddis. For wets, Pheasant Tail, Hare's Ear, Sparkle Pupa, Zug Bugs, and soft hackles are most effective. Long, light leaders are required to catch fish here. The most popular and most easily accessible fishing area on the river is the stretch 2 miles above and 2 miles below the hatchery. Access is easy at Fall River Hatchery and from Forest Route 42 upstream from the hatchery. Catching is tough farther upstream around the campground. There are some good areas below the falls but also an abundance of private property. Be sure to fish undercut banks thoroughly wherever they occur.

Fall River Campground, a Forest Service campground, is the only campground on Fall River. Many others are located nearby along the Deschutes River. Fall River Campground has a picnic area, outhouses, no drinking water, and a fee to camp. Other recreation options in the area include hiking, visiting the hatchery, picnicking, hunting, bird watching, and wildlife viewing.

To find Fall River take the Fall River turn from U.S. Highway 97 18 miles south of Bend and about 14 miles north of LaPine, then follow signs to South Century Drive and County/Forest Route 42. One can turn onto Forest Route 4360 about 3 miles west of the Deschutes River to access Fall River near the falls. Route 42 first parallels the river at Fall River Fish Hatchery about 8 miles west of Highway 97. From the Eugene area via Willamette Pass, follow directions to North Twin Lake (page 86), but instead of turning into the Twin Lakes continue on Route 42 another 10 miles to Fall River Campground.

LEFT: Fall River holds some beauties!

BELOW: Approach and presentation are important when fishing such clear water.
Photos by Brian O'Keefe

FALL RIVER

POINT OF INTEREST

CAMPGROUND

UNPAVED ROAD

LITTLE DESCHUTES RIVER

Size:	approx. 100 miles long
Depth:	water levels fluctuate
Main Catch:	rainbow, brook, & brown trout; whitefish
Best Methods:	shore fishing; floating
Season:	check OSFR
Best Time:	early and late in day; early in season
Tips:	access limited by private land; best fishing from headwaters to Crescent

The Little Deschutes River begins north of Miller Lake in the Mount Thielsen Wilderness and flows nearly 100 miles northeast to merge with the big Deschutes River, 15 miles south of Bend. The Little Deschutes is greatly impacted by irrigation withdrawals from Crescent Creek downstream. The best fishing can be found from the headwaters to the town of Crescent. The Forest Service portion is in the best condition, supporting wild rainbow and brook trout, whitefish, and, below Highway 58, brown trout. Ninety percent of the river is bordered by private land.

Brown trout to 18 inches can be found in the lower river with the average catch 8 to 10 inches in length. Rainbow trout, scattered throughout the length of the river in small numbers, run a maximum of 10 to 12 inches in length. Brookies up to 10 inches are found mainly near the headwaters. Crayfish and whitefish are also present.

Fishing season on the Little Deschutes is open from the Saturday of Memorial Day weekend through October 31. Fishing is by all methods including bait. The catch limit is 2 trout, 8-inch minimum and only one over 20 inches. Rainbow over 20 inches are considered steelhead in streams and must be released. There is no limit on size or number of brook trout or whitefish.

Fishing early in the season and early and late in the day is the best time for catching the brown trout in this river. Small lures can be very productive. Use a careful approach to the browns under banks; the vibrations of your footsteps can spook them. Flies work well for rainbow and brookies in the headwaters and are excellent in the evening for browns farther downstream.

The Little Deschutes is a small, slow, meandering stream with a lot of undercut banks. The headwaters are the most wadable. The lower river has a soft bottom, beaver channels, side meander channels, and some very deep pools. Water levels fluctuate with the irrigation season from Crescent Creek, downstream. The water is tannic stained. Marshy areas border much of the river, and many areas are affected by bank erosion caused by overgrazing, but there are also some healthy, thickly vegetated riparian areas. Mosquitoes can be horrendous. The river is paralleled by roads for most of its length and is flanked mainly by private land. Many homes are situated along the river. Anglers should ask permission to fish from private property. The upper river above the town of Crescent has the least private land. Much of this stretch of the river has good road access north and south of Highway 58. Floating the river is legal, even through private land, and would be the easiest way to fish the river. Unfortunately, put-in and take-out points are restrictively far apart.

The Forest Service's Rosland Campground, a small campground and picnic area with no drinking water and a fee, is the only official campground on the Little Deschutes and is situated about 2 miles north of LaPine. In addition to fishing and camping, the area offers opportunities for bird watching, especially in the spring, a little hunting, trapping, and wildlife viewing. The slow current here is great for floating, swimming, and canoeing.

The upper section of the Little Deschutes River is crossed by State Highway 58, 15 miles southeast of Crescent Lake. Forest roads follow the stream toward its headwaters, and many roads off of Highway 58 and 97 parallel the river downstream to its junction with the Deschutes. Heading south from Bend on U.S. Highway 97 the first public access to the river will be 30 miles south at Rosland Campground, 2 miles west of highway 97 on Route 43. From the south and from Willamette Pass the river can be reached where Highway 58 crosses it, 15 miles southeast of Crescent Lake and 5 miles west of the junction of Highway 58 and Highway 97.

RIGHT: The Little Deschutes meanders and winds through Central Oregon.
Photo by Jim Horyza

BELOW: The river has a lot of undercut banks and a soft bottom. Photo by Geoff Hill

CREEKS

Central Oregon Creeks

Central Oregon has a shortage of healthy, productive creeks. Most small streams here suffer severely from irrigation withdrawals and overgrazing and contain only small fish, at best. Increasing numbers of creeks are closed permanently to protect vital spawning and rearing areas. All are managed for wild fish. Habitat work continues on several important creeks, and efforts to provide better flows are on the rise. Check with ODFW and local fishing tackle outlets for more information about the water you are interested in fishing.

Most creeks are open during the regular angling season, from the Saturday of Memorial Day weekend through October 31, and have a trout catch limit of 2 per day, 8-inch minimum length, with no more than one over 20 inches. Rainbow over 20 inches in streams are considered steelhead and must be released. Many have special regulations, including decreased catch limits and special closures. Be sure to check the current Oregon Sport Fishing Regulations before fishing, since the regulations are continually changing.

BEST BETS:

Tumalo Creek – An excellent stream of great value to Central Oregon fisheries, it has good populations of wild brookies, rainbow and a few brown trout. Thirty miles of abundant, small hungry trout provide excellent fly fishing. Most of the stream is accessible, with road access possible in the burn area, 10 miles west of Bend, and from Shevlin Park, northwest of Bend. Lunkers are 10 inches in length. Tumalo Creek is now open the entire year and is restricted to artificial flies and lures only. Continuing habitat work on the stream insures excellent water quality and fish producing capabilities. Tumalo Creek currently has a reduced catch limit of 2 trout per day, 8-inch minimum. There is no limit on brook trout or whitefish.

Big Marsh Creek – A very stable stream fed by both springs and snow melt, it holds brown trout, whitefish, and small populations of rainbow and brook trout. Located 8 miles south of Crescent Lake, the creek features difficult access through marshy, brushy, and lodgepole-lined banks. Big Marsh is also a recipient of rehabilitation efforts.

Crescent Creek – This outlet of Crescent Lake is also the major tributary to the Little Deschutes River. It is a nice fly fishing stream with good access. It once had a good population of big, wild brown and rainbow trout; fish numbers are currently very low. Irrigation withdrawals leave merely a dribble of water in the creek in the fall. Brown trout are found mainly in the lower stretches of the creek and the rainbow in faster water. Whitefish also populate the creek. Access is available from State Highway 58. Watch for private land. The best fishing for rainbow trout is in the riffles and pools of the canyon section east of State Highway 58. Heavy brush lines the stream from Crescent Creek Campground downstream.

LIMITED POTENTIAL:

Tributaries to Wickiup Reservoir – Browns Creek and Davis Creek. Browns Creek is now closed to angling.

Crane Prairie Tributaries – Cultus Creek, Deer Creek, Cultus River, Quinn River, and Snow Creek. Check OSFR.

Metolius Tributaries – Lake Creek and Spring Creek open to angling. All others are closed to angling. Check OSFR.

Crooked River system – Ochoco Creek, Mill Creek, Deep Creek, Marks Creek.

Odell Creek, outlet of Odell Lake has special regulations. Open June 1–Oct. 31.

Paulina Creek, tributary to Little Deschutes River.

Squaw Creek, Deschutes River tributary.

Three Creek, outlet of Three Creek Lake.

John Day, Klamath, and Malheur Basin Creeks

Quite literally there are more creeks than you can shake a stick at in the John Day, Klamath and Malheur basins. The John Day basin alone probably has 50 fishable creeks. The challenge, as always, is access. Many creeks flow through checkerboards of public and private property. Check with BLM, Forest Service and Fish & Wildlife for detailed maps and specific information. Respect private property boundaries. If in doubt, ask the nearest landowner for permission. Asking permission has become a lost art. It so impresses landowners they may invite you on to some amazing private fisheries. And that's what creek fishing is all about; exploring new areas, catching lots of uneducated fish, and rediscovering oneself amidst the beauty that is unique to small streams. For pure harvest and great eating, help ODFW eradicate brook trout by keeping all you want. Limits on brook trout have been rescinded in most streams to eliminate competition with native species. Make sure you know the difference between brook and bull trout, which must be released. What follows are descriptions of a few of the creeks that intrigued us while expanding Fishing Central Oregon into the John Day, Klamath, and Malheur basins.

Spring Creek (Klamath County) – This gorgeous spring-fed creek flowing past the Collier Rest Area on Highway 97, located 5 miles north of Chiloquin is a very productive fishing hole. Sixteen-thousand legal size rainbow trout are planted annually. They respond readily to drifted worms and salmon eggs; flies and lures are also good. Large native trout are present in the fall. Good trails run along both sides of the creek from the headwaters 2 miles downstream to the confluence with the Williamson. Regulations change in the Williamson so watch for the deadline between the creek and the river. Season is late May until Oct. 31. Limit is 5 trout, 1 over 20 inches. Collier State Park Campground and historic logging museum are next door.

Fourmile Creek (Klamath County) This creek is a very good trout stream flowing into Agency Lake offering a variety of trout, terrain and water types. Paved 3334 road and trail 3703 follow the creek from its source in the Sky Lakes Wilderness, offering good access to brook trout in the upper mountainous reaches. Below Nicholson Road, catch-and-release, flies and lure only regulations protect trophy size rainbow and brown trout in a meandering meadow stream environment. The creek is west of Fort Klamath on Nicholson Road and is open the entire year, one trout per day, no limit on brook trout.

Kiger Creek (Harney County) This offers an opportunity to explore the stunning Kiger Gorge on Steens Mountain, and catch native redside rainbows while doing it. Access is by hiking down from Steens Mountain Loop Rd. or up from Diamond Grain Camp Rd. Good lure and fly fishing are available as is rugged, remote but beautiful desert country for those who like to get away from it all. Similar opportunities await in most Steens Mountain canyons. Season is late May-Oct. 31. Standard regulations apply.

Bridge Creek (Wheeler County) This creek offers spotty fishing but tremendous scenic variety from the north slope of the Ochocos to the impressive Painted Hills near Mitchell to its confluence with the John Day River. Intensive rehabilitation efforts are starting to take effect and fishing should improve. Best angling is after spring run-off in May and June. Standard regulations apply.

Canyon Creek (Grant County) Here, a productive, accessible rainbow trout stream flowing from the Strawberry Mountains into the John Day River at the city of John Day is available. Highway 395, forest roads 15 and 1520 provide access its entire 27-mile length. Wild trout are available above Canyon Meadows Reservoir; mostly planted fish below. Open to all methods with bait most effective until flows drop. Season is late May-Oct. 31. Five trout limit, 1 over 20 inches.

CRANE PRAIRIE RESERVOIR

Size:	over 5 sq. miles
Depth:	11' avg.; deep channels; water levels fluctuate
Main Catch:	native & stocked rainbow; brook trout; kokanee; largemouth bass
Best Methods:	still-fishing with bait; fly fishing; casting lures
Season:	general trout; 4th Sat. in April to Oct. 31; check OSFR
Best Time:	variable depending on weather & water levels
Tips:	best access with boat

For many years Crane Prairie Reservoir has been one of the top producing fisheries in Central Oregon. A variety of fishing techniques are useful here as are a variety of fish; however, most anglers come for the big rainbow trout.

In 1928 the upper Deschutes River was dammed below a meadow named Crane Prairie, forming a reservoir which currently covers over 5 square miles. Trees, previously bordering the channels of the Deschutes, Cultus, and Quinn rivers, were left standing as the reservoir filled and now occupy about 10% of the water's surface as silvered snags. The abundance of deadwood and comparatively shallow water has created an extreme-ly rich environment for insects and plentiful cover for the resident rainbow, brook trout, and largemouth bass, creating an outstanding and unique fishery. One of the largest species of this bird sanctuary, the sandhill crane, for which the area was named, continue to nest here.

Both rainbow trout and kokanee are stocked in Crane Prairie Reservoir every spring. Rainbow trout here can grow up to 2 inches a month during the summer. The largest rainbows extracted from the reservoir push 19 pounds, with most ranging between 14 and 18 inches, and substantial numbers in the 4- to 10-pound range. In addition to trophy rainbow trout, Crane Prairie also has a

LEFT: A lucky angler poses with a Crane Prairie rainbow before releasing it.

BELOW: The calm water and reflected sunlight on this day provide a serene setting at Crane Prairie for this float tuber. Photos by Brian O'Keefe self-sustaining brook trout population, with fish up to 7 pounds and the typical fish, 10 to 14 inches in length.

Sometime around 1980, largemouth bass were illegally introduced to the reservoir. These fish are flourishing and provide exciting fishing for big bass up to 8 pounds. Population surveys have produced bass that would set new state records if ever landed by an angler. Large numbers of smaller bass are also available. Crane Prairie is still primarily managed for trout, but game wardens will check for limits of bass as well as trout. Catch-and-release is now practiced by many anglers, making the game wardens job a little easier.

The ODFW will be phasing out planting of hatchery fish, putting emphasis on all wild trout. Plans are to take eggs from wild spawning fish in the Deschutes River, incubate them in a hatchery, and release them as fingerlings.

Besides the bass, bluegill and crappie were illegally introduced in 1996 and pose an even greater threat to the trout fishery. Fishermen are encouraged to keep all bluegill and crappie caught.

The shoreline of Crane is lined with snags, floating logs, and willows. Wading is nearly impossible on the mucky bottom. Some rocky areas occur where the reservoir can be fished from the bank, mainly along the eastern shore, but overall a boat is neces-

ABOVE: Fishermen and women of all ages have luck here. Photo courtesy of John Garrison.

RIGHT: The scenery is spectacular as well at Crane Prairie. Another Crane Prairie beauty is admired, then released back into the water. Photos by Brian O'Keefe

BELOW: Publisher Geoff Hill got into the action with this nice 20-inch rainbow. Photo by Vicki Hill.

CRANE PRAIRIE RESORT

BOAT RENTALS
Moorage ~ Gas & Oil
Tackle Shop ~ Groceries
Laundry ~ Showers

Full Service RV Park
Large Forest Service Campground

Home of
MICKEY FINN
GUIDES

Oldest Existing & ONLY Resident Guide Service on Crane Prairie Reservoir
For the Serious Fishermen or Family Affairs
We Love to Fish Kids 8 to 80

FLY, SPIN OR BAIT FISHING
Boats to 22' with Padded Arm Chairs

P.O. Box 1171 • Bend, OR 97709 • (541) 383-3939

sary to access the best fishing areas. Weed beds and submerged logs outside of the main channels can complicate boating. A 10 mph speed limit helps reduce casualties. There are many interesting little bays to explore, a few accessible by car.

Since Crane Prairie is an irrigation reservoir, water levels fluctuate, but the change is very gradual over the entire summer. During extreme low water years, some boat ramps may be unusable. The main body of the reservoir averages 11 feet deep at full pool with the river channels, the deepest areas of the reservoir, ranging from 12 to 20 feet in depth.

All fishing methods are used on Crane, but still-fishing with bait and fly fishing are the most popular. For trout, still-fishers most often use Power Bait, or worms and a marshmallow on the bottom, or a worm or dragonfly nymph under a bobber. Some folks troll gold Thomas lures, Rapalas, and flies successfully. It is not necessary to troll very deep. Lures are preferred for bass fishing, and jigging, trolling, and casting are all successful techniques. Flies can be trolled or cast to rising trout with excellent results. The best fly patterns imitate damsel and dragonfly nymphs, mayfly nymphs, scuds, leeches, and midges. If you are planning on fly fishing for trout, be ready with mayfly dries in sizes 12 to 18, Woolly Buggers, and long leaders up to 25 feet in length. When catching and releasing trout, use barbless hooks and make sure you land them quickly and release them as soon as they are fully recovered. Overexertion in the warm waters of the reservoir at Crane Prairie can kill the trophy trout you release.

Fishing strategies at Crane are dependent on water level and temperature. In the early season, the trout tend to be scattered throughout the main body of the lake due to high water levels, with the brook trout favoring the western shoreline where the stream inlets cool the water. Using masses of boats as fish locators works well this time of year. Be sure also to search the edges of the reservoir back in the snags. Later in the year, as

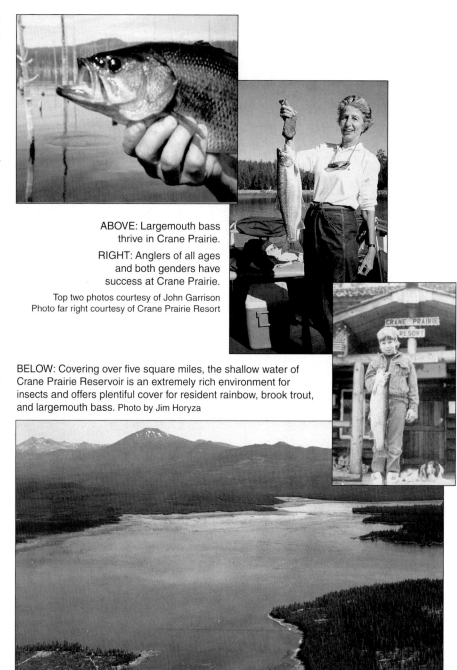

ABOVE: Largemouth bass thrive in Crane Prairie.
RIGHT: Anglers of all ages and both genders have success at Crane Prairie.

Top two photos courtesy of John Garrison
Photo far right courtesy of Crane Prairie Resort

BELOW: Covering over five square miles, the shallow water of Crane Prairie Reservoir is an extremely rich environment for insects and offers plentiful cover for resident rainbow, brook trout, and largemouth bass. Photo by Jim Horyza water levels drop and temperatures rise, the trout will migrate to the deeper and cooler channels and spring-fed bays. The bass will be in shallower, warmer coves early in the season, primarily along the rugged eastern shoreline among the snags. They will disperse to the body of the lake as temperatures rise. When water temperatures reach 65 °F, bass will stay close to cover near their spawning areas in the coves. Often trout and

bass will occupy the same water at Crane Prairie. In the fall look for the bass along the east shore from Big Rock to the dam. At this time of year try crankbait, nightcrawlers, and grubs. Fly fishers, use streamers and nymphs in the fall. In terms of numbers and size of fish, the past few years have been consistently good at Crane.

The reservoir is open to fishing during the general fishing season, with a limit of 5 trout

per day, 8-inch minimum length, no more than one over 20 inches. The limit for bass is 5 per day, no more than three over 15 inches. The reservoir is closed to fishing for all species from one hour after sunset to one hour before sunrise. Always check the current OSFR before fishing. There is a 10 mph speed limit on the lake.

Many campsites are scattered around Crane with facilities ranging from complete-

Crane Prairie Reservoir

Elevation 4,445'

CAMPGROUND

BOAT RAMP

RESORT

POINT OF INTEREST

UNPAVED ROAD

DEAD TREE SNAGS
FALLEN LOG JAMS

ABOVE: Mt. Bachelor still lies under a coat of snow as these early spring anglers try their luck.

CENTER: Crane Prairie Reservoir relinquished another large and beautiful rainbow.

RIGHT: Nesting osprey are a common sight at Crane Prairie. They plunge straight down with an impressive splash and fly away with their catch. An osprey observation point is located on the west bank of the reservoir.

Photos by Brian O'Keefe

ly primitive, to full hookups. The large, paved, Crane Prairie Campground and Crane Prairie Resort (full hookups) are located on the northeast shore of the lake. These have the best boat ramps. Crane Prairie Resort has guide services, rental boats, a store, and RVer's necessities. The resort opens and closes with fishing season.

Additional Forest Service campgrounds on the reservoir are Rock Creek Campground, which has improved toilet and boat ramp facilities, and Quinn River Campground on the west bank (hand pumps for drinking water, camping fees, and concrete boat ramps) and Cow Meadow Campground (no drinking water, ramp suitable for very small boats, camping fee) on the far north shore. Browns Mountain by Crane Prairie Dam in the southeast corner has a small concrete boat launch.

Crane Prairie Reservoir is a picturesque body of water with views of Cascade peaks and common sightings of osprey, bald eagles, sandhill cranes, and a wide variety of waterfowl. Bird watching is a popular activity, especially at Osprey Observation Point on the west bank of the reservoir. A trail out to the water's edge begins at the parking area. Summer months are best for viewing nests and feeding of the young osprey.

Fishing and camping are by far the main reasons to visit Crane Prairie Reservoir. Several fishing tournaments are presented each year by local clubs.

From the Eugene area Crane Prairie Reservoir is reached by taking State Highway 58 east over Willamette pass. About 3 miles past Crescent Lake Junction and .5 mile past milepost 72, turn left onto County Route 61. In another three miles turn left onto Forest Road 46 toward Davis Lake. About 18 miles north, at the junction with Route 42 from the east, you may continue north about 3 miles to Rock Creek Campground and the west shore of Crane or turn right on 42 to access the south shore at Crane Prairie Dam/Brown's Mountain, and the east shore along Road 4270 that leads to the resort.

From Bend the most scenic route is to take Century Drive/Forest Route 46 up and past Mount Bachelor. The shortest route from Bend is to drive south on Highway 97 for 15 miles and turn west at the Sunriver exit onto County Route 40/Forest Route 40. Continue about 22 miles to the junction of Forest Route 4270, turning left and following signs to Crane Prairie Resort. The resort and campground are about 3 miles south of the junction.

From the south, use Forest Road 43 from Wickiup Junction to the junction with Route 42. Continue on 42 to the junction with Road 4270. Bear right and follow signs to the campground and resort.

RIGHT: On a calm day, fly fishing from a boat is a good way to fish the reservoir.
Photo by Brian O'Keefe

BELOW: To enjoy this view of Crane Prairie, one must hike to the top of Cultus Mountain.
Photo by Geoff Hill

WICKIUP RESERVOIR

Size:	10,000 acres
Depth:	extreme water flucuations; deep channels
Main Catch:	brown, rainbow, brook trout; kokanee; whitefish; chub
Best Methods:	shore fishing; trolling
Season:	general trout; 4th Sat. in April to Oct. 31; check OSFR
Best Time:	just after ice-out for browns; through July for salmon
Tips:	best access with boat

The very rich, highly productive, relatively warm water and cooler deep channels of Wickiup Reservoir generate some of the finest fishing in Central Oregon. Wickiup is renowned for its brown trout over 20 pounds and normal catches in the 5- to 8-pound range. Many large brown trout are brought into Twin Lakes Resort to be weighed and photographed, but most people never see the largest fish they hook. Long distance releases are routine. Wickiup also has a reputation for good numbers of kokanee and decent populations of rainbow trout, brook trout, whitefish, and the unwanted chub. Large numbers of fishermen and women are entertained here each year. At full pool, Wickiup Reservoir covers 10,000 acres and is the largest of all the Cascade lakes. Located along the Deschutes River, it is the second irrigation reservoir on the Deschutes, about six miles downriver from Crane Prairie Reservoir.

The largest trout each year are usually caught the first two weeks of fishing season when the big browns are ravenous after a long winter under the ice. There are some true giants in here; a former state record brown trout from Wickiup weighed 24 pounds, 14 ounces. A brown trout caught opening day of 1998 weighed over 26 pounds. Larry Marecek of Salem caught the monster brown using a rainbow-colored Rapala. They are mostly natural reproduction, although fingerlings are stocked every spring. Numbers are excellent. There are anglers here whose lives are dedicated solely to fishing for the brown trout at Wickiup. One should try using lures or plugs that imitate fleeing baitfish to entice these predatory browns.

Very early in the season the trick to hooking the big guys is to fish fast, using floating Rapalas so that they run 2 to 3 feet deep. The best areas early are in the flats from Round Swamp to the dam and near Reservoir Campground and the Davis Arm. Later on in July, the fish move into the deep channels, and it is important to get tackle down near the bottom. Flies can produce excellent results; use streamers, Muddler Minnows, sculpins, or anything that imitates a tasty chub or salmonid fingerling. Leeches and Woolly Buggers will produce smaller browns. Use sinking lines along the points, ledges, and shallower areas at low light. Shore fishing is popular and can be very productive early in the season along the base of the dam, in the Round Swamp area, and along the edges and ledges of the channels. Gold or bronze minnow imitations and crayfish imitations can be effective from shore.

Fishing for kokanee is the most popular pastime on Wickiup next to pursuit of lunker browns. Fishing for these salmon with spinners or bait is especially good through late

LEFT: This beautiful brown trout was caught in Wickiup Reservoir by John Bratton.
Photo courtesy of John Bratton

BELOW: Photographed looking south, this aerial shows North and South Twin lakes adjacent to the Deschutes Arm of Wickiup.
Photo by Jennifer Emmert

WICKIUP RESERVOIR

July near the dam. Still-fishing with a "Wickiup Sandwich" of a piece of worm, a section of crayfish, one red salmon egg, and a single piece of white corn is a popular plan of attack. Other bait variations including red eggs work well too, fished a few feet off the bottom. Kokanee are schooling fish. Look for them in the channels and in the cooler water near Gull Point later in the year when trolling bait behind spinners and flashers will attract them. White corn and Buzz Bombs for jigging are an essential part of your tackle this time of year. Try different depths until you locate a school. Kokanee spawn in the Deschutes River and move closer to the river late in summer. The Deschutes above Wickiup closes September 1 to protect spawning fish. Once the kokanee have

changed to their red spawning colors, they are no longer good eating. Kokanee in Wickiup are now all natural reproduction. Sizes and numbers of these small salmon fluctuate over a 3 to 4-year cycle with numbers increasing as size decreases and vice-versa. Kokanee vary from 12 to 18 inches and occasionally up to 20 inches.

Rainbow are not often fished for in Wickiup but are usually taken by kokanee and brown trout anglers. They are no longer stocked but seem to be doing just fine. An average catch will be 2 to 7 pounds but they get a lot bigger with fish up to 16 pounds. Dark Rooster Tails fished along shorelines seem to work best. Fish the channels midday and shorelines early and late in the day. Bait commonly used in the channels

includes worms, eggs, Power Bait, and crayfish. Fly fishers cast or troll nymphs near shorelines early and late in the day.

Wickiup has an abundant population of native whitefish up to 4 pounds. Monsters can be seen cruising the bottom near channel mouths. Whitefish are excellent eating and a delicacy smoked. They are good fighters and often easier to catch than the trout. They prefer the clear, cold water of the Davis Arm, where they gather before spawning. A fly fisher can have a lot of fun with a Hare's Ear. Whitefish have small mouths so use smaller bait and insect imitations.

Brook trout are not in the reservoir proper, but are concentrated toward Sheep Bridge on the Deschutes Arm. The average brookie is 10 to 14 inches, and they go up to

5 pounds. There are also largemouth bass in Wickiup that have escaped from Crane Prairie Reservoir. Bass up to 5 pounds are found around Goose Island and in the Deschutes Channel.

Wickiup experiences extreme water fluctuations due to irrigation drawdowns. Over half of the reservoir's water can disappear over the fishing season. The deepest point in the reservoir, at the intersection of the Deschutes and Davis Channels, is 60 feet maximum depth. Heavy drawdowns and very low water does not seem to have any adverse effect on the fishery. In fact, the brown trout may be even fatter after having their finny food source concentrated for them.

A boat is necessary to fish most effectively at Wickiup, although early in the season shore fishers do all right. The best boat ramp is at the west end of Gull Point Campground with another good one just east of the campground. The character of the shoreline at Wickiup is as variable as the water level. At full pool, Wickiup is a beautiful, pine-edged lake, with some willows and sandy beach

areas. At low water, steep soil and gravel banks drop abruptly to the water. Other banks become mucky hazards. Obstacles emerge at low water including many stumps and structures added in the Deschutes and

Davis arms by ODFW.

Four Forest Service campgrounds are located on the shoreline of Wickiup: Gull Point Campground at the north end has drinking water, fees, boat ramps, and fish

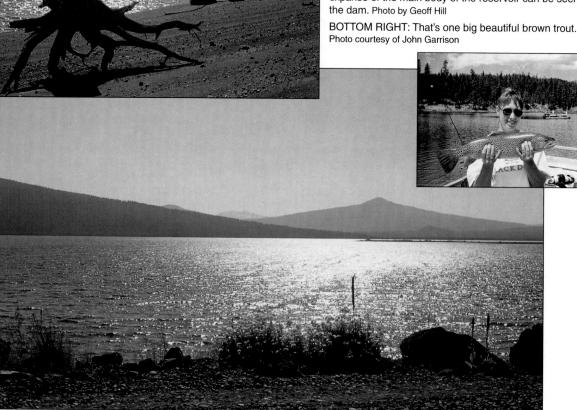

TOP: This photo of the Deschutes Arm of Wickiup was shot looking north, with South Twin Lake in the foreground and North Twin off to the right. Photo by Geoff Hill

CENTER: The character of the shoreline at Wickiup is as variable as the water level. Many stumps were left when the reservoir was filled … this one appears to be an octopus running along the beach. Photo by Don Burgderfer

BOTTOM: At full pool, Wickiup Reservoir covers 10,000 acres and is the largest of all of the Cascade lakes. The wide expanse of the main body of the reservoir can be seen from the dam. Photo by Geoff Hill

BOTTOM RIGHT: That's one big beautiful brown trout.
Photo courtesy of John Garrison

cleaning stations; Wickiup Butte Campground at the east end has a camping fee but has no drinking water; Round Swamp Campground in the southeast corner has no drinking water and no fee; and Reservoir Campground, with a boat ramp and fee and no drinking water, is located on the southwest corner. In addition, there are South Twin and West South Twin Campgrounds (water, fee), Sheep Bridge Campground (hand pump, fee, small boat ramp), and Twin Lakes Resort, with cabins and a full hook-up RV campground on the Deschutes Arm, and North Davis Creek (water, fee, concrete boat ramp) on the Davis Arm. Most campgrounds have boat ramps, but some may not be usable in extremely low water. Camping is also allowed above the high water mark on the west side of the Deschutes Arm and on the south side of the Davis Arm.

LEFT: Almost as big as she is! Photo courtesy of John Garrison

BELOW: A boat is necessary to fish most effectively at Wickiup, although early in the season shore fishers do all right. This view is of the Deschutes Arm of the reservoir. Photo by Geoff Hill

Wickiup has a bonus limit on kokanee of 25 fish with no size limits, in addition to the trout limit. The trout catch limit is 5 per day, 8-inch minimum length and no more than one over 20 inches. There is no limit on whitefish. The bass limit is 5 per day with no more than 3 over 15 inches.

Be aware of a special closure on the Deschutes Arm September 1. Watch for the deadline markers near West South Twin Campground. General fishing season opens the fourth Saturday of April and is open through October 31 each year. One should always check the current OSFR before fishing. There is no boat speed limit on the main body of the reservoir, but boats are limited to 10 mph on the arms. Boat rentals are available on the Deschutes Arm of Wickiup

at the Twin Lakes Resort.

Wickiup is a popular waterskiing and jet-skiing lake and is considered one of best areas in the county to windsurf with a sure bet for afternoon winds along the east end. These same afternoon winds, of course, rough up the water for waterskiers and anglers. Swimming, and relaxing along the beaches at the many campgrounds are favorite pastimes for non-fishing visitors.

The easiest way to get to Wickiup Reservoir is to take County Route 42 off of U.S. Highway 97 south of Bend or County Route 43 just north of LaPine which merges with 42 in about 12 miles. Six miles west of the junction of 42 and 43 turn toward Twin Lakes Resort and Wickiup Reservoir on Forest Route 4260. 4260 reaches the

Deschutes Arm of Wickiup at Gull Point Campground in about 3 miles and continues along the northern edge of the reservoir to the dam. Other Forest Service roads can be picked up south of the dam to continue along the southern shore and eventually to a junction with County/Forest Route 46.

From the Eugene area take State Highway 58 east over Willamette Pass. About 3 miles past Crescent Lake Junction turn left onto County Route 61. In another 3 miles turn left onto County/Forest Route 46 toward Davis Lake. About 13 miles north you reach the junction to the unpaved routes along the south shore of Wickiup. The junction with Route 42 is another 7 miles north. A turn to the east on 42 brings you to the turn to Wickiup Reservoir in about 5 miles.

LAKE BILLY CHINOOK

Size:	3,997 acres
Depth:	max. depth 415'
Main Catch:	bass; kokanee; rainbow & bull trout
Best Methods:	shoreline trolling for bull trout; still-fishing for other species
Season:	special regulations; check OSFR
Best Time:	April through June and fall for kokanee
Tips:	Crooked & Deschutes arms open year-round; popular recreation area

In the middle of some of the best agricultural land in Central Oregon and at the bottom of 400 feet of basalt rimrock lies Lake Billy Chinook. This is big water: 3,997 surface acres and 415 feet deep, formed by Round Butte Dam. The lake has filled the canyons of the Crooked, Metolius, and Deschutes rivers, forming the three "arms" of the reservoir. Each arm is 6 to 12 miles long, creating 72 miles of shoreline at full pool. Lake Billy Chinook holds largemouth and smallmouth bass, kokanee, and rainbow, brown and bull trout to test your angling skills year-round. Whitefish, a few land-locked chinook salmon, a very small population of bluegill and black crappie, pikeminnow, chiselmouth chubs, and two types of suckers complete the species list.

Lake Billy Chinook is best known for its trophy bull trout of over 20 pounds. The first-, second-, and third-place bull trout state records have all come out of Lake Billy Chinook in recent years. All were over 20 pounds; the largest was 23 pounds, 2 ounces. The average bull trout caught is 14 to 20 inches in length and 4 to 5 years old. At the age of 7 or 8, these fish should weigh 10 to 20 pounds; they can live to be 10 to 12 years old. The bull trout, with a federal listing as a "threatened and endangered" species, currently holds a "sensitive" status in Lake Billy Chinook. A small but stable spawning population survives in the lake. Anglers are encouraged to release all bull trout unharmed. Currently, the catch limit on the lake is 1 bull trout over 24 inches per day.

Lake Billy Chinook is also well-known for its large numbers of kokanee. The cyclical abundance of kokanee results in good years, with many fish of a smaller size, and less productive years, with fewer but larger fish. Currently, kokanee average 12 to 14 inches and range up to 16 inches and 1 pound. The kokanee are all naturally reproducing fish.

Smallmouth bass grow slowly in the cool waters of Lake Billy Chinook. Most fish are about 10 inches in length and weigh around

Looking downriver at the Crooked River Arm of Lake Billy Chinook. File by George W. Linn

LAKE BILLY CHINOOK
Elevation 1,945'

WARM SPRINGS INDIAN RESERVATION

METOLIUS RIVER

⑩

Monty

Perry South

Chinook Island

Three Rivers Marina

Three Rivers Recreation Area (Private)

Gatekeeper

Round Butte Dam

Round Butte

COVE PALISADES STATE PARK

Cove Palisades Restaurant & Marina

To Culver

CROOKED RIVER

DESCHUTES RIVER   ⑩

⑩

△ DAY USE AREA

▲ CAMPGROUND

◣ BOAT RAMP

■ RESORT

● POINT OF INTEREST/VIEWPOINT

🐟 BANK FISHING

⑩ 10 MPH ZONE

⎯⎯ PAVED ROAD

- - - UNIMPROVED ROAD

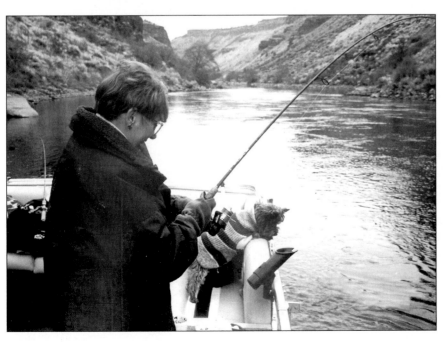

Glen Baker of Bend with his 30" bull trout.
Photo courtesy of Glen Baker

one pound, with a few in the 2- to 4-pound range. The Crooked Arm tends to have a lot of little smallmouth, with the biggest, but fewer, in the Metolius Arm. Largemouth bass are present but not in great numbers and prefer weedy, brushy habitat. Rainbow and brown trout reach 20 inches in the reservoir, with the average trout 12 to 13 inches. A few browns up to 10 pounds are in the lake but are few and far between. The best fishing for all of the species and for the largest of all the fish is in the Metolius Arm.

For bull trout, the most commonly used lure is a Rapala, split back or not, up to 8 inches in length. Shoreline trolling, especially around the head of Metolius, is most effective. Several different colors of Rapalas work well. The largest fish are usually deepest.

For the kokanee salmon, the most important fish-finding factor is to get the lure down to 45°F water. The river channels hold the coldest water, and the Metolius is the coolest of the three. The kokanee follow the plankton, their food source, which are usually found at depths of 60 to 100 feet as water warms. One popular area to fish for kokanee is at the confluence of the Deschutes and Metolius arms. Usually, the best fishing for kokanee, which prefer cold water, occurs in April through June, when the fish are in relatively shallow water, and again in the fall. Early in the year, use small lures, such as red wedding rings with white corn, or troll hard-

The Family pet enjoys the action at Lake Billy Chinook as well.
Photo courtesy of John Garrison

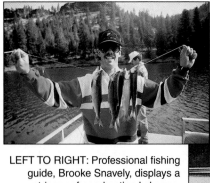

LEFT TO RIGHT: Professional fishing guide, Brooke Snavely, displays a stringer of good eating kokanee.

These anglers have located a school of kokanee on the upper end of the Metolius Arm. Brooke Snavely photos

Trolling lures produced this beautiful bull trout.
Photo courtesy of John Garrison

ware; Ford Fenders are preferred. Troll as slowly as possible in S-curves until you catch one, usually indicating that you have located a school. Once you find the school, continue to troll in that area. During the kokanee's spawning run, the last week of August and the first week of September, bait is not needed to hook these feisty little salmon. Often a Buzz Bomb or treble hook with different color weights in 15 to 20 feet of water is adequate. This method only works during the two weeks of spawning. Jigging with Buzz Bombs and white corn is the most popular method for catching kokanee late in the year. The Metolius Arm, with its cleaner, cooler swifter water, is usually the best arm for kokanee.

Smallmouth bass and rainbow and brown trout are found mostly along the shorelines in all three arms. The best trout stretches are at the heads of each of the three arms. Another good spot is at the confluence of the Deschutes and Crooked arms. About the only place to fish from shore on Lake Billy Chinook is between the two boat ramps on the Deschutes Arm and near bridges and docks. Most of the shoreline is pretty steep elsewhere on the reservoir. Still-fishing a nightcrawler under a bobber or fishing a nightcrawler or Rooster Tail with a slow retrieve is the most successful method for smallmouth bass and rainbow and brown trout. Trolling with a nightcrawler or Rooster Tail is also effective. Fly fishers need to hike up the arms and fish the rivers before they hit the reservoir or work submerged structure along shorelines in the reservoir. The best bass catching is along the shoreline, casting plugs and lures. Look for rocky points, submerged rocks and bars, and grassy shorelines as cover for smallmouth bass. Lures and flies imitating crawfish and fingerlings of any species present in the lake will usually interest the bass. Rapalas work well. Some fishermen successfully pop plugs along the cliffs, but this is not nearly as effective as the other methods.

Water levels fluctuate very little at Lake Billy Chinook and change no more than 10 to 15 feet during wintertime drawdown in the worst of the drought years. The lower elevation of this area and protection from wind make for warm, pleasant days on the lake. Waterskiing, boating, swimming, picnicking, and sightseeing are popular activities. The area has interesting geological features, the Palisades being named for distinctive columnar basalt formations. There is a petroglyph site between the Deschutes and Crooked arms. Sandy beaches, excellent campgrounds, picnic areas, and houseboats for rent add to the many recreational opportunities.

The Crooked and Deschutes arms of Lake Billy Chinook are open year-round. The Metolius Arm is administrated by Warm Springs Confederated Tribes and is open to fishing only from March 1 to October 31 each year. A tribal permit is required to fish the Metolius Arm. It is illegal to land a boat on reservation land which lies along the north shore of the Metolius Arm. The Metolius Arm is also closed to the taking of crayfish, except for tribal members.

The generous kokanee limit throughout the reservoir is 25 per day with no size limit,

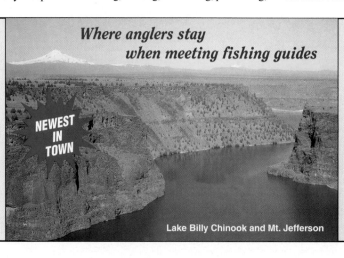

in addition to the trout limit. The trout limit is 5 per day, 8-inch minimum length, with no more than one over 20 inches, including bull trout (minimum 24"). There is a possession limit of one bull trout, and no live bull trout may be held while angling. If you catch a bull trout with a tag, leave the tag in the fish if you are releasing it but write down the information from the tag and turn it into the Oregon Department of Fish and Wildlife. If you keep the fish, the tag needs to be returned to ODFW. A special sanctuary for bull trout, managed by the CTWS, extends 350 yards downstream from the cable crossing on the Metolius Arm. Bull trout caught in the area must be released unharmed; however, kokanee may be kept. Always check the current OSFR before fishing. A speed limit of 10 mph is in effect above the bridges on each arm of the reservoir. There is also a speed limit on the waterskiing course on the Crooked River Arm.

Cove Palisades State Park begins at the top of the rimrock and extends down to Lake Billy Chinook. There are approximately 300 campsites in the state park, a trailer dump, and boat launches (one on the Crooked Arm and two on the Deschutes Arm). The state park also offers picnic areas, swimming beaches, and fish cleaning stations. Supplies and boat rentals are available at the Cove Palisades Restaurant and Marina which opens about April 15 each year and closes in mid-October. The Three Rivers Recreation Area is a day-use area and private marina on the Metolius Arm. Perry South Campground, on the upper-end of the Metolius arm, is a primitive Forest Service campground. Perry South has a boat ramp, drinking water, and a fee to camp. Monty Campground is 3 miles farther up on the

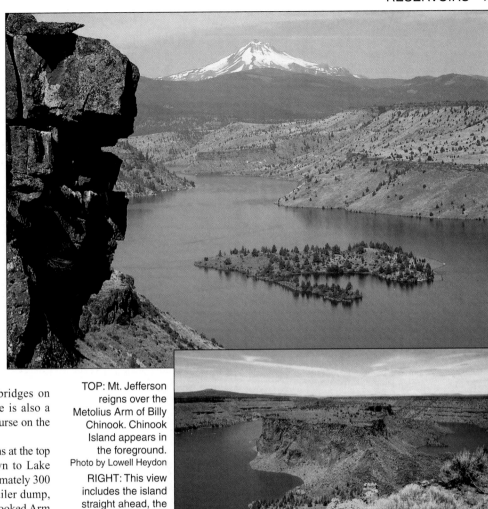

TOP: Mt. Jefferson reigns over the Metolius Arm of Billy Chinook. Chinook Island appears in the foreground.
Photo by Lowell Heydon
RIGHT: This view includes the island straight ahead, the Deschutes Arm to the left, and the Crooked Arm to the right.
Photo by Scott L. Staats

Metolius River and also offers primitive camping with drinking water and no fee.

From the Portland area, take U.S. Highway 26 to Madras. From Madras follow the Cove Palisades Tour Route from the south end of town for an enjoyable 11-mile drive to the lake.

From Bend, drive north on U.S. Highway 97 through Redmond and Terrebonne. Take the left turn to Culver, about 10 miles south of Madras, and follow the Cove State Park/Tour Route signs about 8 miles to the lake.*

From the Eugene area, take U.S. Highway 20 to Sisters, then State Route 126 to Redmond, and U.S. Highway 97 north through Terrebonne to the turn to Culver.

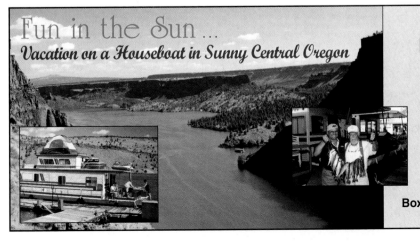

LAKE SIMTUSTUS

Size:	7 miles long
Depth:	very deep
Main Catch:	stocked kokanee and rainbow, brown trout, and stocked steelhead
Best Methods:	still-fishing & trolling from a boat
Season:	general trout; 4th Sat. in April to Oct. 31; check OSFR
Best Time:	early & late in season
Tips:	boat necessary for access; tribal permit required

Lake Simtustus is a deep, cold, and narrow body of water 7 miles long, formed by Pelton Dam on the Deschutes River, backing up to Round Butte Dam below Lake Billy Chinook. It has good fishing for kokanee, massive rainbow and brown trout, bull trout, steelhead, smallmouth bass, and pikeminnow. The reservoir was named after a Warm Springs warrior who served as an Army scout in the Paiute wars of the 1860s and lived on the Warm Springs Reservation until his death in 1926. The lake is located 7 miles west of Madras.

The main fishery here is for kokanee, but there are also some huge rainbow and remnant brown trout that mostly hang out at the upper end of the lake. The last brown trout were stocked in 1996. In 1997, annual stocking of hatchery steelhead began. Simtustus is stocked annually with kokanee and legal size rainbow trout. A few bull trout immigrants from Lake Billy Chinook, smallmouth bass, and a profusion of pikeminnow round out the menu. Fishing is usually best early and late in the season. Angling is almost entirely from boats; the steep, rocky gorge makes shore fishing possible only at the two campgrounds on the lake.

Two-pound kokanee are common at the log boom on the upper end of the lake. Trolling is the most popular technique for taking them, although some anglers jig at the boom with bait combinations. The average kokanee is in the 15- to 22-inch range

TOP: Located just north of Lake Billy Chinook, this deep, narrow reservoir passes through some beautiful high desert scenery. Photo by Jennifer Emmert.   BOTTOM: Catching this beautiful brown trout in Simtustus made young angler happy. Photo courtesy of Don Ratliff

and is included in the trout catch limit. Rainbow trout average 12 to 16 inches, but Simtustus holds the runner-up state record for rainbow trout at 24 pounds, 2.25 ounces, and there are more like it lurking in the depths. In fact, another 24-pound rainbow was caught in the summer of 1996. The 1998 season produced a 17-pound German brown and a 14-pound rainbow, plus many more over 5 pounds. The big fish are usually deep and toward the head of the reservoir, where they feed on the remains of the not-so-lucky that have gone through the turbines of Round Butte Dam. The "big lures for big fish" principle holds true on Simtustus. A #9 count-down, rainbow Rapala is a favorite for browns. Any color of Nordic works for jigging. A fish finder can be a blessing.

Bull trout are occasionally taken by trolling or still-fishing bait. As of 2001, brown trout were still present in good numbers, and angling for them can be fair in the colder and more turbid water conditions of spring. Browns from 10 to 15 pounds are not uncommon: the average being 14 to 20 inches. Pikeminnow on the dry fly can be great sport for beginning fly fishers.

The upper section of the reservoir is known as "the narrows" as the near vertical canyon walls come together. It is quite spectacular, and numerous picturesque waterfalls cascade out of seams in the shear rock.

A tribal permit is required to fish Lake Simtustus. These are reasonably priced and can be purchased at any outlet for fishing licenses in Central Oregon for the day or the entire season. Fishing season opens the last Saturday in April and is open through October 31 each year. The trout limit is 5 per day, with a 8-inch minimum length, and of these no more than 1 over 20 inches, including bull trout (minimum 24"). There is a possession limit of one bull trout, and no live bull trout may be held while angling. Kokanee are part of the trout limit. Always check the current OSFR before fishing.

A 10 mph speed limit is in effect on the upper 6.5 miles of the reservoir. Boat landing on the western shore (Warm Springs Reservation) is prohibited except at Indian Park. Boat launches are available at Pelton Park, Lake Simtustus RV Park, and Indian Park.

Other recreation on the lake includes jetskiing, waterskiing, picnicking, swimming, and lounging. There is a small wading area at Indian Park. Water fluctuations are minor, and there are fewer waterskiers than at Lake Billy Chinook and less wind. Occasional algae blooms turn the water to pea soup.

The camping experience at Indian Park on the Warm Springs Reservation includes pit toilets, a hand pump for drinking water, a fee to camp, and a long bumpy ride along the west side of the Deschutes River. You must have tribal fishing permits to camp here. Camping is also available at Pelton Park on the east side of the lake. This campground is run by Portland General Electric and has drinking water, a picnic area, modern bathrooms (some with pay showers), a boat launch and dock, boat rentals, and a fee for camping. There is also a small store nearby. In addition, a privately operated RV park and campground is situated along a cove on the east side of the reservoir. This facility has a boat launch and dock, boat rentals, showers, and a bait and tackle shop. All parks are open during the general fishing season.

To reach Lake Simtustus from Bend drive north on U.S. Highway 97 to Madras, connecting with U.S. Highway 26 toward Warm Springs at the north end of town. The turn toward Pelton Park is about 7 miles north of Madras. From the Portland area take Highway 26 to Warm Springs. The turn to Pelton Park is 3 miles south of town. From the Eugene area take U.S. Highway 20 to Sisters, then State Highway 126 to Redmond and Highway 97 north to Madras. The Pelton Park turnoff gives access to the east shore. The west shore access road to Indian Park begins on the west side of the bridge over the Deschutes River at Warm Springs. This gravel road heads back upstream and reaches the lake in 15 miles.

A boat is required to get to the best fishing areas in this 7-mile long lake. Photo by Geoff Hill

PRINEVILLE RESERVOIR

Size:	3,000 acres at full pool
Depth:	60' average; extremely variable
Main Catch:	stocked rainbow trout; bass; brown bullhead; black crappie
Best Methods:	shore fishing; trolling
Season:	entire year; check OSFR
Best Time:	bass & bullheads in early spring; trout when water levels lower mid-summer
Tips:	popular for ice fishing

Prineville Reservoir is situated 15 miles south-southeast of the town of Prine-ville in the heart of high desert juniper and sage country. This irrigation and flood-control reservoir is 15 miles long and .5 mile wide, covering about 5 square miles at full pool. The reservoir averages 60 feet in depth, and, at the dam, is over 130 feet deep. Planted rainbow trout, large- and smallmouth bass and brown bullhead are the main game here. The reservoir also has pikeminnow and crayfish to amuse the visitor. Black crappie, extremely competitive with trout, were illegally introduced to the reservoir and may affect the trout fishery in years to come.

In mid-May of each year, 170,000 rainbow trout fingerlings are stocked in Prineville Reservoir. The average size trout caught by the angler is 10 to 12 inches with the largest up to 16 inches in length. There are believed to be larger ones lurking about. Both species of bass naturally reproduce in the reservoir, and 6- to 7-pound fish are taken out every season. Brown bullheads up to 12 inches are available, and pikeminnow are always a possibility on the end of your line. Crappie are averaging 6 to 7 inches. Crayfish are abundant enough to be harvested commercially, but numbers have decreased in recent years.

Most folks on the reservoir fish for trout with some sort of cheese combination. Some swear that garlic flavored cheese is the best, and others combine it with a worm or egg. Shore fishing is easy and very productive. Trout fishing gets better as the water level lowers in the summer. Trolling catches trout, too, using flashers and worms or lone spinners. Some of the more popular areas to fish for trout are along the cliffs across from the resort and around Big and Little Island. Fly fishers troll black Woolly Worms, scud imitations, and Prineville Specials, trolled shallow with a lot of line out. As the water warms, the trout move to deeper water. In the fall, the channel above the 5 mph markers in the upper mile of the reservoir can be very good. A fish finder is a very useful item to have when cruising Prineville's 3,000 acres of water.

Prineville Reservoir has a very good bass fishery. The reservoir formerly held the state record for smallmouth bass with a 6-pound, 6-ounce entry. Largemouth reach 8 pounds, with fair numbers in the 4- to 6-pound range caught every year. Bass fishing is often best early in the spring in the upper end of the reservoir where the largemouth are spawning in the shallower, brushy, warmer water, like around Owl Cove. Throughout the year, look for largemouth in submerged brush and stumps and in the willows along shorelines. Smallmouth bass prefer cooler temperatures than the largemouth and live and breed along rocky points, rocky shorelines, and submerged gravel bars. One of the best smallmouth bass spots is right at the base of the dam, although a lot of these will be small fish.

Plugs, spinnerbaits, flies, real and artificial worms, and spinners will all catch bass at one time or another. Keep trying different methods until you find the one they want that day.

More cover-oriented than the trout, the brown bullhead and the bass tend to be found along the edges of the reservoir. Fishing for bullheads is usually best March through June when they are spawning in the shallower, warmer water coves. Another very good time to fish for bullheads is when

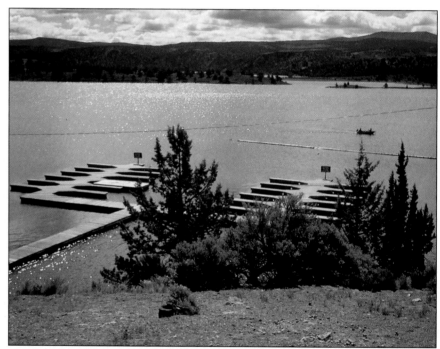

Boat docks at the State Park get heavy use during the busy summer season. This photo was taken during the off-season. Photo courtesy of Oregon Department of Transportation

the pool is rising and the water is warming. Look for them in mud-bottom bays and in the upper end of the lake in 2 to 4 feet of water. Worms are the most commonly used bait. Bullheads here average 8 to 10 inches, with an occasional one up to 12 inches in length. Their population numbers tend to fluctuate, with some years of great production and others not so great. Currently, their size is stable, and numbers are good.

Prineville Reservoir is a popular ice fishing spot in the winter for rainbow trout. The most commonly used method is some kind of bait combination of cheese, eggs, and worms. Day Beach, Jasper Point, the county boat ramp, the state park and resort areas on the north shore, and Powder House Cove and Bowman Dam at the west end of

ABOVE: A view of Prineville Reservoir in the area of the Prineville Reservoir Resort.
Photo courtesy of Prineville Reservoir Resort

RIGHT: Bass fishing has become increasingly popular at this body of water.
Photo by Brian O'Keefe

the reservoir are all good ice fishing areas.

Much of the shoreline of Prineville Reservoir has a gradual slope. There are a few areas of steep cliffs and talus. Some of the most popular shore fishing areas are at Jasper Point, the state park, and Bowman Dam. As many people fish from shore as from boats most of the year, although more people fish from shore in the fall. Water levels are extremely variable due to irrigation drawdown, and as water levels fall, many boat ramps become unusable. The best boat ramps are at Jasper Point and the state park. Primitive boat ramps exist at Roberts Bay on the south shore across from resort, Powder House Cove on the west end, and Prineville Resort and Crook County Park on the north shore.

The reservoir has some good beaches, and quite a few people boat into secluded areas for a day of sunbathing, picnicking, and waterskiing. Visitors enjoy sailing on the lake or showing up for a bass tournament. There are many primitive campsites along the banks of the reservoir. The best camping facilities on the reservoir are at the resort and Prineville Reservoir State Park. Advanced reservations are necessary for both. The state park has campsites, a boat ramp, drinking water, restrooms (some with showers), and a camping fee. The resort offers rooms, camping, RV hookups, a store, restaurant, boat rentals, and boat moorage. It opens the first of April and closes around the end of September. Jasper Point, in the same area, has a primitive camping area.

Prineville Reservoir is open to fishing year-round. The catch limit for trout is 5 per day, 8-inch minimum length, and of these no more than 1 over 20 inches. For bass, the limit is 5 per day, no more than 3 over 15 inches with a minimum length of 12 inches on largemouth bass. In addition, all smallmouth bass between 10 and 14 inches must be released. Always check the current OSFR before fishing.

To reach Prineville Reservoir from the Portland area, travel U.S. Highway 26 east through Madras to the town of Prineville.

LEFT: Prineville Reservoir has good beaches and campsites, as well as boat ramps, and day-use areas. File photo

BELOW: Fishing the many coves at Prineville Reservoir can often be productive. Photo by Bruce Holt

PRINEVILLE RESERVOIR

RESORT
△ **DAY USE AREA**
▲ **CAMPGROUND**
◢ **BOAT ACCESS**
〜 **PAVED ROAD**
- - - **UNPAVED ROAD**

From the Eugene area take U.S. Highway 20 east to Sisters, then State Route 126 through Redmond to Prineville. From Bend drive U.S. Highway 97 north to Redmond and then State Route 126 east to Prineville.

From the town of Prineville there are several routes to the reservoir. From Third Street in the middle of downtown Prineville take the turn onto Main Street at the sign to Bowman Dam and follow the Crooked River upstream 19 miles to the west end of Prineville Reservoir. At the eastern edge of Prineville, past the turn to Bowman Dam, turn right on Combs Flat Road toward Paulina and in a few miles turn right toward Prineville Resort on Juniper Canyon Road. It's 14 miles on this paved road to the northern shore of the reservoir and Prineville

Reservoir State Park and 16 miles to Prineville Resort. There is a primitive, unmaintained road into the extreme upper end of the reservoir farther east off of Combs Flat Road and the Paulina Highway, but at times this access road is impassible even with 4-wheel drive.

There are also several routes into the southern shore of the reservoir off of U.S. Highway 20 east of Bend. About 30 miles east of Bend take a left turn onto State Route 27 to the reservoir. This gravel road (being considered for paving) ends up at the dam in around 20 miles. There are a couple of turns off of Route 27 that lead to Roberts Cove and Bear Creek along the south shore of the reservoir. It's a good idea to have a BLM map to follow these circuitous routes.

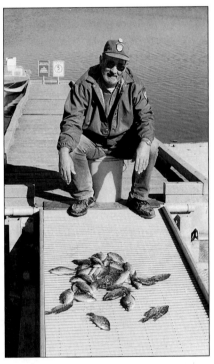

The upper end of Prineville Reservoir near the resort is a popular place to catch the tasty crappie. Photo by Scott Staats

OCHOCO RESERVOIR

Size:	surface acreage varies from 120-1,200 acres depending upon irrigation draw-off
Depth:	30' average; 100' max.
Main Catch:	stocked rainbow trout
Season:	entire year; check OSFR
Best Methods:	trolling
Best Time:	early spring
Tips:	popular for ice fishing

RIGHT: Ochoco Reservoir, seen here from the air, is only about half full. At full pool, the reservoir is 3 miles long and about a half-mile wide. Photo by Lyle Cox, *The Bulletin*

BELOW: Camping facilities on the reservoir cater to all outdoor enthusiasts.
Photo by Roger & Donna Aitkenhead, courtesy of USFS/Ochoco National Forest

At full pool, Ochoco Reservoir is 3 miles long and about .5-mile wide and is open to fishing year-round. Fishing is excellent for stocked rainbow trout. The average catch is 12 to 14 inches with lunkers up to 6 pounds. Ice fishing is very popular at Ochoco, especially down by the dam and near the state park. Ice fishers use cheese, eggs, worms, and Power Bait successfully, fishing just off the bottom. At ice-out until water levels start to rise in the spring, fishing is very good along the north shore using bait, but trolling is the most productive method year-round. Rooster Tails, Mepps, and flashers are good choices on Ochoco. As the year progresses, the water warms, and the trout move into deeper water. Anglers will have better success fishing nearer the dam with flashers and bright lures close to the bottom. Some folks jig in the deepest areas of the reservoir near the dam.

Crayfish and a small number of brown bullhead are the only other game in Ochoco Reservoir. Also present are non-game species, such as suckers. The trout limit is 5 per day, 8-inch minimum, and of these no more than 1 over 20 inches. Always check the current OSFR before fishing.

Because it is an irrigation reservoir, water levels at Ochoco change dramatically over the year, and surface acreages vary from 120 to 1,100 acres. At full pool, Ochoco averages 30 feet in depth with a maximum of 100 feet near the dam. A few lava outcroppings occupy the banks but, because of lowering water levels, shorelines will usually be composed of exposed silty bottom and muddy flats. Mill Creek and Ochoco Creek form channels in the reservoir. In the spring and summer afternoon winds, can be substantial.

There are two boat ramps on the reservoir, one at Ochoco County Park and one at Lakeshore RV Park. Anglers manage to get small boats in the reservoir during low water, but it takes much caution on muddy approaches and can require 4-wheel drive.

Although most visitors fish, others come to bird-watch, photograph, swim, sun, picnic, hunt, or sailboard. At full pool, a few waterskiers or jetskiers may be on the water.

Anglers may want to be aware of elevated mercury levels at Ochoco. Fish have not exceeded DEQ standards for mercury, but you might not want to feast regularly on your catch from this site.

Camping facilities on Ochoco Reservoir include Ochoco Lake Campground, open from April though October, which charges a fee and has drinking water, flush toilets, showers, a boat ramp, and a day-use area. The Crystal Corral has an RV park with 17 full hookups, a cafe, and a store. Lakeshore RV Park and Store offers full hookups, a marina, store, boat rentals, and a boat ramp.

Ochoco Reservoir is located 6 miles east of Prineville on U.S. Highway 26.

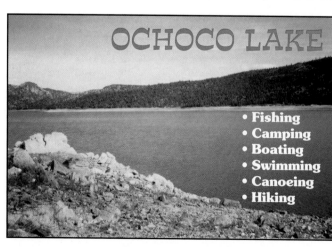

HAYSTACK RESERVOIR

Size: 240 acres
Depth: 27' average
Main Catch: brown & rainbow trout; kokanee; bass; crappie
Best Methods: trolling deepest areas; shore fishing
Season: entire year; check OSFR
Best Time: spring & summer
Tips: fish shallows for brown trout in early spring

Haystack Reservoir is a re-regulation facility, situated 8 miles south of Madras in the juniper and sage desert. Most of the fishing at Haystack is for kokanee, rainbow trout, and bass, but there are also trophy-size bullhead, black crappie, brown trout, and bluegill.

Haystack is open to fishing year-round, but the angling is usually on the slow side. Water quality is good, and fish grow fast, but continual losses through the unscreened outlet and nearly daily influx of cold water take a bite out of fish numbers and successful reproduction. Ice fishing is not very good here, as the climate is too mild for good ice formation. Spring and summer are the best times to fish for the warm water species, and the salmonids can be caught year-round. Maximum depth of the reservoir is 75 feet with an average depth of 27 feet. There are great views of Mt. Jefferson from the water.

Kokanee catches range from 2 to 3 pounds, 14 to 18 inches in length, with catches up to 20 inches. Thirty-thousand kokanee fingerlings are planted each year. Trolling the deepest areas of the lake with flashers, a Wedding Ring, and a piece of corn or worm is the most effective technique. Vary the trolling depth until a school is located and then stay in the school. Still-fishing with bait can be productive once a school is located. Kokanee are also caught from shore using a variety of bait, including worms, white corn, and red eggs.

Legal-size rainbow and brown trout are planted annually. Fishing is usually pretty slow for the trout, but it is possible to catch them from shore year-round on Power Bait, eggs, cheese, or worms. From the west boat ramp around to the inlet and near the dam are the best areas for shore anglers. Try for the browns and rainbow early in the spring while they are still cruising the shallows and ravenous after the long, cold winter. Trollers will occasionally take rainbow while fishing for kokanee.

Fishing for largemouth bass is fair. Most bass anglers here use spinnerbaits, plugs, spoons, and worms. The best bass catching areas of the reservoir are in the shallow bays along the south shore, particularly near the vegetation in the southeast and southwest corners. The best time to fish is mid-spring. An average catch is 12 to 14 inches, with the largest bass ranging from 3 to 5 pounds.

Haystack is one of the few fishing spots in Central Oregon with black crappie. These sunfish reach admirable sizes up to 12 inches in length, with the average catch at 8 to 10 inches. The best fish are taken near vegetative cover in the southeast corner of the reservoir in late May through June. Bluegill transplanted into Haystack in the summer of 1993 are hanging on, but their numbers are small. The few bullheads in Haystack are usually caught from shore by anglers fishing for other species. Nightcrawlers are the standard bait for those intending to catch the catfish. The bullhead average 1 to 2 pounds with the big guys at 3 pounds.

The trout and kokanee catch limits are 5 per day, with an 8-inch minimum, and of these no more than 1 over 20 inches. The catch limit for bass is 5 per day, with no more than 3 over 15 inches. There is no limit on bluegill, crappie, or bullhead.

An excellent Forest Service campground occupies the east shore and has a boat ramp, drinking water, and facilities for day-use and overnight camping (with fees). In mid-summer, Haystack becomes a center for water-skiing, and anglers disappear to avoid conflicts. Even though there is a 5 mph speed limit in the west corner of the lake, the reservoir really is not large enough to handle both forms of recreation. There are two good boat ramps on the lake. As the water level drops over the summer, the east shore ramp may become unusable. The west shore ramp is good year-round.

Haystack is located 7 miles south of Madras and about 2 miles east of U.S. Highway 97. From the Portland area take U.S. Highway 26 to Madras, then Highway 97 south 7 miles to the turn toward Haystack. To get there from the Willamette Valley take U.S. Highway 20 east to Sisters, then State Route 126 through Redmond to U.S. Highway 97. Drive north on Highway 97 through Terrebonne. The turn into Haystack is about 8 miles north of Terrebonne. From Bend take Highway 97 north to Redmond and continue on as described above.

TOP: A fisherman works the shallow south end of Haystack for the warm water species.
Photo by Anne E. Davidson, courtesy of USFS/Ochoco National Forest

RIGHT: An aerial view of the reservoir.
Bend Mapping & Blueprint file photo

Ana Reservoir

Ana Reservoir is a 60-acre reservoir located 5 miles north of the community of Summer Lake. It is open year-round and remains ice-free due to the constant inflow of 58°F water from springs.

Ana is stocked each year with legal-size rainbow trout, but the most exciting residents are the hybrid white bass, stocked every other year, which grow fat on the abundant chub population. The original stocking of these bass was in 1982, and it's believed that those fingerlings are now rewriting the record books. The state record for hybrid white bass was set three times within a two-month period. The new state record hybrid white bass of 18 pounds, 8 ounces was taken out of Ana in February, 1996.

Bait, lures, and flies are all effective here, but still fishing with prawns catches most of the bass. Casting or trolling rapala-type minnow imitations work well as the bass feed on the chub. Most fish are caught from the bank, but one can get a small boat in the water. It's OK to camp here, although there is no official campground, and the one existing outhouse may return to the dust at any time.

To get to Ana, take County Route 31 off U.S. Highway 97, 3 miles south of LaPine. Five miles north of the town of Summer Lake, there is a small sign indicating the left turn toward Ana. It's then about 2 miles to the reservoir

Thompson Valley Reservoir

Located 14 miles south of State Highway 31 and the town of Silver Lake, Thompson Valley Reservoir holds planted rainbow trout, cutthroat trout, largemouth bass, and hybrid white bass. The reservoir's surface acreage varies from 2,550 acres to a low of 210 acres, due to irrigation drawdowns. Maximum water depths range from 34 feet down to 7 feet.

Wildlife abounds at Thompson Reservoir. Bald eagles and osprey nest in nearby trees. Excellent habitat for grebes and migratory shorebirds is found around the reservoir along with habitat for white pelicans, sandhill cranes, and migratory waterfowl. Mule deer and antelope are often seen as well.

Two boat ramps are available on the reservoir, and there is a 10-mph boat speed limit. Thompson Valley is open to angling year-round. Two Forest Service campgrounds are situated on the lake.

Follow signs to the reservoir from the town of Silver Lake along either County Route 4-11, which becomes Forest Route 27 and leads to the north shore, or take County Route 4-12 which becomes Forest Route 28 and ends up on the east shore.

Ana Reservoir remains ice-free and open for fishing year-round. Pictured here is the Ana River, about one mile downstream from the reservoir. Photo by Brian O'Keefe

Thompson Reservoir

To Hwy 31

To Silver Lake Hwy 31

SILVER CREEK

N

28

27

Thompson Reservoir

DAM

△ CAMPGROUND

◣ BOAT RAMP

— PAVED ROAD

East Bay

SQUAW CREEK

28

Antelope Flat Reservoir

Located in the Ochoco National Forest 30 air miles southeast of Prineville, Antelope Flat Reservoir offers good fishing for stocked rainbow trout. The reservoir is open year-round to angling.

When full, it covers 170 acres and has a maximum depth of 28 feet. There is a concrete boat ramp and a nice Forest Service campground on the reservoir.

From Prineville, take the Post-Paulina Highway, turning south onto Forest Route 17 about 6 miles east of Post. Follow signs to the reservoir, about 13 miles south and about a mile off Route 17.

Delintment Lake

Delintment Lake is one of several popular reservoirs in the southern part of the Ochoco National Forest. Delintment covers 50 acres when full and has a maximum depth of 15 feet. The lake is surrounded by ponderosa pine forest and has an attractive Forest Service campground.

Stocked annually with fingerling rainbow trout, this rich reservoir grows them fast, but is prone to winter kills. The reservoir becomes very weedy by mid-summer. Average fish are 8 to 14 inches with the rare hold-overs to 3 and 4 pounds. There is good opportunity for bank fishing, a gravel boat ramp, and a 5-mph boat speed limit. Delintment also has a universally accessible fishing dock.

There are three major access routes; one from Hines, just west of Burns: another through Paulina, if coming from the west; and along Silver Creek, just west of Riley on U.S. Highway 20. See Ochoco National Forest maps for details.

Walton Lake

Walton Lake is a popular put-and-take fishery, nestled high in the Ochoco National Forest. In the 1940s, the Isaac Walton League dammed spring-fed Ochoco Creek, creating this 18-acre lake with constant water levels and clear, green water.

Walton Lake has a maximum depth of 21 feet, with an average depth of 12 feet and .8 mile of shoreline. Stocked several times a year with rainbow trout, the lake offers catches averaging 8 to 11 inches, with a few holdovers of up to 19 inches. A few accidental brook trout also inhabit the lake.

A trail circling the lake provides good bank fishing opportunities. Fishing from float tubes and small rafts is popular, and only electric motors are allowed. There is a gravel boat ramp, handicapped fishing access, and a small beach and swimming area located near the boat ramp. As of 2001, concessionaires are charging fees for both campsites and for day-use.

Take U.S. Highway 26 east out of Prineville for about 14 miles, then take the right-hand fork onto Forest Route 22 toward Walton Lake. Take a left-hand turn in another 8 miles to continue on Road 22, following signs to the lake for another 7 miles. The road is paved all the way to Walton and continues clear around the lake.

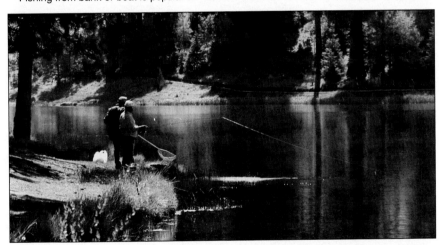

Fishing from bank or boat is popular at Walton Lake in the Ochocos. Photos by Tim Cochran

PAULINA LAKE

Size:	1,320 acres
Depth:	max. depth 250'
Main Catch:	kokanee; rainbow & brown trout
Best Methods:	trolling; still-fishing; jigging; fly fishing
Best Time:	varies each of "four seasons" – ice-out, spring, summer, fall
Season:	general trout; 4th Sat. in April to Oct. 31; check OSFR
Tips:	renowned for trophy browns

In May of 1993, a 27-pound, 12-ounce brown trout was pulled out of Paulina Lake, setting a new state record. But that's not all. That 27- pound fish was only a runner-up. Paulina first grabbed the state brown trout record in 1965 with a 35-pound, 8-ounce behemoth and has held it ever since. However, there is an asterisk behind that record, indicating it was not a legal catch … It was wallowing in the lake with a broken line and tackle hanging from its mouth and was scooped up with a net. Earlier, a fisherman had hooked the fish and tired it out before it broke the line. But wait, there's more. The state record kokanee is also from Paulina Lake, captured by a 4-pound, 2-ounce entry in 1989.

Paulina Lake shares the caldera of Newberry National Volcanic Monument with East Lake. This is a fascinating geologic area formed by the collapse of Mount Newberry 10,000 years ago and includes the largest obsidian flow in North America, pumice fields, and cinder cones. Paulina Peak, the remnant rim of Mount Newberry, overlooks the crater from 7,998 feet above sea level. After Mount Newberry's collapse, the two craters filled with snow-melt, rainwater, and seepage from hot springs to form two fishless lakes. Many years of stocking have created two of Central Oregon's finest lake fisheries.

Paulina is a big lake, covering about 1,300 surface acres and obtaining depths to 250 feet. Fish of each species are stocked every year. Paulina is mainly a kokanee fishery, with fish up to 23 inches in length.

Brown trout catches typically range

INSET: This view is from Paulina Lake Resort moorage looking east.

BELOW: Paulina Peak, the remnant rim of Mount Newberry, rises in the background.
Photos by Geoff Hill

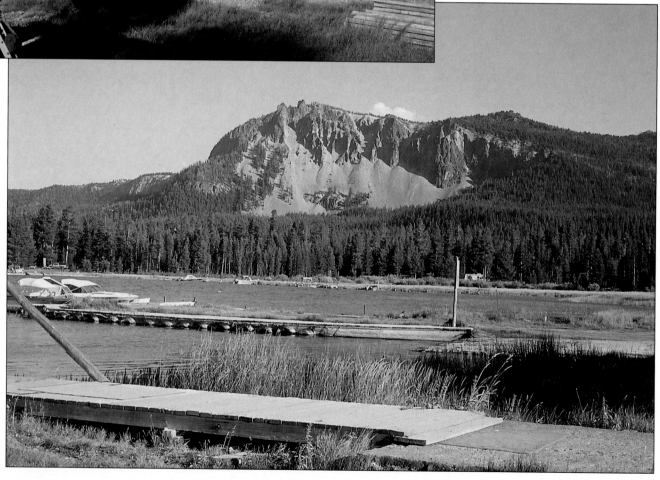

between 12 and 20 inches, with fish in the 7- to 10-pound range not uncommon. The lake also holds rainbow trout averaging 10 to 14 inches and a few larger.

Fishing techniques in the Newberry Crater revolve around four "fishing seasons:" ice-out, spring, summer, and fall. These "seasons" will affect one's trolling speed, leader length, depth, presentation, and location. Ice-out is the time to pursue big browns by trolling big plugs. Anglers should try different depths and various parts of lake. In the spring, kokanee schools are scattered in 24 to 100 feet of water. Trolling with bait and jigging are the most popular techniques for catching kokanee this time of year. Still-fishing, trolling or casting close to the shoreline are the best bets for the early season. Anglers should concentrate their efforts close to the bank and within 35 feet of the surface for the rainbows and browns. Casting lures from shore in early spring and in the fall is an effective method for catching large brown trout and rainbows. Use a 3- to 4-inch P.J. Shiner or a Krocodile spoon. The Kroc is a favorite in windy conditions because of its tremendous castability. Change the speed of the retrieve often, as a stop-and-go technique is very enticing to large, predator fish. Spinners, such as brown Rooster Tails with a gold blade, are good for catching browns; and black Rooster Tails, with a silver blade, are good for rainbows.

When still-fishing for rainbows, one should fish near the bottom with salmon eggs, worms, Velveeta cheese or Power Bait in green or rainbow colors. Dodgers, Cowbell, or Bear Valley lake trolls make excellent attractors. Probable the most critical aspect of setting up a trolling outfit is to use a rather long leader from the attractor to the lure or bait. Because of the lake's crystal-clear water, a longer leader is needed between lake troll flasher and lure or bait. A leader length of at least 30 to 72 inches is recommended.

The hot summer days push fish into deeper water but fishing remains good if anglers concentrate their efforts where the fish con-

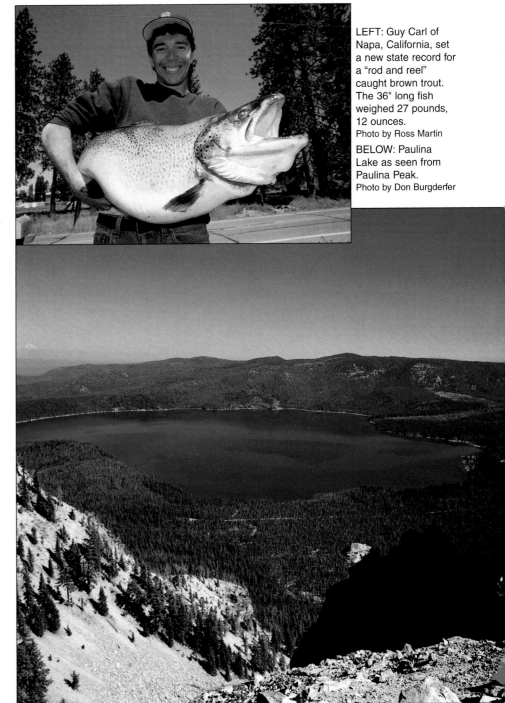

LEFT: Guy Carl of Napa, California, set a new state record for a "rod and reel" caught brown trout. The 36" long fish weighed 27 pounds, 12 ounces.
Photo by Ross Martin
BELOW: Paulina Lake as seen from Paulina Peak.
Photo by Don Burgderfer

Big Bay   Red Slide

Hot Springs

MOSS BEDS

S

F

ELEVATION 6,331'
DEPTH 250'

Black Slide

MOSS BEDS

F

Old Log

S
T

Paulina Lake

T
S

Rocky
Points

S

Paulina Creek Falls

Paulina
Lake
Lodge ■

Big
Point

T

USFS
Guard
Station

Main
Campground

Road to
Paulina
Peak

Little Crater
Camp

F

MOSS BEDS

Summer
Homes

⌒ PAVED ROAD

▲ CAMPGROUND

■ RESORT

◤ BOAT RAMP

● POINT OF INTEREST

F Fly Fishing

S Still Fishing

T Trolling

BT Brown Trout

RT Rainbow Trout

K Kokanee

To Depth 250'

To Depth 20'

gregate. Rainbows can be caught from mid-depth (20–60 feet) and browns caught shallow in the early morning and late evening. They are found around steep drop-offs, rock shelves in 40-ft. or deeper water. Kokanee will school up, usually at or around the 40-ft. depth and may be found throughout the middle of the lake.

Fall fishing finds cooler water conditions and more active fish as winter approaches. Spring tactics again become most popular as the fish move into shallower water to feed, in preparation for the cold weather ahead. German browns and kokanee spawn in the fall, so efforts should be concentrated in shallower water areas. Gravel lake bottom or underwater springs and creeks are the best bets. Fish at this time of year become very irritable and will strike out at anything that passes near them.

Trolling flashers is by far the most popular fishing method on Paulina Lake, still- fishing the second, and fly fishing third. For kokanee, trolling a Wedding Ring with corn or a piece of worm on the end is very effective. Jigging is increasing in popularity, using Buzz Bombs, Zingers, Crippled Herring, and Nordic lures. Another kokanee-producing method is to first locate schools with a fish-finder and, depending on their depth, troll with a downrigger, flashers and corn, or red flies.

Along Paulina Lake's 8 miles of shoreline, the easiest bank fishing is in the northeast corner of the lake by the black slide. Weedbeds often offer excellent fishing in front of Paulina Resort on the southwest shore of the lake, in front of the summer homes on the south bank, and in front of the black slide. Logs along the east shore and logs and stumps close to shore on the west side create good cover for shy fish. Wading is not easy along Paulina's shores; float tubes are very popular. Water levels fluctuate little.

Opening day is with the general trout season, the last Saturday in April. However, anglers should check to be sure the ice has thawed enough to allow open fishing water. The fishing season remains open through October 31. The catch limit is 5 trout per day, with a 8-inch minimum length and no more than 1 over 20 inches. The lake has a 10 mph speed limit. Several boat ramps are available. Also note that

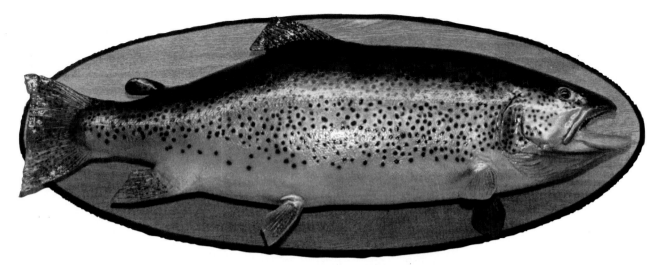

The world's third largest brown trout (35 lbs., 8 oz.) came from Paulina Lake.
The mounted fish is now back home at Paulina Lodge restaurant. Photo by Diane Kulpinski

winds can be bad especially in the afternoon.

Other recreational opportunities in Newberry National Volcanic Monument include sightseeing, photography, bird watching, hiking, and canoeing in the summer; and snowmobiling and cross-country skiing in the winter. There are several good hiking trails in the Newberry Monument, including one which traverses the entire rim of the crater. A road leads to the top of Paulina Peak, where there are fantastic views of the Cascade Mountains to the west, the high desert to the east, and the entire Newberry volcano.

Several good Forest Service campgrounds are located on the lake. These include Paulina Lake Campground on the southwest shore (drinking water, fees, picnic facilities, and boat launch), North Cove Campground on the north shore (primitive, boat or hike-in), Little Crater Campground on the east shore (drinking water, fees, picnic facilities, boat ramp), and Newberry Group Camp on the south shore (water, fee, picnicking, reservations). In addition, there is Paulina Creek Falls picnic area just west of the lake and Chief Paulina Horse Camp

just across the highway from the lake. More campgrounds are located around East Lake.

Paulina Lake Resort has a store, restaurant, cabins, moorage, boat rentals, and a fee boat ramp. The resort is open late April through October 31 and mid-December through mid-March.

To get to Paulina Lake drive south on U.S. Highway 97 from Bend about 22 miles, or about 6 miles north of LaPine if coming from the south. Turn east on County Route 21 to East Lake, Paulina Lake, and Newberry National Volcanic Monument. Paulina Lake is 13 miles up the road, East lake an additional 5 miles.

From the Eugene area take State Highway 58 east over Willamette Pass, then County Route 61 to the town of Crescent and Highway 97 north to LaPine. Continue north of LaPine to County Route 21 and turn east to the lakes.

John Hofferd shows off his 24-pound brown trout taken in 1998 from Paulina.
Photo courtesy of John Hofferd

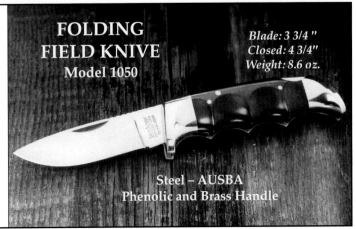

EAST LAKE

Size:	1,050 acres
Depth:	max. depth 200'
Main Catch:	brown & rainbow trout; kokanee; Atlantic salmon
Best Methods:	still-fishing; trolling; fly fishing; jigging; casting
Season:	general trout; 4th Sat. in April to Oct. 31; check OSFR
Best Time:	early & late for trophy browns; all season for other species
Tips:	best fished from a boat or float tube

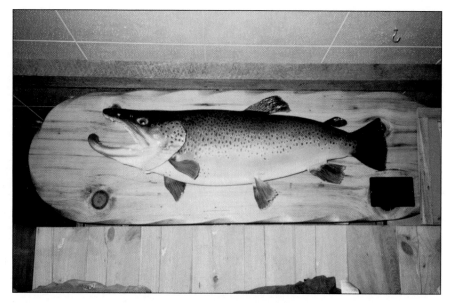

East Lake is one of two exceptional trout lakes nestled in the caldera of the Newberry National Volcanic Monument, the largest ice-age volcano in Oregon. About 37 miles south of Bend, East Lake occupies 1,050 acres and has a maximum depth of 200 feet. East Lake shares this outstanding geologic area with Paulina Lake, both well-known for their large brown trout.

East Lake is 6,381 feet above sea level, is approximately a mile in diameter, and the average depth is just over 67 feet. The lake is fed by snow-melt and underground springs.

Covering over 500 square miles, Newberry Volcano is one of the largest shield volcanoes in the lower 48 states. The area was named after J. S. Newberry, a scientist attached to the 1853 railroad surveying party. The volcano's summit contains a sev-

TOP: This 16.5-pound brown trout, was caught September 22, 1992 by John Hofferd.

CENTER: Even with 6.5 miles of shoreline, most of the fish at East Lake are caught from a floating device.

BOTTOM: In this aerial, Paulina (front) and East lakes are viewed from the southwest.
Photos by Geoff Hill

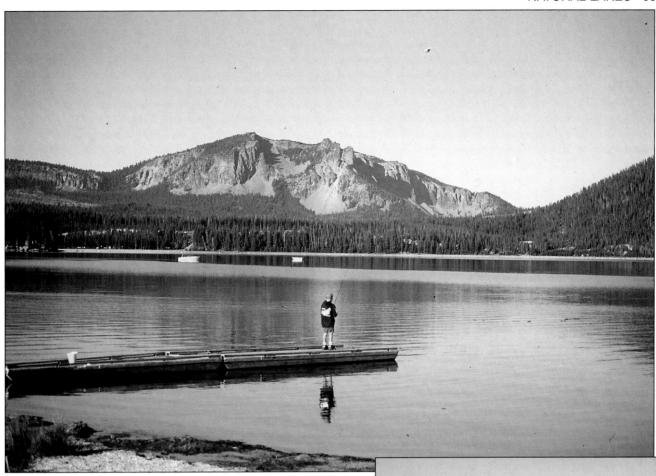

enteen square mile caldera, formed as the top of the volcano collapsed when the magma chamber beneath emptied out. The caldera, also referred to as Newberry Crater, may have once contained only one lake, like Crater Lake. However, more recent eruptions divided the crater into two crystal clear lakes, separated by pumice, ash, and lava flows.

East lake is one of the finest and most traditional fisheries in Oregon, regularly producing brown trout over 10 pounds. The lake record is a 22-1/2 pound Brown. Rainbow trout are the backbone, being brought in using all techniques: trolling,

TOP: A number of boat ramps, docks, and campgrounds are available at this outstanding geologic area.
RIGHT: Views of Paulina Peak are visible from many points along the shoreline.
Photos by Geoff Hill

still-fishing, wet and dry flies, jigging, and casting. Kokanee, introduced in 1993, have been caught up to 20 inches. Atlantic Salmon, one of the few lake trout species that will rise on a dry fly, are particularly popular with flyfishers. Unfortunately, chub have become a pest ... but then, they are the food source for the big brown trout.

The catch limit at East Lake is 5 trout per day (any species) and two catches in possession. The minimum length is 8 inches, and only one fish over 20 inches is allowed. Because of East Lake's high altitude, it may be partially ice-covered at season opening. The ice recedes from the southeast corner where an underground hot springs warms the water a few degrees providing the angler the best chance of catching a trophy-sized brown trout. The wily browns prowl the south and east shores. Casting and retrieving or trolling minnow-type lures such as floating Rapala minnow imitators in the perch, rainbow, gold or silver color, or 1/4 or 3/8 oz. Krocodile spoons imitating chub patterns, in shallow water, should produce.

The early season is also an excellent time to fish for the other species. Rainbows, especially, are found in large numbers along the ice's edge until the lake has completely thawed, at which point they disperse more evenly throughout the lake. Trolling is probably the most effective means of catching fish at East Lake. Ford Fender, Cowbell, Flashlites, Dodgers, and Jack-O-Diamonds make excellent attractants. The most critical aspect of setting up a trolling outfit is to use at least four to six feet of 4 lb. test leader.

East Lake is very clear. A bare worm will catch fish, but Number 1 and 2 Needlefish, Wedding Ring, Triple Teazer can also be productive, especially when augmented with a worm. Try Kwikfish or Flatfish in Frog, Coach Dog, and Black Glitter patterns, too.

Still-fish with Velveeta cheese, Power Baits (rainbow, chartreuse, pink or orange), worms, single eggs, or canned shrimp. Anglers can enhance their success by anchoring boats from both ends facing into the wind to reduce movement. Try to keep bait just off of the mossy, weed-covered lake bottom. Use a 2-pound leader with number 14 to 18 hook. Doughbait treble hooks for cheese and Power Bait, or a single hook tucked completely inside a salmon egg, are recommended. Either split shot or sliding sinkers should be used to maintain the bait from 18 to 24 inches off of the bottom.

The prize catch during the summer months is the Kokanee. This red meated, land-locked sockeye is the most delicious freshwater fish available, especially when smoked. Kokanee fishing is exciting, as they are fighters, but very soft mouthed. It takes skill to land Kokes. By mid-summer, the Kokanee will be deep, sometimes 40 to 50 feet. To reach that depth without a downrigger, one must troll with up to four ounces of lead. Stick to the northern half of the lake where water depth exceeds 80 feet. Trolling outfits for Kokanee are similar to those used for Rainbow, with the addition of white shoepeg corn to the bait. Try Kokanee King or Krocodile, without the worm, but with the corn. Jensen Dodgers in size 000 and

Flashlights make excellent attractants for the Kokes because their low drag does not require as much weight to get deep. Jigging with a Nordic Jig or Buzz Bomb can also be deadly against Kokanee, especially with the aid of a fish-finder.

Ounce for ounce, and sometimes pound for pound, there isn't a better fighting fish than the Atlantic Salmon, especially on the end of a fly rod. Unlike any other lake in Oregon, this species can be kept here — if you can land them. Slim-bodied, silver-sided with a black spot or series of spots on the gill plate, and forked tail, Atlantic Salmon may be caught still-fishing, casting or trolling, but for pure sport, go after them with flies. Adams, midge, mosquito, mayfly, and callibaetis are the preferred dries, and nymphs, leeches, Hare's Ear, and Woolly Buggers are the best wet flies.

There are some excellent midge hatches early and callibaetis hatches throughout the summer, especially in the northeast corner of the lake. Often there is decent fly fishing within wading distance of the northeast shore in late afternoon to evening. Generally, nymph patterns are most often used throughout the lake.

For casting, Super Dupers, Bang Tails, and Rooster Tails in frog, white, and black are recommended. Although 95% of the fish caught at East Lake are from boats, casting from shore can be effective. The three best shore fishing spots are off the launching dock at the Hot Springs Campground, as close as one can get to the bluff on the north shore (hike from the Cinder Hill Campground), or all along the

Joe Shockley with his 30", 10-pound brown trout caught in July of 1998 with an AP Olive Emerger fly pattern. Mom and dad proudly look on.
Photo courtesy of Sunriver Fly Shop

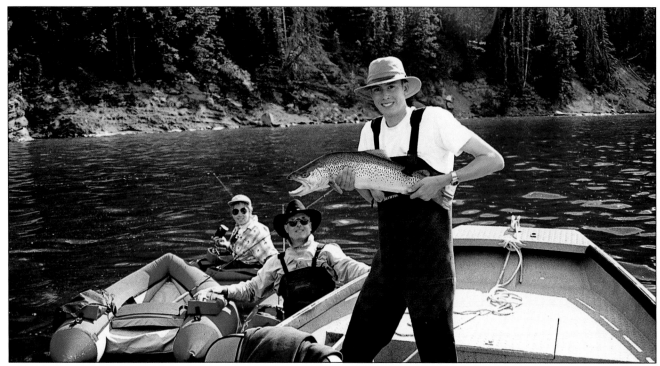

East Lake
Elevation 6,371'
Maximum Depth 200'

Red Fissure

Rock Cliffs

Cinder Hill
Forest Camp

N

White
Pumice
Slide

East
Lake
Resort

Hot Springs

East Lake
Forest Camp

Hot Springs
Forest Camp

**To Hwy 97
and Paulina Lake**

S STILL FISHING

F FLY FISHING

T TROLLING
Flashers for Rainbow
& Kokanee

T TROLLING
Rapalas for Browns

▲ CAMPGROUND

◄ BOAT ACCESS

■ RESORT

● POINT OF INTEREST

⌇ UNPAVED ROAD

DEPTH BELOW 50'

DEPTH OVER 50'

DEPTH OVER 100'

DEPTH OVER 150'

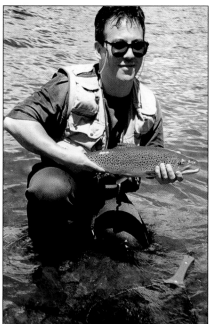

This brown trout is a fine example of the
beauties to be found in East Lake.
Photo courtesy of Sunriver Fly Shop

west shore where the white slide is located. The west shore can even produce browns late into the season, and has the added advantage of having the predominately westerly wind at the fisher's back to aid in casting.

East Lake has many weedbeds located near the hot springs, in front of the white slide and along the cliffs on the north side. These weedbeds, full of freshwater shrimp, are good sites for both trolling and still-fishing. Shoreline character of the lake varies from gradually sloping beaches and weed-clogged shallows to steep, rocky cliffs. Winds can be bad in the afternoon.

Three Forest Service Campgrounds on East Lake have nearly 200 campsites. East Lake, Hot Springs, and Cinder Hill Campgrounds have overnight camping, drinking water, toilets, boat launches, and day-use picnic tables. Reservations are not required in these National Forest campgrounds, but can be made (for an additional fee) by calling 1-800-280-CAMP. East Lake Resort, on the east shore, features rustic cabins, an RV

park with electricity and water hook-ups, rental boats (with or without motors), laundromat, public showers, gasoline, propane, cafe, and a store with sundries, snacks, bait, tackle, and fishing advice.

There is a 10-mph speed limit for motor boats on East Lake. Anglers should be aware of a mercury advisory for East Lake. Water levels fluctuate 2 to 3 feet over the year, changing the configuration of boat ramps, docks, and fishable shorelines. The weather is extremely variable at this altitude (6,380 feet), so be prepared. Opening day is the last Saturday in April; closing is October 31. Always check the current OSFR before fishing. Roads are usually plowed into East Lake Resort prior to opening day. The resort is open mid-May each year and closes in early October.

To reach East Lake travel 22 miles south of Bend on U.S. Highway 97 (9 miles beyond the Sunriver turn-off), then 18 miles east on East Lake-Paulina Lake Road.

THREE CREEK LAKE

Size:	28 acres
Depth:	28' max.
Main Catch:	stocked rainbow trout; brook trout
Best Methods:	shore fishing; trolling & still-fishing from a boat
Season:	entire year; check OSFR
Best Time:	mornings & evenings after ice-out

Three Creek Lake, elevation 6,550 feet, is an alpine gem resting at the base of Tam McArthur Rim south of Sisters. This 28-acre lake has planted rainbow trout and a self-sustaining population of brook trout, ranging from 8 to 15 inches. Most catches average around 10 inches. Trolling flies and lures, fishing from shore, and still-fishing with bait are all successfully used methods.

The shoreline of Three Creek Lake varies from gentle slope to rocky cliff, surrounded by old growth forest. Maximum depth is 28 feet down the center and near the cliff on the south end of the lake. Early in the season, many logs lie in the water along the west shore. As summer progresses, weed beds begin to appear along the edges of the lake, water level lowers gradually, and the logs become high and dry

Most of the lake is easy to fish from shore or by wading, but fishing from a boat is by far the most popular method. Motors are not allowed on Three Creek Lake, contributing to the serenity of the setting. There is a prim-itive boat ramp on the east shore as well as a small store which rents boats.

Soon after the lake is stocked every spring, spin and bait fishermen do well near the dam on the northeast corner of the lake. A little later in the season, try still-fishing the deep water along the cliffs on the south end of the lake and along the campground on the southeast shore. The largest fish are usually taken from these areas. Trollers do well near the dam, the boat ramp, and along the south end with both spinners and lures. The west shoreline between the two inlet creeks is also a popular trolling lane. Fly fishing can be rewarding during evening hatches or while trolling nymphs along the west shoreline. Try black and green streamers or large Gold Ribbed Hare's Ears. Zigzag trolling patterns and changes in speed can sometimes entice otherwise wary brook trout. Morning and evening are the best times to fish water this clear.

There are two primitive Forest Service campgrounds: Three Creek Campground and Driftwood Campground on the lake. These sites have outhouses but no drinking water, and a fee is charged. Another similar campground, Three Creek Meadow, is a mile back toward Sisters.

The most popular activities at Three Creek Lake are camping, fishing, and swimming, but there are also excellent hiking trails near the lake. Several trailheads originate on the perimeter of the lake as well as back along the road toward Sisters.

From Highway 20 in Sisters turn south onto Elm Street which becomes Forest Route 16. The road is paved for about 15 miles and is one of the most beautiful drives in Central Oregon, climbing 2,400 feet through towering ponderosa pines and past vistas of Cascade peaks. The last 2 miles to the lake are on a fair gravel and cinder road. Due to the elevation the road is often not open until July. Call the Sisters Ranger District of the Deschutes National Forest for information regarding road conditions and progress of ice-out on the lake.

LITTLE THREE CREEK LAKE

A .5-mile trail leads from Driftwood Campground on the north shore of Three Creek Lake to Little Three Creek Lake. This modest lake is 14 acres, about 10 feet deep, and holds a good population of wild brook trout, averaging 10 inches in length. Casting from shore is possible, but the fish are often out of range. Packing in a lightweight tube or raft makes access to fish complete. Due to a large number of small fish, spinners, attractor dry flies, and nymphs in the 12 to 16 size range are most successful.

Surrounded by old growth forest, Three Creek Lake is easy to fish from shore; however, fishing from a boat is the most popular method. INSET: A trail along the Tam McArthur Rim offers a nice view of Little Three Creek Lake.   Photos by Geoff Hill

BIG LAKE

Size:	225 acres
Depth:	max. depth 66'
Main Catch:	stocked rainbow trout, brook trout, kokanee, & cutthroat
Best Methods:	still-fishing from a boat or the bank; trolling
Season:	entire year; check OSFR
Best Time:	early spring for cutthroat & rainbow; fall for brook trout & kokanee

Big Lake is perched at the top of Santiam Pass at 4,645 feet elevation, right next to Hoodoo Ski Area. The lake covers 225 acres and has a maximum depth of 66 feet. Water levels fluctuate a few feet during the year, with the lowest point in September, at which time the boat ramp may not be useable by big boats. Big Lake has gently sloping shorelines surrounded by forest. Winds can get nasty in the afternoon.

Fishing is not the biggest draw at Big Lake; most people come here to enjoy the cool mountain air, the camping and nearby hiking on the Pacific Crest Trail, swimming, waterskiing, and jetskiing.

Nonetheless, Big Lake holds decent numbers of kokanee, cutthroat, rainbow, and brook trout. Kokanee are stocked every year and rainbow and brook trout every few years. In 1995, 2,200 rainbow trout fingerlings were planted, 2,000 kokanee, and 1,400 brook trout. Cutthroat were last planted in 1993. Brook trout average 12 inches in length, rainbow trout 6 inches, and kokanee 11 inches in length. The catch limit is 5 per day, 8-inch minimum length, and of these no more than 1 over 20 inches. The fishing season is open year-round.

Big Lake is what is known as an "oligotrophic" lake in the trade, meaning that it is less than rich and doesn't grow fish very well. Fishing, or catching, is only fair. Instead, the water is very clear, and there are few weedbeds or other obstructions in the water. The main catches are cutthroat and rainbow trout, and the best time to catch them is in early spring, although access by car can be impossible at that time of year. Big Lake is easy to fish from either the bank or from a boat, using the usual methods: still-fishing with bait and casting and trolling lures or flies. Fall is the best time to catch the brook trout and kokanee. Trolled flashers work best for the kokanee.

There is an excellent campground here with tremendous views of 7,794-foot Mt. Washington. Big Lake Campground has over 60 sites, 5 day-use sites and charges a fee to camp. It has a pressurized water system, swimming area, and picnic area and is entirely paved except for the gravel boat ramp.

To get to Big Lake, take U.S. Highway 20 from either the east or the west to the turn into Hoodoo Ski Area, Big Lake Road, and Benson Sno-Park at the top of Santiam Pass. It's 3 miles into Big Lake Campground on Road 2690 which is paved all the way.

TOP: Mt. Washington dominates the view at Big Lake. Photo by George Linn
BELOW: From the sky, the forested shoreline is apparent. Photo by Jennifer Emmert

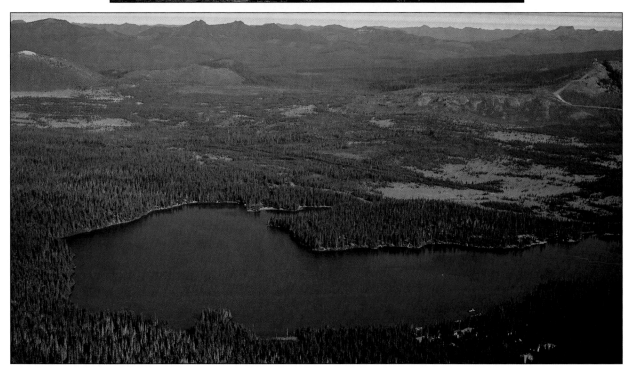

SUTTLE LAKE

Size:	250 acres
Depth:	75' maximum
Main Catch:	kokanee; brown trout; whitefish
Best Methods:	still-fishing from boat; fly fishing
Season:	entire year; check OSFR
Best Time:	kokanee: May & June trout: early & late in season

Fifteen miles northwest of Sisters and easily accessible from U.S. Highway 20, Suttle Lake sits in a pretty setting of mixed conifer forest with views of Cascade peaks. The 250-acre lake is 75' deep at its maximum depth and has an excellent population of naturally reproducing kokanee, plus brown trout, whitefish, and crayfish.

Kokanee fishing at Suttle Lake is best in May and June using bait. The most commonly used baits are periwinkles and caddis larva, but nightcrawler and red egg combinations are also popular. Kokanee sizes currently average 9 to 10 inches with the numbers of kokanee up and sizes down. Still-fishing from a boat is the best approach, fishing closer to shore early in the season and in the deeper water during mid-summer. The same baits work throughout the season when presented just off the bottom. It is possible to fish from the bank for kokanee near the Suttle Lake picnic area on the northeast corner of the lake.

Brown trout from 10 inches to 10 pounds hide out here, with many in the 3 to 5 pound range. Most are taken early in the season trolling a Rapala near the surface. Late in summer, the brown trout head for the depths. Flashers, lures, and Rapalas need to run deep this time of year. Late in the season is another good time of year for catching brown trout. When late in the day, or anytime light intensity is low, chances of catching a big brown increase. Mid-summer fly fishers troll nymphs and Woolly Buggers near the surface. Early evenings are especially good fly fishing. Any lure, spinner, or fly that looks like a succulent kokanee fin-

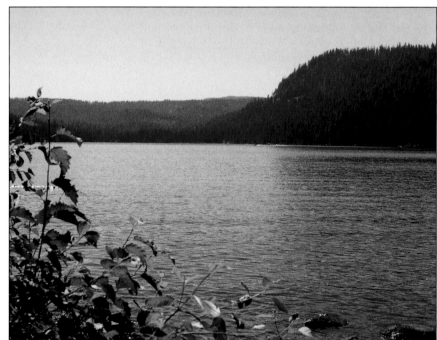

Located northwest of Sisters, Suttle Lake is surrounded by forest. To take advantage of the lake's wide expanse, fishing by boat is the most productive method. Photos by Geoff Hill

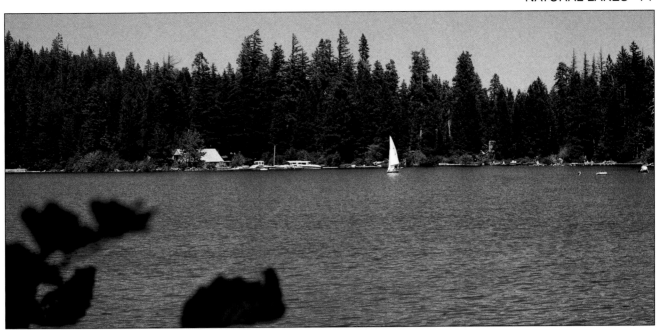

Aside from fishing, Suttle Lake offers numerous other activities including camping, hiking, sailing, and waterskiing. Photo by Geoff Hill

gerling will appeal to the big browns. Crayfish patterns are worth a try, too.

Native whitefish of 10 to 12 inches are usually an incidental catch when fishing for the other species. The fry are a favorite snack of brown trout.

Boats are most commonly used on Suttle Lake, float tubes are adequate, and wading is possible in some areas. There are few areas fishable from shore. Suttle Lake has a kokanee catch limit of 25 with no size limits, in addition to the trout limit of 5 per day, with an 8-inch minimum, and of these no more than 1 over 20 inches. There is no limit for whitefish. Check the current OSFR before fishing.

About 1.5 miles long and half-a-mile wide, Suttle Lake is a great place for family outings. Excellent campgrounds and boat ramps and opportunities for horseback riding, hiking, sailing, and windsurfing give the visitor a wide choice of activities. Good swimming areas and designated areas for waterskiing round out the excellent recreational facilities at Suttle Lake. Other fishing opportunities are nearby.

Three Forest Service campgrounds are located on the lake: Blue Bay Campground, South Shore Campground, and Link Creek Campground. All three have drinking water, boat ramps, and charge camping fees. Suttle

Lake Picnic Area is on the northeast corner of the lake. Scout Lake Campground is about .5 mile south of Suttle Lake. Suttle Lake Resort, on the east end of the lake, offers cabins, camping, boat rentals, a restaurant, and store. (Nearby Blue Lake is no longer open to the public.)

To reach Suttle Lake from the Willamette Valley take U.S. Highway 20 east over Santiam Pass. About 7 miles east of Hoodoo Ski Bowl take the Suttle Lake turn south off of Highway 20. From Bend take Highway 20 west through Sisters and about 16 miles west of Sisters turn left at the Suttle Lake sign. The entry road to the resort is just to the west.

TODD LAKE

Size: 45 acres
Depth: 56' max.
Main Catch: stocked brook trout
Best Methods: shore fishing; trolling from float tube or raft
Season: entire year; check OSFR
Best Time: just after ice-out

Todd Lake is the first of many lovely alpine lakes accessed from the Cascade Lakes Highway west of Mount Bachelor. At 6,150 feet, it is also the highest. Lying near the base of Broken Top mountain a half-mile off the highway, the 45-acre lake is encircled by alpine meadows and fir forests and is dominated by spectacular views of Broken Top and Mount Bachelor.

Stocked brook trout are the only game here, but the angling can be invigorating. Fish average 8 to 10 inches with some as large as 15 inches. The best action is usually right after ice-out, a late event at this elevation, but it's also possible to hit some lively fishing anytime during the season.

Small spinners, bait, and flies are all effective on Todd Lake. It is a very pleasant experience to carry in a float tube or small raft and slowly troll around the lake on a warm summer evening. Fly fishers, try trolling green Woolly Buggers if nothing is rising.

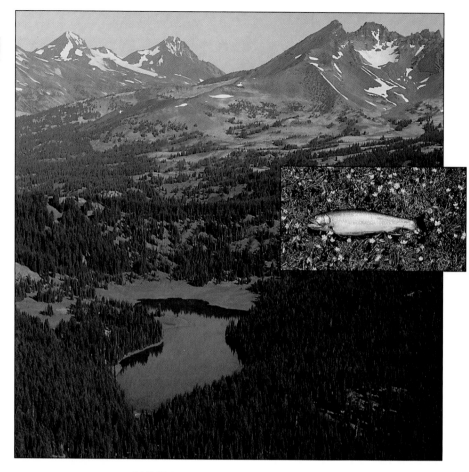

ABOVE: Looking north in this aerial view, Broken Top (right), Middle and North Sisters loom above Todd Lake. INSET: Stocked brook trout are the only game here. Photos by Geoff Hill

LEFT: A float tuber enjoys the solitude at Todd Lake. Photo by Brian O'Keefe

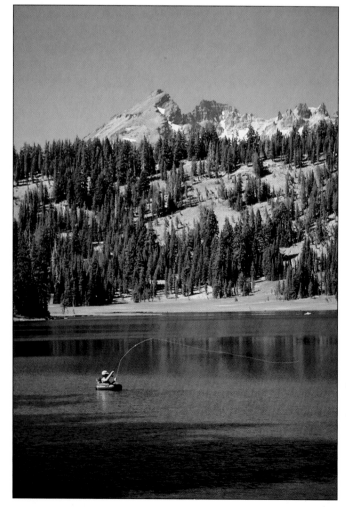

Most of the shoreline of Todd has a very gentle slope and can be fished from shore or easily waded. Rock outcroppings are rare. No major obstacles occupy the water, and the nourishing weed beds are always a good place to fish. A decent trail runs around the lake, but swampy areas exist in the north meadow. There is a small campground with four tent sites and a picnic area on the west shore of the lake. No fee is charged to camp here.

Catch limits on Todd Lake are 5 trout per day, 8-inch minimum length, and of these no more than 1 over 20 inches. Motors are prohibited on the lake. Always check the current OSFR before fishing.

To reach Todd Lake from Bend, follow the signs 22 miles to Mount Bachelor on Forest Road 46 (Century Drive). Two miles past Mount Bachelor Ski Resort, turn right onto Road 370 and drive .5 mile on the gravel and cinder road to a large parking area. The trailhead to the lake (and several other destinations) starts here. It's a .25-mile hike into the lake. Early in the season the road past Mount Bachelor may still be blocked by snow, and Todd Lake will not be accessible by car. To check whether the roads are clear of snow, call the Bend Ranger District of the Deschutes National Forest or Deschutes County Highway Maintenance.

Coming into Todd Lake from the south, take the turn to Sunriver from Highway 97, 15 miles north of LaPine. Follow County Route/Forest Route 40 west to Forest Route 45, follow 18 miles to its junction with County Route 46. Turn left (west) and drive about 5 miles to the turn into Todd Lake on Road 370.

From the Eugene area take State Highway 58 over Willamette Pass, turning left toward Crescent on County Route 61. In approximately 4 miles turn left (north) onto Forest Route 46 toward Davis Lake. It's a long (nearly 50 miles) and very scenic drive up most of the length of the Cascades Lakes Highway to Todd Lake.

SPARKS LAKE

Size: 400 acres
Depth: 10' max.; levels fluctuate
Main Catch: cutthroat & brook trout
Best Methods: fly fishing only with barbless hooks
Season: entire year; check OSFR
Best Time: just after ice-out
Tips: canoes helpful

A large, shallow, trout lake located on the northwest edge of Mount Bachelor, Sparks Lake is the first of the high lakes you see from the Cascade Lakes Highway west of Bend. Views of South Sister, Mount Bachelor, and Broken Top are breathtaking. Prior to 1997, Sparks Lake was a brook trout fishery and, although brookies may still be available, the lake's stocked and featured species is cutthroat trout.

Sparks Lake covers 400 acres and has a maximum depth of 10 feet. The lake is surrounded by fascinating lava formations. At several points along the shore, the lake's water disappears into the edges of the lava,

producing exotic noises as the water drains out. The deepest area of the lake is the far south end.

Brook trout average 11 inches with a few to 18 inches, but numbers are small. The main (northern) body of the lake is very shallow, and the extremely clear water requires long, light leaders and stealth.

A narrow channel about a half-mile long connects the north and south portions of the lake. Smaller fish are usually caught in the channel and larger fish in the lower lake. A 2.5-mile trail leading to the southern portion of the lake starts near the highway. This lower portion of the lake is almost completely surrounded by lava flows, making shore access difficult except by the trail. Sparks is most easily accessed by boat.

Sparks Lake is open to fly angling with barbless hooks only. Debarbing hooks helps reduce injuries to released fish. Streamers are frequently fished during the day and dry flies in the evenings, with bucktails and Mickey Finns popular for trolling. The brook trout often prefer the brighter colors of yellow and orange tied-down Caddis in sizes 8 to 14; Royal Wulffs, Royal Coachmen, Adams, and Humpys in sizes 12 to 18, all fished with fast retrieves. Sometimes realistic nymphs are more effective. Mornings and late afternoons usually provide the best results, and during some late afternoons, there are often some good hatches.

At an elevation of 5,400 feet, access to Sparks Lake

can can be blocked by snow until quite late in the year. Like most of the high lakes, some of the very best fishing is right at ice-out, and some fly fishers will don snowshoes or skis in order to take advantage of hungry trout.

Low water levels at Sparks Lake late in the season can cause difficulties for boaters. Motors are allowed on the lake but cannot be operated while fishing. Consequently, canoes are a popular form of transportation. A good boat ramp is located at the end of the main road into the lake but may not be usable during low water. There is a 10 mph speed limit for motor boats. The catch limit is 5 trout per day, 8-inch minimum, and of these no more than 1 over 20 inches. Always consult the current OSFR before fishing.

There are two small campgrounds on the lake: Soda Creek Campground and Sparks Lake Campground, with no drinking water and no fees. Many people come to Sparks Lake just to canoe, picnic, hike, or camp, and to enjoy the beautiful surroundings. The trailhead located .1 mile off the highway is also a designated mountain bike trail. The Ray Atkeson Memorial offers a barrier-free interpretive trail, wayside, and toilet.

From downtown Bend follow the signs 22 miles to Mount Bachelor on Forest Route 46 (Century Drive). About 4 miles past the ski resort a small sign indicates a left turn to Sparks Lake, onto spur road number 400. After the turn a fork to the right continues .2 mile in along Soda Creek to several primitive campsites. Along the left fork you will reach the trailhead in .1 mile and the first primitive campsites of Sparks Lake Campground are 1 mile down the road. The road ends in 1.7 miles at the boat ramp and turn-around.

For access from the Eugene area, see directions to Todd Lake (page 72).

TOP: South Sister dominates the horizon at Sparks Lake, a shallow lake open for fly fishing only.
Photo by Geoff Hill

RIGHT: A fly angler tries his luck in one of the narrow, shallow channels winding through the Sparks Lake area.
Photo by Brian O'Keefe

DEVILS LAKE

Size:	35 acres
Depth:	9' max.
Main Catch:	stocked rainbow trout; brook trout
Best Methods:	still-fishing from floating device; shore fishing
Season:	entire year; check OSFR
Best Time:	summer season
Tips:	good place for children

Devils Lake is first glimpsed from the Cascade Lakes Highway 1 mile west of Sparks Lake. Its extraordinary turquoise color will stop you in your tracks. Fortunate-ly, there is a large pull-out along the highway designed for this purpose. Spring-fed Devils Lake is absolutely crystal clear, giving the viewer an eerie feeling of looking deep into another world. Both brook and rainbow trout inhabit that world.

One reason these 35 acres of water are so clear is lack of nutrients. The second reason is that it is shallow, 9 feet at its deepest. This cold, clear lake does not grow fish rapidly, and the self-sustaining brook trout are quite small, averaging 6 to 7 inches. Rainbow trout are planted several times during the summer, making this an excellent place to take chil-dren. The average size rainbow trout in the lake is 8 to 11 inches in length.

Devils Lake has very little bottom struc-ture, making fishing both easy (nothing to hang up on) and difficult (spooky fish). Light leaders are essential. Small spinners, bait, and flies will all work here; these hatchery fish are not picky. For spinners, try gold Thomas lures, Mepps, or yellow Roost-er Tails. Red salmon eggs work well for the rainbow and worms for the brookies. Fly fishers cast Adams or attractor dries if fish are rising, caddis, mayfly or damsel nymph imitations if they're not. The northern shore of the lake can be fished from the bank. Most fish are caught in the northeast corner, the deepest part of the lake.

The catch limit is 5 trout per day, 8-inch minimum length, and of these no more than 1 over 20 inches. Always consult the current OSFR before fishing. No motors are allowed on the lake. This is a great place to take a small boat or raft.

Devils Lake Campground offers walk-in tent sites along a winding, wooded trail by the lake. No drinking water is available, but there are outhouses. There is no charge to camp here. Picnic facilities are also available.

Several trailheads nearby include one to the south shore of the lake and several oth-ers that take off into the Three Sisters Wilderness (overnight wilderness camping permit required). There is also a horse camp, parking for stock trailers, and horse access to the wilderness trails at Wickiup Plains trailhead.

To find Devils Lake from downtown Bend drive on the Cascade Lakes Highway 6.5 miles past Mt. Bachelor Ski Resort to the left turn into the Devils Lake Camp-ground/Wickiup Plains Trailhead. From the Eugene area and areas south of Bend, see directions to Todd Lake (page 72).

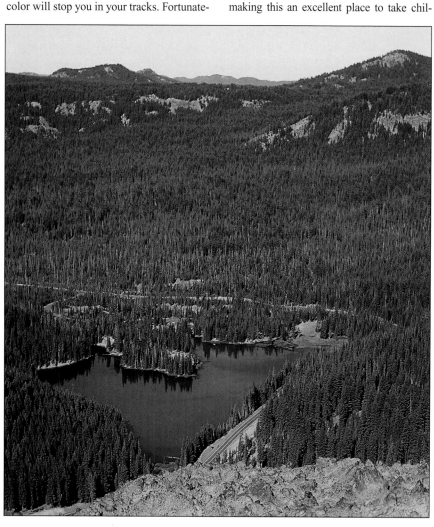

Easily viewed from the Cascade Lakes Highway, this cold, clear, blue lake is a popular wayside attraction as well as a scenic place to fish. Photo by Geoff Hill

ELK LAKE

Size:	390 acres
Depth:	25'–35' avg.; 75' max.
Main Catch:	kokanee; stocked brook trout
Best Methods:	still-fishing and trolling from boats
Season:	entire year; check OSFR
Best Time:	early season (June) for brook trout; late fall evenings for fly fishing

Most visitors come to Elk Lake for the beauty of its cold, clear, deep blue water, views of South Sister, Broken Top, and Mt. Bachelor, sandy beaches, and afternoon winds. Little is heard about the fishing at Elk Lake, which is actually alive and well. The lake has a surface area of 390 acres, a maximum depth of 75 feet, and supports both stocked and naturally reproducing kokanee and brook trout. Elk Lake is located 4 miles south of Devils Lake.

Elk Lake is not a rich lake but, instead, is so transparent you can see the bottom clearly from any location on the surface. It has an average depth of 25 to 35 feet. The many kokanee in the lake, commonly 7 to 10 inches in length – not large but abundant – make excellent eating because of the cold water. These fish are mainly found in the "Kokanee Hole" at the south end of the lake near the lava flow, also the deepest part of the lake. Nightcrawlers, eggs, and periwinkles; still-fishing, wind drifting, and jigging are the methods most often used. Few kokanee are caught elsewhere on the lake.

Twenty-thousand brook trout fingerlings are planted every summer. The average catch is about 12 inches in length with fish up to 18 inches, and good numbers in the 2- to 3-pound range. Commonly used methods are still-fishing worms, trolling, or fly fishing with black flies and lures. Gold flashers with worms on a long leader works well, never silver. Ask at the lodge for tips. The best shore fishing is off the south end using worms.

Early season fishing for brook trout is best – these fish are wonderfully hungry in June. Most are caught in shoal areas, usually in water no deeper than 20 feet. Late fall evenings can be very good fly fishing.

Catch limits on Elk Lake are 25 kokanee per day with no size limit, in addition to a trout limit of 5 per day, 8-inch minimum length, and of these no more than 1 over 20 inches. Always check the current OSFR before fishing. There is a boat speed limit of 10 mph.

The water level at Elk can fluctuate as much as 15 feet through the year, but the boat ramps remain usable. There are no obstacles to boating on the lake, and the few weed beds stay pretty short. Summer homes line the north and northwest shores. Boat launches can be found at Elk Lake Resort, Little Fawn Campground, and Point Campground.

As mentioned before, fishing is not the main activity on Elk Lake. The sandy beaches, good breezes, and great scenery are con-

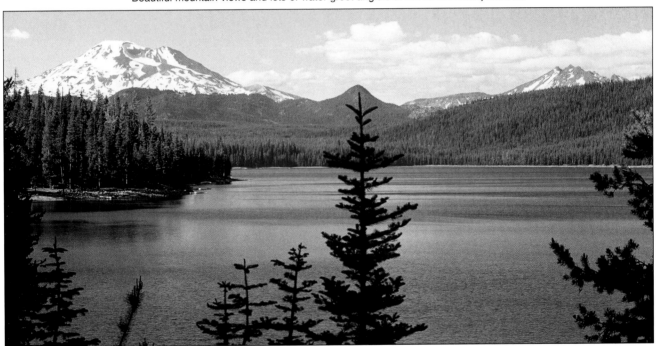

Beautiful mountain views and lots of water greet anglers at Elk Lake. Photo by Geoff Hill

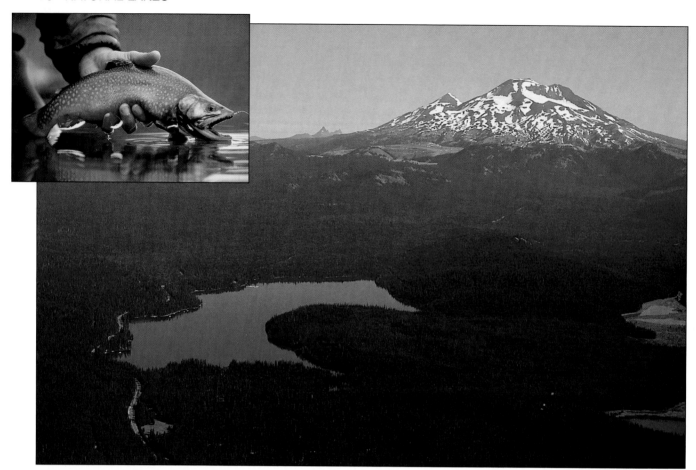

ducive to sailing, windsurfing, picnicking, swimming, and just plain relaxing. The Pacific Crest Trail is 1 mile to the west of Elk Lake. Trailheads are just on the other side of the Cascade Lakes Highway from the lake. Hosmer Lake and many other excellent fishing spots are close by. In the winter, Elk Lake is a popular destination for cross country skiers and snowmobilers.

Forest Service day-use facilities on the lake include Beach on the southwest corner, Little Fawn on the southeast corner, and Sunset View on the east shore. Three campgrounds are on the lake: Elk Lake Campground and Point Campground on the west shore, both with pressurized water systems, latrines, and use fees; and Little Fawn

Campground on the southeast corner with a hand pump, latrines, and fees. Little Fawn also has a group camp that can be reserved in advance. Elk Lake Resort on the west shore is open year-round.

Four miles south of Devils Lake (directions on page 74), a turn east on Forest Route 4625 will bring you to Sunset View in a little over a mile of bumpy gravel road. In another mile you will arrive at the turn into Little Fawn. The turn into Elk Lake Resort off the Cascade Lakes Highway is a .5 mile south of the turn to Sunset View. Elk Lake Campground is .1 mile south of the resort, Point Campground 1 mile farther, Beach Day Use Area another .3 mile south. About a mile south of Beach, turn onto Forest Route

ABOVE: Though most well-known for its sandy beaches and beautiful views, Elk Lake offers some excellent fishing opportunities. Photo by Geoff Hill

INSET: This late fall brook trout was fooled by an artificial fly, photographed and released only to be fooled again.
Photo by Brian O'Keefe

4625 toward Hosmer Lake and East Elk Lake to reach Little Fawn in 1.7 miles. The pavement ends 1.2 miles off the Cascade Lakes Highway.

Coming from the south the turn to East Elk Lake on Forest Route 4625 is 5 miles north of Lava Lake (directions on page 80).

HOSMER LAKE

Size:	160 acres
Depth:	8 1/2' max.
Main Catch:	Atlantic Salmon
	brook & rainbow trout
Best Methods:	fly fishing only
	with barbless hooks
Season:	entire year; check OSFR
Best Time:	good hatches generally
	all season
Tips:	floating devices useful

Hosmer Lake, just east of Elk Lake, is 160 acres of water well-known for its big fish and its beautiful surroundings. This is an idyllic setting with views of Cascade peaks, heather-covered islands, and abundant wildlife. Eight and one-half feet at its deepest, the lake attracts anglers who are often heard muttering to themselves as monster brook trout and Atlantic Salmon cruise in the crystal clear water a few feet below their rod tips. Of course, the fish can see them too. Hosmer Lake is restricted to fly fishing with barbless hooks only and catch-and-release on all salmon.

The average brook trout catch here is 14 inches and many have grown into lunkers over the years. The second place state record brook trout, at 6 pounds, 12 ounces, came out of Hosmer in 1977, and there are more like it still in there. The landlocked Atlantic Salmon in Hosmer average 16 inches in length, with the largest currently about 22 inches. Three-thousand half-pound Atlantic Salmon are planted annually. The stocking of brook trout was discontinued in 1997. Catching fish is a challenging proposition at Hosmer, particularly as its popularity continues to increase. These are double PhD fish.

There are good hatches most of the time on Hosmer. Nonetheless, nymph patterns are used 90% of the time. Leech, damsel, mayfly, and scud imitations are best. For dries, be prepared with Elk Hair Caddis in sizes 8 to 14. Tied-Down Caddis and Salmon Candy patterns are good when used with a floating line. Use a sink tip or full intermediate sinking line when fishing nymphs.

Hosmer Lake's two major pools are connected by a weed-lined channel nearly a mile

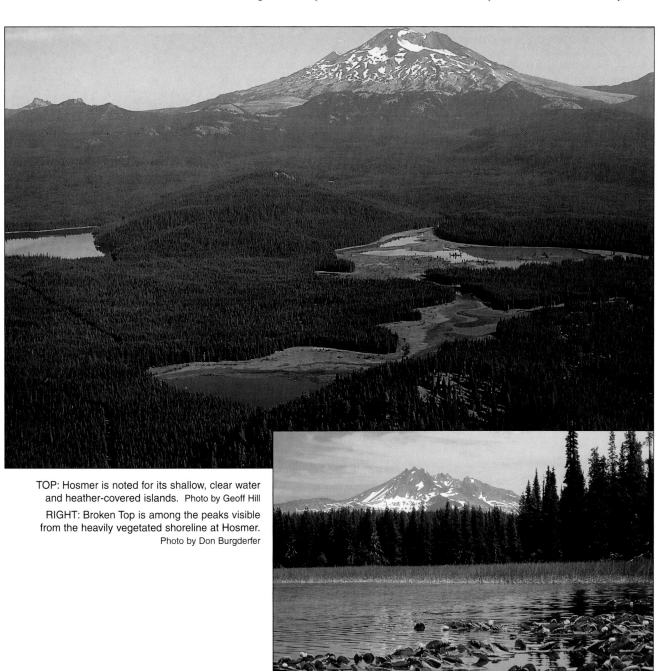

TOP: Hosmer is noted for its shallow, clear water and heather-covered islands. Photo by Geoff Hill

RIGHT: Broken Top is among the peaks visible from the heavily vegetated shoreline at Hosmer. Photo by Don Burgderfer long. The channel runs from the northern portion of the lake down through Mallard Marsh to the southern pool. About halfway down the channel, there is a small cove with an outlet into a lava flow where a rock dam has been built to keep the fish in. Besides the massive amount of shoreline vegetation, there are very few obstacles in the water.

The northern pool is the largest and also the shallowest part of Hosmer Lake, averaging 3 to 4 feet deep. It is fed by Quinn Creek, a crystal clear spring-creek. The bottom has very little structure. A channel running through this portion of the lake is the deepest area within it. The smaller southern pool has the deepest water in all of Hosmer. Water levels are very stable, even in low water years.

The shoreline of Hosmer is heavily vegetated, and there are only a few spots where one can fish from shore with difficulty. However, the fish are seldom anywhere close to shore. It is by far best to fish from a boat. Float tubes and canoes are very popular here. In the fall, many fish move down into the deeper southern portion of the lake. A good caster could conceivably reach fish with a long cast from the boat ramp.

Canoes are the most popular method of conveyance on Hosmer Lake. As many people come to canoe as to fish. It's a pleasant lake to paddle; watch otter, osprey, and endless waterfowl; and drool over big fish.

The catch limit on Hosmer is 5 trout per day, 8-inch minimum length. All Atlantic salmon must be released unharmed. Only fly angling is allowed. Angling from motor-propelled craft while the motor is operating is prohibited, and only electric motors are permitted. Check the current OSFR before fishing.

There are two good campgrounds on the lake. South Campground along the southern portion of the lake has outhouses, a concrete boat ramp, and some pull-throughs. Mallard Marsh Campground is a little farther north with similar facilities and a small slip in the weeds to launch canoes or other small boats. No drinking water is available at the Hosmer campgrounds, and fees are charged to camp here. The nearest drinking water is at Little Fawn Campground on the southeast shore of Elk Lake, about a mile away.

From Bend, travel the Cascade Lakes Highway past Mount Bachelor about 13 miles to milepost 35. Turn left onto paved Road 4625 at the East Elk Lake/Hosmer Lake sign. In just over a mile, take the right hand turn toward the boat ramp, the southern end of Hosmer Lake and South Campground. The turn toward Mallard Marsh Campground on Road 600 is another .1 mile down Road 4625. The pavement ends here.

For access from the south, see directions to Lava Lake (page 80). The turn into Hosmer is 3 miles north of Big Lava Lake.

TOP: Hosmer is noted for its shallow, clear water and heather-islands. Photo by Geoff Hill

BOTTOM: Canoes and float tubes are the most popular method of conveyance for anglers and sightseers on Hosmer Lake. Photo by Rodger Carbone

LAVA LAKE

Size: 1/2 sq. mile (320 acres)
Depth: 30' max.
Main Catch: stocked rainbow & brook trout; chub
Best Methods: still-fishing with bait; fly fishing
Season: general trout; 4th Sat. in April to Oct. 31; check OSFR
Best Time: early and late in season
Tips: floating devices useful

"Big" Lava Lake is one of several high Cascade lakes with excellent trout fishing as well as beautiful surroundings. The view from the lake is dominated by Mount Bachelor, South Sister, and Broken Top. Lava Lake is located about six miles south of Elk Lake along the Cascade Lakes Highway, a National Scenic By-Way.

Big Lava Lake covers approximately one-half square mile and is 30 feet deep, maximum. This rich, spring-fed lake grows fish rapidly. As of 1997, brook trout are no longer stocked, and the lake will be managed primarily for rainbow with annual plantings. Rainbows are currently the most plentiful species, the fish ranging from 6 inches to 5 pounds, averaging 13 to 15 inches with generous numbers in the 16- to 17-inch range.

Brook trout in the lake run to 19 inches, averaging 12 inches in length.

Peak fishing at Lava Lake takes place early and late in the season. Still-fishing with bait is the most popular fishing method throughout the season, and Power Bait or cheese are most often used. One particular brand of cheese is so popular here that a peninsula on the northeast shore is known locally as Velveeta Point. Trolling with Thomas brand and FlatFish lures, about 50 feet off shore, is another productive method in the spring and fall. Fly fishing is most effective these same times of year, when fish are in the abundant shoal areas of the lake.

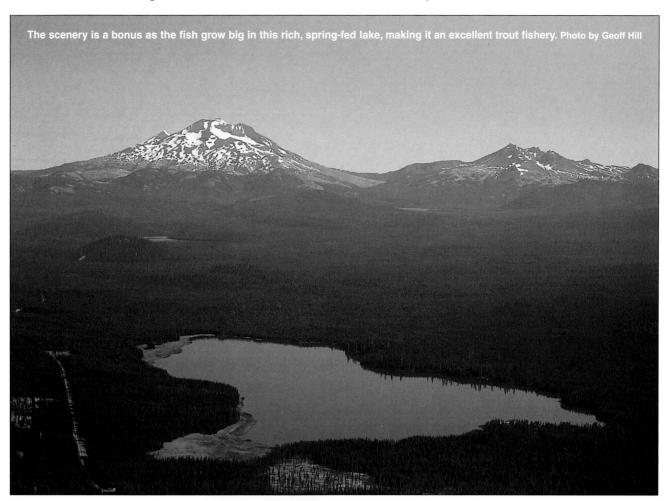

The scenery is a bonus as the fish grow big in this rich, spring-fed lake, making it an excellent trout fishery. Photo by Geoff Hill

Try Careyflashers any time of year or Mickey Finns in the fall, especially in the southeast corner of the lake and along the bull rushes around the lake. When in doubt, try green lures and flies.

Small hooks are a must with all methods, and when trolling, leaders up to 7 feet long and not over 4-pound test should be used. Be forewarned, the Lava Lake fish seem to have a particular dislike for brown leader material. But the most important fact to consider when fishing this lake is that the fish are almost always right on the bottom.

Rushes line most of the shore of Lava Lake, and plentiful shoal areas are easily accessible from the water. Most fish are caught from floating devices. A few rock outcroppings around the lake and the shallow area on the north end of the lake can be fished from shore.

The water level of Lava Lake fluctuates with annual snow melt, the lowest level occurring in April and the highest water levels in early September. The deepest area of the lake runs from the northernmost point of the lake along the east shore down two-thirds the length of the lake.

There is a 10 mph speed limit on the lake.

The view from the boat dock at Lava Lake Resort is worth the trip. Photo by Geoff Hill

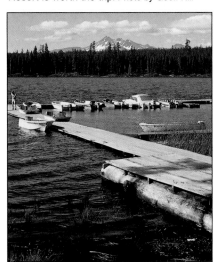

Fishing season begins the fourth Saturday in April and is open through October 31. The catch limit is 5 trout per day, 8-inch minimum, and of these no more than 1 over 20 inches. Always check the current OSFR before fishing.

Most visitors at Lava Lake come to fish, although some come just to camp, enjoy the sights, or canoe this popular scenic area. There are several trailheads near the lake for those who wish to do some hiking. Lava Lake Resort is open during fishing season when the snowpack permits. The resort offers an RV park with full hookups. A Forest Service campground on the lake has drinking water, latrines, a fish cleaning station, and a good boat ramp. There is also a Forest Service campground on Little Lava Lake, a half-mile off the access road into Lava Lake.

From downtown Bend, the turn into Lava Lake on Road 500 is at milepost 38, 16 miles south of Mount Bachelor. The lake is 1 mile in on a paved road. Lava Lake is just as easily reached from Bend by taking the turn to Sunriver off of Highway 97, 15 miles south of Bend and 15 miles north of LaPine. Follow County Route/Forest Route 40 west 22 miles to its junction with County Route 46. Turn right (north) and drive about 6 miles to the turn into Lava Lake.

The lake can also be accessed from the Eugene area via Willamette Pass. See directions to Todd Lake (page 72).

LITTLE LAVA LAKE

Size: 130 acres
Depth: 20' max.
Main Catch: stocked rainbow trout; brook trout; whitefish; chub
Best Methods: still-fishing; trolling
Season: entire year; check OSFR
Best Time: variable
Tips: most fish from boats

Little Lava Lake is a small forest lake about a half-mile south of "Big" Lava Lake. This 130-acre lake has a maximum depth of 20 feet and supports planted rainbow trout, some brook trout, and self-sustaining populations of whitefish and chub. The fishing here is not as good as at Lava due to competition from the chub population. Rainbow trout average 6 to 12 inches. Little Lava has a catch limit of 5 trout per day, 8-inch minimum length, and no more than one over 20 inches. Always check current OSFR before fishing.

All fishing methods work here: bait, lures, and flies, both still-fished and trolled. Trolled flies are often most effective. As in Big Lava, lead or sinking lines are mandatory. The shoreline is similar to big Lava's with bull rushes and some lava outcroppings, surrounded by forest. The best spot to fish from shore is just north of the boat ramp, but most people fish from a boat. There is a 10 mph speed limit on the lake.

Little Lava's biggest claim to fame may not be its fishing, but that it is the source of the mighty Deschutes River which, at this stage of its life, emerges from Little Lava Lake as a demure brook. Occasionally larger fish from the river will migrate into Little Lava Lake. The state record brook trout, at 9 pounds, 6 ounces, was taken from the river below the lake in 1980.

There is a small Forest Service campground at Little Lava with a hand pump, outhouses, and a small concrete boat ramp. This is a good lake for small boats and rafts. It also has a shallow wading area for children near the boat ramp. Additionally, there is a trail head about .1 mile south of the junction with the road to Lava Lake.

To get to Little Lava Lake from downtown Bend, follow the directions to Lava Lake (page 80). About a half-mile in toward Lava Lake on Road 500, turn right toward Little Lava Lake on Road 520. The graveled road reaches the lake in another .5 mile.

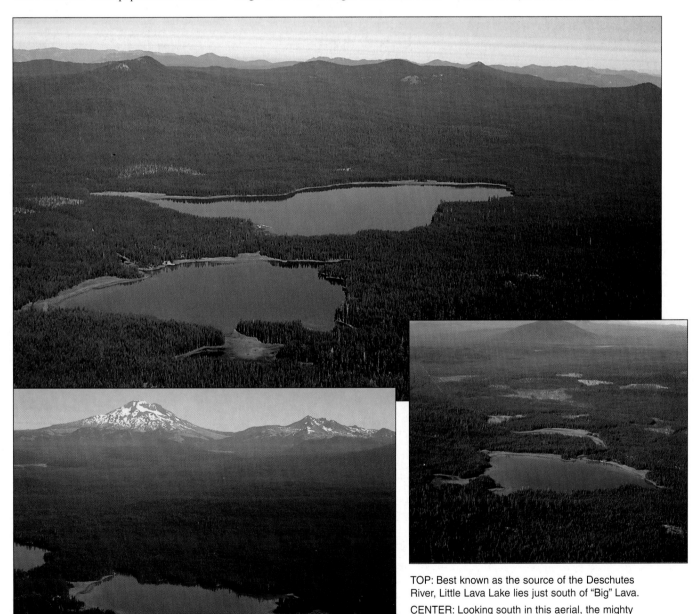

TOP: Best known as the source of the Deschutes River, Little Lava Lake lies just south of "Big" Lava.

CENTER: Looking south in this aerial, the mighty Deschutes is seen emerging from Little Lava Lake as a demure brook.

LEFT: The Cascades dominate the skyline in this view looking north. Photos by Geoff Hill

LITTLE CULTUS LAKE

Size:	175 acres
Depth:	60' max.
Main Catch:	rainbow & brook trout
Best Methods:	trolling; bank fishing
Season:	entire year; check OSFR
Best Time:	early & late in day

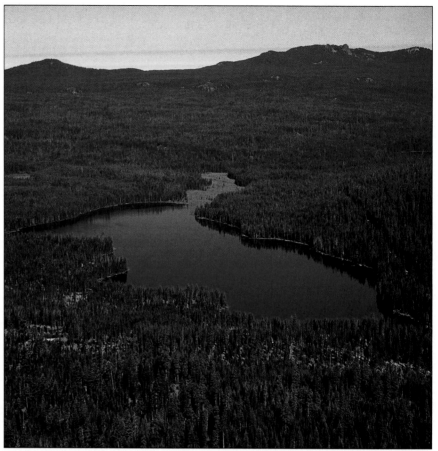

Little Cultus Lake is a 175-acre lake nestled in the pines a few miles off the Cascade Lakes Highway, 2 miles south of ("Big") Cultus Lake. With good fishing for rainbow and brook trout, Little Cultus is a great place to take the family for a quiet weekend of fishing and camping. Rainbow trout, 11–17 inches, are the primary fishery. Brook trout stocking ended in 1997; however, some up to 16 inches are still available.

Little Cultus' gently sloping shorelines are easily wadable. The deepest spots, up to 60 feet deep, are in the center of the lake. Trolling flashers with a trailing nightcrawler or single lures, such as a gold Thomas lure or yellow Rooster Tail, along drop-offs is a commonly used technique here. Anglers should troll slowly to get down to the fish. Bank fishing is best along the north shore of the lake, using bobbers and worms or spinners, spoons, or a marshmallow and worm fished near the bottom. The fish at Little Cultus Lake often surface feed on emerging damselflies and mayflies. Fly fishers can be well-prepared with mayfly dries, ant imitations in sizes 10 to14, damsel nymph imitations, and Woolly Buggers. Searching the shallower areas of the lake with wet flies, early and late in the day, is especially effective.

Catch limits on the lake are 5 trout per day, 8-inch minimum length, and of these no more than 1 over 20 inches. Always check the current OSFR before fishing. There is a 10 mph speed limit on the lake.

Little Cultus Lake offers a quiet, wooded area with primitive camping. Road surfaces are dirt or gravel. Little Cultus Campground, on the southeast corner of the lake, charges a fee and has a picnic area, outhouses, a hand pump for drinking water, and a paved boat ramp. There are more primitive campsites farther west. Part of the northeast shore of Little Cultus Lake, with a few additional campsites, is accessible by the road into Deer Lake. There is no fee to camp in the primitive areas. In addition to fishing, the lake is a popular spot for swimming and boating.

To find Little Cultus Lake follow directions to Cultus Lake (page 84). About 1.5 miles in toward Cultus Lake on Road 4635, turn left onto Road 4630, following signs to Little Cultus Lake and Irish and Taylor Lakes. Little Cultus Lake is about 3 miles, at the junction with Road 640 to Deer Lake. Turn left to reach Little Cultus Campground (.5 mile).

Off the beaten track, nestled in the forest, Little Cultus Lake offers a quiet, peaceful setting for some good fishing for brook and rainbow trout. Photo by Geoff Hill

CULTUS LAKE

Size:	791 acres
Depth:	200' max.
Main Catch:	mackinaw; rainbow & brook trout
Best Methods:	trolling the depths for mackinaw & shallower areas for trout
Season:	entire year; check OSFR
Best Time:	just after ice-out
Tips:	very popular summer recreation area

Cultus Lake is known throughout the state for the trophy mackinaw (lake trout) lurking in water up to 200 feet deep. This 791-acre lake is located in the heart of the high Cascades 50 miles southwest of Bend and 4 miles east of the crest of the Cascade Mountains. Cultus Lake's sapphire blue water is surrounded by pine and fir forest and is bordered on the north and west by the Three Sisters Wilderness.

The mackinaw here range from 12 inches in length to over 20 pounds in weight, with many fish over 10 pounds taken every season. Early in 1996, a 17.5-pound mackinaw was recorded at the resort. In addition to those naturally reproducing, rainbow trout are planted every spring and average 8 to 11 inches throughout the season. Occasionally, a few larger holdovers are taken. A small population of self-sustaining brook trout reach lengths of 10 inches and average 6 to 7 inches. Whitefish are also available.

The water level in Cultus Lake fluctuates about 3 feet every year from its low at the end of winter to a high around the beginning of September. The "mack zone," the deepest water in the lake, runs in a line between the mouth of the big bay on the north shore to the cabins just east of the resort's lodge. Many of the big macks landed come from this part of the lake. Water up to 120 feet in depth runs down the center of the lake from west to east and is also fished for mackinaw. The most popular methods for catching macks are flasher systems trailing a worm, or downrigger systems with a FlatFish or Rapala trolled at depths of 100 to 200 feet. At ice-out, large mackinaw are known to prowl near the edge of the ice, feeding in the ice-free shallows. Every spring, some big fish are taken after the angler has struggled through remaining snow to reach the lake. Any lure or fly resembling a minnow is a good bet to initiate violent strikes at this time of the year.

For rainbow trout, fish in the shallower shoal areas. Try trolling and casting small green or black lures early in the season and switch to silver and gold in the fall. Lures such as Rooster Tails and Mepps can be productive. Another good method is to troll, wind drift, or use a very slow retrieve with trout Power Bait, flies, worms, or red eggs. Still-fishing bait with a bobber is a good bet. Fly fishers, try trolling Woolly Worms or Hare's Ears, and for dries, Elk Hair Caddis, ants, or Comparaduns, again, in the shoal areas. Catch limits on Cultus Lake are 5 trout per day, 8-inch minimum length, and of these no more than 1 over 20 inches, including mackinaw (minimum 24 inches). Always check current OSFR before fishing.

Cultus Lake is a very popular summertime recreation area with large campgrounds and a good boat ramp. Long, sandy beaches with shallow water along the eastern and western shores are ideal for sunbathing and swimming. The lake is a very popular waterskiing area in mid-summer. Trailheads nearby offer opportunities for horse-packing, backpacking, and day-hiking in the Three Sisters Wilderness. Many other good fishing spots are close to Cultus. Also popular at Cultus are windsurfing, kayaking, canoeing, sailing, and nature photography.

Two Forest Service campgrounds rest under large conifers along the shore of the lake. Cultus Lake Campground is a 55-site drive-in campground with drinking water, boat ramp, trailer parking, and a picnic area. There is a fee for camping. West Cultus Lake Campground, at the far west end of the lake, is accessible only by boat, hiking, or horseback. There is a fee to camp there. The 3-mile trail into West Cultus begins at the north end of Cultus Lake Campground. Cultus Lake Resort also has accommodations, plus boat rentals, a store, and a restaurant.

To reach Cultus Lake take the turn to Sunriver off of Highway 97, 15 miles south of Bend and 15 miles north of LaPine. Twenty-two miles west of Sunriver, Route 40 reaches a junction with Route 46. Turn left (south) here and in a little over a mile turn right onto Road 4635 toward Cultus Lake Resort and Cultus Lake. It's about 3 miles into Cultus Lake.

For access from the Eugene area, see directions to Todd Lake (page 72) via Willamette Pass. It's about 32 miles north on Route 46 from County Route 61 to the left turn into Cultus Lake.

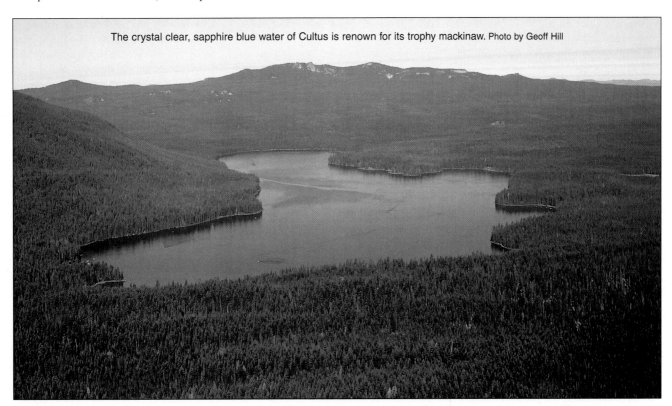

The crystal clear, sapphire blue water of Cultus is renown for its trophy mackinaw. Photo by Geoff Hill

SOUTH TWIN LAKE

Size:	120 acres
Depth:	55' max.
Main Catch:	stocked rainbow trout
Best Methods:	trolling & still-fishing with bait; fly fishing
Season:	general trout; 4th Sat. in April to Oct. 31; check OSFR
Best Time:	variable
Tips:	bait fishing from boats most popular method

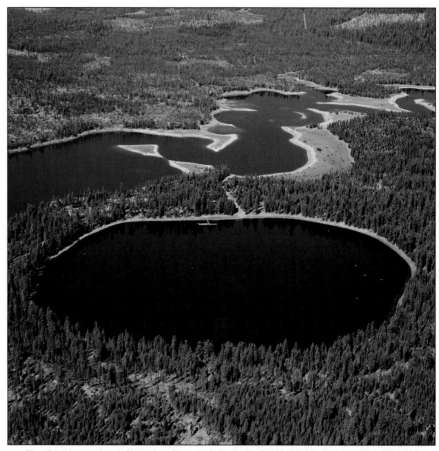

The Deschutes Arm of Wickiup Reservoir flows by South Twin Lake. Photo by Geoff Hill

A lure's toss from the Deschutes arm of Wickiup Reservoir, less than a mile south of North Twin, pinpoints South Twin Lake. The fishing at South Twin has improved tremendously in the past few years after a 1987 poisoning by ODFW to eliminate rough fish. Consistent stocking of fingerlings and legal-size rainbow trout several times a year since then has resulted in an excellent fishery. The largest recorded rainbow to come out of South Twin was over 13.5 pounds.

The trout average 10 to 14 inches, with 18- inch fish common. Most anglers fish from boats and use bait. The deeper south end of the lake, the northeast corner, and the entire north shore along the weedbeds are especially good areas. Ten feet off of the resort's dock is another excellent spot. Depths of 15 to 30 feet are the best producers. The 120-acre lake has a maximum depth of 55 feet. Trolling slowly with a flasher and a piece of worm or egg or with a very small lure are productive methods throughout the season. Still-fishing with eggs, worms, and a marshmallow or Power Bait far enough off the bottom to stay out of the weeds is also a popular method. Successfully used lures are FlatFish, Rooster Tails and various small spoons, or small lures like Needlefish.

For best results, fly fishers use sinking or sink-tip lines and sizes 10 and 12 dark nymphs, including Hare's Ears, Twin Lakes Specials, or dark leech and streamer patterns. Nymph fishing is good all day around the edge of the lake. Make sure you try the shallows near the campground, too. The best fly hatches usually occur mid-day.

One more winning characteristic of South Twin Lake is its calm water when winds are howling over other Cascade lakes. South Twin is completely tree-lined except for the beach day-use area. Water levels vary just a little over the season. The lake is rich with weedbeds. No motors are allowed on the lake. Fishing season opens the last Saturday of April and is open through October 31 each year. The trout catch limit is 5 per day, 8-inch minimum length, and no more than one over 20 inches. Always check the current OSFR before fishing.

South Twin is a more "developed" lake than North Twin. South Twin Campground on the lake and West South Twin Campground on the Deschutes arm of Wickiup Reservoir both have drinking water, boat launches, toilets, beach areas, and fees. South Twin Campground also has a day-use area. Twin Lakes Resort on South Twin Lake is a cozy resort with cabins, a restaurant, store, marina, and full RV hookups. Mountain bike trails originate near the resort. There are also excellent hiking opportunities, wildlife viewing, and good swimming beaches at South Twin. Exceptional fishing opportunities are close-by at Crane Prairie Reservoir and Wickiup Reservoir.

To get there, follow directions to North Twin Lake (page 85). Instead of turning onto the spur road into North Twin continue on Forest Route 4260, 2 miles farther to South Twin Lake.

NORTH TWIN LAKE

Size:	130 acres
Depth:	60' max.
Main Catch:	stocked rainbow trout
Best Methods:	shore fishing; fly fishing
Season:	entire year; check OSFR
Best Time:	early & late in day
Tips:	limited space for backcasting

The near-perfect circles of North Twin Lake and South Twin Lake were formed in prehistoric times by explosive volcanic eruptions when molten lava met ground water. The filled crater of North Twin, at 130 surface acres and a maximum depth of 60 feet, is slightly larger than South Twin. North Twin is ringed by pine forests with the only open area at the beach and boat ramp on the north shore. The lake harbors healthy numbers of stocked rainbow trout and illegally introduced bullhead.

Fishing for rainbow trout here can be very good. The average catch is 8 to 12 inches in length, due to competition with the catfish.

Occasionally a larger fish is extracted. Locals do well angling near the shorelines early and late in the day using bait, flies, or lures. The best bait fishing is along the west shore in the deeper holes using red eggs, Power Bait, or marshmallows and worms suspended just off the bottom. Rooster Tails, Panther Martins, and dark flies trolled slowly or cast toward shore catch many fish. Fly fishing is most effective near shore. There are some good hatches of mayflies, caddis, damsels, and flying ants. A boat or float tube is best for fishing on the lake, due to limited space for backcasts.

Water levels fluctuate slightly during the year but not enough to affect fishing. The lake supports extensive weedbeds, prime trout territory. The majority of shore fishing is done from the west shore where the drop-off is steepest. No motors are allowed on the lake. The trout catch limit is 5 per day, 8-inch minimum length, and no more than one over 20 inches. Always check the current OSFR before fishing. Additionally, ice fishing may

be a possibility when access is available.

North Twin offers quiet, primitive camping in the pines, a good swimming beach, a dirt boat ramp, and other excellent fishing opportunities nearby. North Twin Campground has latrines, no drinking water, and charges a fee. The closest resort is at South Twin.

North Twin Lake is located about 45 miles southwest of Bend. From U.S. Highway 97 take the Fall River turn 3 miles south of Sunriver onto County Route 42, or 2 miles north of LaPine turn onto County Route 43 at the sign to Wickiup Reservoir. The two routes merge 6 miles east of the turnoff onto Forest Route 4260 to Twin Lakes Resort/ Wickiup Reservoir. A dirt spur road turns into North Twin Lake about 100 yards off the highway and reaches the lake and campground in about .25 mile.

From the Eugene area over Willamette Pass, follow directions to Todd Lake (page 72). About 20 miles north of County Road 61, turn east onto Route 42. The turn into the Twin Lakes is about 5 miles east.

Ringed by pine forests, the only open area at North Twin is the beach and boat ramp on the north shore. Photo by Geoff Hill

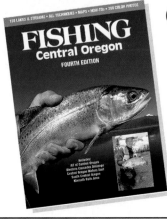

DAVIS LAKE

Size:	3,000 acres at full pool
Depth:	very shallow; max. 25'
Main Catch:	Klamath rainbow; largemouth bass
Best Methods:	fly fishing only with barbless hooks
Season:	entire year; check OSFR
Best Time:	spring & fall
Tips:	floating devices useful

After being hammered by drought in the early 90s, Davis Lake approaches the millennium as a ribbon-trophy trout lake. At full pool, this large, shallow lake located 10 miles south of Crane Prairie covers 3,000 acres and is 25 feet at its deepest. At its best, 2- to 5-pound rainbow are common. Davis Lake is open to fly fishing only with barbless hooks.

Klamath rainbow trout have been planted annually to supplement natural reproduc-tion, which was successful until the drought. Chub have been a problem in the lake, and it is hoped that the piscivorous Klamath trout are dining on the chubs. The stocking of Klamath strain rainbows will be discontin-ued in 1999. The wild rainbow populaton seems to be doing fine since habitat and structure restoration work in Odell Creek. Atlantic Salmon plantings were discontin-ued in 1995, and Atlantic Salmon are no longer found in the lake. Largemouth bass were illegally introduced in 1995 and seem to be thriving.

Fishing at Davis is usually good through-out the season, although some fishermen would say it's a little better in the spring and fall. Some of the most popular flies on the lake are black and dark olive Woolly Bug-gers in sizes 4 to 10, Peacock Herl nymph patterns, Black Montana Nymph, and leech and damsel imitations in black, drab olive, and brown. For hatches, be prepared with Pale Morning Dun and Callibaetis imita-tions. The lake usually fishes well through-out the day.

Reeds, marsh grasses, and other thick vegetation along the shoreline, plus a mucky

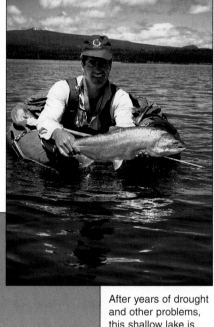

After years of drought and other problems, this shallow lake is finally returning to its former excellence as a fishery. Float tubing is a popular method to access the abundant Klamath rainbows.
Photos by Brian O'Keefe

LEFT: Open for fishing year-round, the Davis Lake area is home to a healthy eagle population (center) and some big rainbows (bottom).
Photos by Brian O'Keefe

bottom, make it very hard to wade and difficult to fish Davis from shore. (It also makes for a very rich aquatic life). A person could fish from the lava flows if the fish are in shallow water, but normally the fish will be nowhere near shore. Float tubes are good here, and some sort of boat or floatation device is normally necessary to fish effectively. There previously was very little structure in the lake, but recently the Forest Service and ODFW added logs to the creek channel to provide cover for fish.

Davis Lake was formed by a huge lava flow less than 300 years ago which blocked Odell Creek, forming a shallow lake with a surface area of 5 square miles. The deepest part of the lake is along the northeast shore against the lava. Odell Creek feeds the lake, along with two other small creeks, and the Odell Creek channel is the second deepest area in the lake. Leaks into the lava cause quite a bit of water fluctuation. Algae blooms can sometimes slow fishing.

Davis is open for fishing year-round. The catch limit is 2 trout per day with an 8-inch minimum length, and of these no more than 1 over 20 inches. There are no bag limits on warm water fish. Watch for the angling deadline signs at the West Davis Campground boat ramp. Motors are allowed on the lake, and fishing is allowed with the motor running.

There is a primitive boat launch at West Davis Campground and a good boat ramp at Lava Flow Campground on the northeast corner of the lake. However, due to nesting eagles, Lava Flow is open only from September 1 to December 31 of each year.

The Davis Lake area is a pretty one, with very good campgrounds. East and West Davis Campgrounds are located on the south end of the lake and have drinking water and camping fees. Lava Flow Campground has no drinking water, no fee, and a boat ramp. Waterfowl abound here, and bird watching is a popular pastime. The grebes do their dance on Davis Lake. A hiking trail runs along the west shore of the lake.

From the Eugene area Davis Lake is reached by taking State Highway 58 east over Willamette Pass. About 3 miles past Crescent Lake Junction turn left onto County Route 61. In another 3 miles turn left onto Forest Route 46 toward Davis Lake. The turn toward West Davis Campground is in another 3 miles onto Forest Route 4660. After traveling about 3 miles on 4660, make a right turn onto Forest Route 4669 which reaches West Davis in about 2 miles. East Davis Lake Campground and Lava Flow

Campground are both accessed 5 miles farther north on Forest Route 46 (a total of about 8 miles from County Route 61) by turning left onto Forest Route 62 to spur road 855. East Davis is then about 2 miles south (left) and Lava Flow is 3 miles north on the 855 spur.

From Bend take U.S. Highway 97 south about 18 miles to the turn to Fall River on County Route 42. Follow 42 west to its junction with County Route 46, about 26 miles. A left onto 46 will bring you to the turn into East Davis and Lava Flow Campgrounds in about 10 miles.

CRESCENT LAKE

Size: 3,600 acres
Depth: 280' max.
Main Catch: kokanee; mackinaw; rainbow & brown trout; whitefish; chub
Best Methods: trolling
Season: entire year; check OSFR
Best Time: early in the season
Tips: fish finders helpful in mid-summer

Crescent Lake is a popular recreation area in an attractive setting of wooded shorelines and sandy beaches. Its brilliant blue-green water shelters kokanee, mackinaw, rainbow trout, brown trout, whitefish, and chub, all waiting to tease your tackle. The lake covers 3,600 acres and is 280 feet deep. Numerous picnic, camping, and swimming areas sprinkled along the shoreline make this a great family spot. Crescent Lake is located 60 miles southwest of Bend and 75 miles southeast of Eugene.

The best fishing at Crescent Lake is early in the spring. At ice-out, the mackinaw (lake trout) are in very shallow water near the resort on the northern tip of the lake. As the season progresses, the fish move deeper, eventually cruising at depths as great as 180 feet by mid-summer. The lake is being managed as a trophy mackinaw fishery. An average mackinaw is in the 8- to 9-pound range, and there's a very good chance of landing one over 10 pounds and even connecting with something over 20 pounds. In 1996, a fish of 31 pounds is rumored to have been pulled out of Crescent Lake.

To catch mackinaw, most anglers troll Rapalas and FlatFish. By July, the fish are in water deep enough that downriggers, lead lines, and heavy weights are necessary. Effective trolling depth depends on the bottom structure and time of year; in mid-summer, the macks can be anywhere from 60 to 180 feet down. Fish finders are very helpful, to put it mildly. Popular fishing areas for mackinaw are along the northwest shore near the summer homes and along underwater ledges near Spring and Contorta Point Campgrounds on the south side of the lake. Jigging with lures, such as Nordics, once the fish have been located is growing in popularity. Also, locating a school of kokanee and jigging underneath them for mackinaw can achieve results, as the big macks feed on the kokanee. A less common technique is casting spoons or Rapalas from shore early in the spring, but bank fishing is mainly limited to two rocky points near Simax Beach. Fly anglers can use big streamers successfully on Crescent Lake.

Kokanee are stocked annually and currently average 14 inches in length, with a few up to 20 inches. Again, early season offers the best fishing, and trolling the usual kokanee lures is the most popular method. Jigging in pinpointed schools and trolling spinners and flashers can also be effective. Running a downrigger at depths of 35, 60, and 90 feet is another method to try. A few of the best kokanee catching areas are off the resort along the northeast shore and out from the summer homes near the island. The larger-than-usual size of these little salmon make this lake a popular kokanee fishing spot.

Annually stocked brown trout average 16 to 24 inches in Crescent Lake, and there are some large browns up to 12 pounds. Fishing the shorelines early and late in the day and trolling Rapalas or Rebels are the most common techniques, but all methods are used to catch the brown trout. Rainbow trout naturally reproduce in Crescent Lake and are stocked annually as well. The numbers are not large, and the average size is around 16 inches with a few as large as 6 to 8 pounds. Techniques are the same as for brown trout. Anglers should look for the rainbow near the creek inlets on the south shore.

Whitefish abound in Crescent Lake. This native species can grow to be quite large. They are good eating, especially delectable when smoked. There is no catch limit on whitefish. They are liable to end up on the end of your line when you are fishing for any of the other species.

Catch limits on Crescent Lake are 5 trout per day, 8-inch minimum length, and of these no more than 1 over 20 inches, including mackinaw (30-inch minimum). One should always check the current OSFR before fishing.

Steve Kroll holds this 9.5-pound brown trout before releasing it. Photo by Rick Arnold

Crescent Lake is used for irrigation and suffered from low water levels for many years. It has been slow to refill and 1996 was the first year that the fishing resumed its usual quality. Some boat ramps which are unusable at low water include Spring Campground and Crescent Lake Campground's new ramp, although the old one at Crescent can still be used successfully. A few obsta-

CRESCENT LAKE
Elevation 4,839'

N

BT Brown Trout
K   Kokanee
M   Mackinaw
R   Rainbow Trout

▲ CAMPGROUND
△ DAY USE AREA
◤ BOAT RAMP
– – – UNPAVED ROAD

Depth up to 80'
Depth 80' to 160'
Depth 160' to 200'
Depth over 200'

Forest Road 60 to Hwy 58
Crescent Lake Junction

CRESCENT CREEK
60
6015
247
480
60

Crescent Lake Lodge
Crescent Lake
Zims Point
summer homes
Tandy Bay Picnic Area
SUMMIT CREEK
Tranquil Cove Picnic Area
Spring Creek
Contorta Point
RAINBOW CREEK
Rainbow Point
Crescent Lake (Boy Scout Camp)
Simax Beach

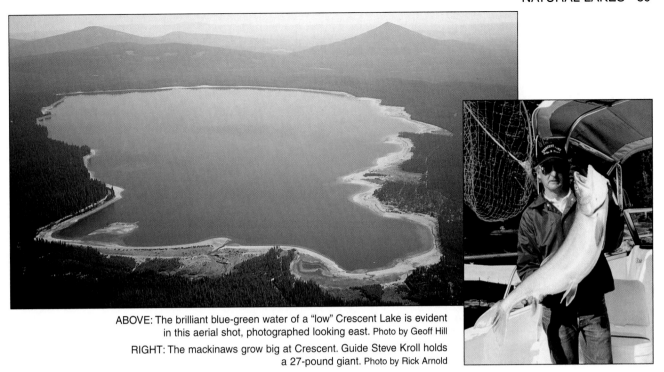

ABOVE: The brilliant blue-green water of a "low" Crescent Lake is evident in this aerial shot, photographed looking east. Photo by Geoff Hill

RIGHT: The mackinaws grow big at Crescent. Guide Steve Kroll holds a 27-pound giant. Photo by Rick Arnold

cles in the form of protruding rocks are present at low water, near the points off of the summer homes and Contorta Point.

The bottom structure of Crescent Lake is a variable topography of humps and bumps that are great for hiding mackinaw. The wind can be bad here, though not quite as strong as at Odell Lake. The north shore is the most sheltered, and the lake's west end tends to have the calmest water. Summer homes line much of the northern shore. Makualla Boy Scout Camp resides on the south shore.

Hobie cats are prevalent on Crescent Lake as are jetskis, swimmers, and windsurfers. Gently sloping, sandy beaches have pleasantly warm water for swimming in the summer. Trailheads located at Crescent Lake Campground and Tranquil Cove lead into the Diamond Peak Wilderness. Trailheads near Spring Campground give access to the Oregon Cascades Recreation Area where mountain bikes are allowed, unlike in the Wilderness Area. Bikes are not allowed on the

Pacific Crest Trail regardless of its location. In the winter, cross-country skiing and snowmobiling are popular activities, although Crescent Lake tends to have more snowmobilers, and Odell Lake is more attuned to cross-country skiers. Good Forest Service roads circle the lake but, at times, are quite a distance from the shore.

Five Forest Service campgrounds are on the lake: Crescent Lake Campground on the northern tip of the lake and Spring Campground on the southwest corner of the lake, both with boat ramps, drinking water, and fees; Contorta Point Campground on the south shore, a small, primitive campground with no fee, no drinking water, and no boat ramp; and Whitefish Horse Camp on the west end where campsites can be reserved. Simax Group Camp on the northeast shore is paved; has electricity to all sites, flush toilets, showers, and a reservation system. Picnic facilities are available at Crescent Lake Campground and Simax Beach on the north-

east shore, at Spring Campground, and at Tandy Bay and Tranquil Cove on the west end. Crescent Lake Lodge and Resort is situated at the most northern point of the lake.

Crescent Lake lies 75 miles southeast of Eugene just off State Highway 58 about 10 miles east of Willamette Pass. At the small community of Crescent Lake Junction, National Forest Route 60 heads southwest and reaches the lake in 2 miles, then runs along the northwest and south shores for about 11 miles to its junction with Forest Route 6015. Forest Route 6015 then heads north to join back with Route 60 near the northern tip of the lake.

Coming from Chemult, Crescent Lake Junction is 18 miles northwest of the junction of Highway 58 and Highway 97. A shortcut from Bend is available by turning west onto County Route 61 at Crescent and following Route 61 to its junction with Highway 58 in 12 miles. It is then 3 miles west on Highway 58 to Crescent Lake Junction.

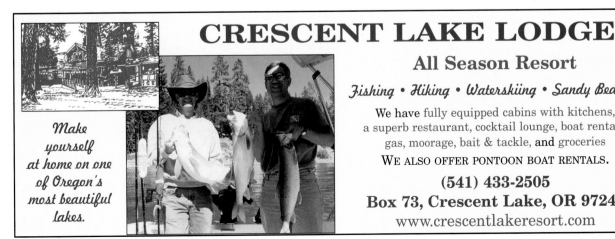

ODELL LAKE

Size:	3,600 acres
Depth:	305' max.
Main Catch:	kokanee; mackinaw; rainbow trout; whitefish
Best Methods:	trolling or jigging for kokanee & mackinaw; still-fishing, fly fishing, & casting spinners or lures for rainbows
Season:	end of April to Oct. 31; check OSFR
Best Time:	mackinaws best April, May, early June & October
Tips:	fish finders, depth gauges & downriggers helpful

Diamond Peak stands as a sentinel over Odell Lake, one of the blue giants of the Deschutes National Forest. A twin to Crescent Lake just a few miles east, Odell Lake covers 3,600 acres, and its cold waters reach a maximum depth of 305 feet. Surrounded by beautiful campsites in thick forests, Odell Lake offers camping, fishing, and windsurfing. Mackinaw, rainbow trout, kokanee, bull trout, and whitefish all naturally reproduce in the lake. Odell Lake is being managed as a trophy mackinaw fishery and holds the state record for mackinaw (lake trout) with a 40-pound, 8-ounce entry in 1984. The fish was 45.5" long and was caught with a homemade jig by Kenneth Erickson, fishing in water 100 to 110 feet deep. The previous state record also came from Odell Lake, a 36-pound, 8-ounce entry in 1976.

A mackinaw weighing 37 pounds was taken out of Odell Lake during the 1998 season, and the lake holds many more in that size range. The average catch is 8 to 9 pounds with many larger. The mackinaw have lots to eat in Odell, preying on smaller fish, including kokanee and whitefish. Many anglers use the strategy of locating the kokanee schools first to find the macks they are really after. Mackinaw should be fished for just below the school of kokanee, on which they may be feeding. The macks also prowl along humps and ledges. Some good mack areas are located east of Princess Creek boat ramp, east of the Highway 58 viewpoint, east of Chinquapin Point boat ramp on the east end, near the railroad slide on the south shore east of Serenity Bay, and off Burley Bluff near Shelter Cove. These fish are found deep most of the year, at depths up to 160 feet. Productive tackle includes weights up to 8 ounces or downriggers (weighted with balls up to 8 pounds) with terminal Rebels, Rapalas or FlatFish in red, fluores-

Surrounded by beautiful campsites in thick forests, Odell Lake is one of the blue giants of the high Cascade lakes.   Photo by Geoff Hill

Odell Lake Resort

Hwy 58, East Exit Odell Lake

P.O. Box 72 • Crescent Lake, OR 97425

541-433-2540

Spectacular Fishing
Spectacular Scenery

Mackinaw • Kokanee • Rainbow Trout

Fishing Guide Service
Cabin & Lodge Rooms
Restaurant
Marina & Moorage
Boat Rentals • Tackle • Licenses

www.odelllakeresort.com

In this view of Odell Lake looking south toward Shelter Cove, Diamond Peak dominates the horizon. Photo by Geoff Hill
INSET: Sometimes even a smooth water day will produce a prize catch. Photo by Del Stephens
RIGHT: Before releasing his trophy bull trout, an endangered species, this angler posed for the camera. Photo by Steve Kroll, Odell Guide Service

cent colors, blue, or green. Troll off shoals and bottom contours at the correct depth.

One technique perfected by the Luhr Jensen fishing team which has produced consistent mackinaw results (after a concentration of fish has been located using a depth sounder) is jigging with the Nordic or Crippled Herring jigs. Some of the team's favorite jigging areas are out from Princess Creek, viewpoint, and the railroad slide. Glo/Fluorescent Green Stripe and Chartreuse/Green Stripe have been the top colors. See the diagram for jigging instructions.

Strikes which come when working a jig almost always occur as the lure is falling.

Hesitation in the descent of the jig, a twitch of the line, a "tap" or anything else unusual as the lure is falling is immediate reason for setting the hook. Many times it is not possible to detect a "strike" but resistance is felt when the rod is raised. This, too, signals "set the hook." The use of a premium quality, high-visibility line such as Trilene XT (which also has high knot strength and thin diameter in relation to pound test) is one thing that will aid anglers in detecting strikes as the jig is falling.

The success rate averages 2 mackinaw per day for those with the know-how, with fish finders, and experience. There are many

good mack areas in the center of the lake. Look for the right depth once you know how deep they are holding. The fish will move deeper as the water warms in spring. At first ice-out, try north of the lodge where they will be in relatively shallow water. Mack fishing is usually best early in the spring, mainly in April and May, sometimes into June, and will pick up a little again in October. In October, the lake trout spawn near the dock at the lodge.

Kokanee average 10 to 12 inches with a few up to 14 inches in length. The year 1995 was one of the best years ever for kokanee, but since then, numbers are down. Most fishermen jig lures or troll flashers followed by a lure with corn or worm. Ford Fenders, Wedding Rings, and Nordics are popular. A fish finder helps to locate schools.

Trolling techniques work well, with most anglers using lead core line, a lake troll, and a small spoon such as Needlefish, Super Duper, or Kokanee King.

Odell has very clear water, so it is recommended to use a 24- to 48-inch, 4- to 8-pound test leader between troll and lure. During warm weather, when kokes can be found near the bottom, a size 025 Nordic jig or Crippled Herring in Mother-of-Pearl, Silver/Blue Stripe/Silver Prism-Lite or Chartreuse/Green Stripe can be very effective. Seasons seem to change the color schemes. Early in spring, most success is with flame orange; late in the summer, it is pink and white.

One of the biggest mistakes made by anglers is working a lure too fast. Most will not perform correctly at fast speeds and kokanee generally will not hit a fast-moving lure … they need to be tantalized by it. The best advice is to troll S-L-O-W-L-Y — the slower the better.

Kokanee have very delicate and tender-mouths. Care must be taken to make sure the shock of the initial strike is absorbed by using a rubber snubber or having a flexible rod tip and that they are carefully played and landed with the aid of a net to prevent hooks from tearing out.

Early in the spring, the kokanee will be in water 10 to 30 feet deep often along the north shore and can be caught with worms and corn. In late summer, downriggers may be necessary as the fish are often as much as 100 feet down. The kokanee prefer water temperatures of 60°F or cooler, so be looking for these temperatures as water warms throughout the season. The best fishing for kokanee is usually early and late in the day. In fall, toward their spawning season, the kokanee move into shallower areas of the lake seeking inlets.

Odell has a good population of rainbow trout averaging 12 to 16 inches with some to 18 inches and over. In 1996, a 22-inch, 5-pound rainbow was recorded; and in 1998, several over 20 inches were caught. Good techniques include fishing along the shorelines trolling spinners, Wedding Rings with corn or worm, or Rooster Tails in brown or black. Still-fishing with crayfish is also an effective method. There is good fly fishing for rainbow trout around the edges of the lake, near Odell Lake Resort, and on the extreme east end of the lake. The rainbow are active all day; and some mornings and evenings, there is dry fly action in the shallows. They can also be caught off the dock on the east end with worms and bobbers or a fly with a bobber. The south shore can be fished for rainbow from the bank.

Odell Lake is closed to the taking of bull trout throughout the season, but they are sometimes caught by mack fishermen. Please release the bull trout carefully. They are listed in the state of Oregon as a threatened and endangered species, and only a small population survives in Odell Lake.

There generally is not much shore fishing at heavily forested Odell Lake. A boat is necessary to fish most effectively. Small boaters beware of the afternoon winds; the lake can get dangerously rough.

Water levels vary little over the year, with many springs and creeks continually feeding the lake. Average depth is 80 to 120 feet. Algae blooms can sometimes slow fishing.

Odell Lake is open late April to October 31. Catch limits are 25 kokanee per day. The trout catch limit is 5 per day, 8-inch minimum length and no more than one over 20 inches. This includes mackinaw (30-inch minimum). Odell is closed to the taking of

RIGHT:
Anglers proudly display a 32 lb., 8 oz. BIG MACK.

FAR RIGHT:
A happy fisherman has this catch to smile about … a 28-pounder!

Photos by Del Stephens

bull trout and is closed to angling within 200 feet of the mouth of Trapper Creek. Always check the current OSFR before fishing.

Odell's dependable afternoon winds make it an excellent and popular windsurfing area. An annual canoe race is sponsored by Odell Lake Resort. The lake is bordered on the south by the Diamond Peak Wilderness, with trailheads along the south shore. Skyline Trail skirts the west end of Odell Lake.

Forest Service campgrounds on the lake include Sunset Cove Campground on the northeast corner of the lake with picnic and camping facilities, a boat ramp, drinking water, and fees; Odell Creek Campground on the southeast corner with a trailhead, drinking water, camping, and fees; Trapper Creek Campground on the southwest corner with a boat ramp, camping, water, fees, and a trailhead; and Princess Creek Campground on the north shore with camping, picnicking, drinking water, a boat ramp, and a fee. Pebble Bay Campground, on the south shore, is accessible by boat only and has a very small picnic and camping area, no drinking water, and no fees. During the winter, the area is enjoyed by cross-country skiers.

Odell Lake Resort on the southeast corner of the lake has accommodations, restaurant, marina, guide service, and boat rentals and is open year-round. Shelter Cove Resort, also open year-round, offers a restaurant, cabins, a marina, an RV park, and a store.

Odell Lake is situated along State Highway 58 about 70 miles southeast of Eugene and just a few miles west of Crescent Lake. Highway 58 parallels the northern shore for most of the length of the lake. There are two roads into Odell Lake: the farthest west, Forest Route 5610, leads from Willamette Pass to the west end of the lake and continues along 1/3 of the southern shore; on the east end of the lake, a well-marked paved road leads into Odell Lake Resort and Odell Creek Campground.

Coming from the east, follow directions to Crescent Lake Junction but continue on Highway 58 for 2 miles farther to Odell Lake.

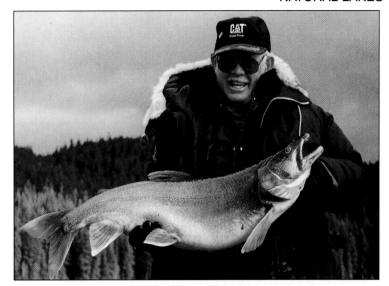

Dean Lewis proves the fishing is great when it's cold and miserable with this 34-pound Mack. Photo by Del Stephens

GOLD LAKE

Size: 96 acres
Depth: 43'; 12' average
Main Catch: brook & rainbow trout
Best Method: fly fishing
Season: Saturday of Memorial Day weekend to October 31
Tips: fly fishing only

Gold Lake
Elevation 4,800'
Maximum Depth 45'

N

5897

To Highway 58

SALT CREEK

Gold Lake

▲ CAMPGROUND
◀ BOAT RAMP
— PAVED ROAD

DEPTH UNDER 20'
DEPTH UNDER 30'
DEPTH ABOVE 30'

Named for its brown stained water that looks gold in certain conditions, Gold Lake is a productive fly fishing lake on the Willamette Pass just west of Odell Lake. Small, easily accessible, loaded with spunky brook and rainbow trout and constantly changing insect hatches, Gold lends itself to fly fishing from float tubes, canoes and rowboats. Fly fishing only with barbless hooks and no boat motors (gas or electric) are allowed, preserving the serenity of the high Cascade setting.

At 96 acres, Gold Lake is big enough to accommodate a fair number of anglers, but small enough to fin all the way around in a float tube, although it will take awhile. With trees and brush to water's edge, the shore is not very friendly to bank fishers. Likewise, the lakebed's soft muddy bottom make wading difficult. The best fishing is from boats around the lake's extensive weed beds and in the 40-foot depths.

With only the Salt Creek outflow breaking its otherwise oval shape, Gold Lake is pretty easy to read. Just go to where fish are rising, typically along the deep edges of weed beds, and fish with floating lines, dry flies and nymphs. If there is no rise activity, use Woolly Buggers on full sink lines in the center of the lake to reach fish resting near the bottom.

The catch rate is about 2-to-1 brookies over rainbows. The brook trout average 12

inches stretching beyond 20. Rainbows run 11-22 inches with a 13-inch average. Both species are fat, hard fighting fish. Gold Lake is a good place to keep some fish. ODFW wants the brook trout eliminated, so there is no size restriction. Even if everyone caught and kept that many, it will take awhile to trim down the brook trout population. Rainbows must be released unharmed. Apparently, the state is trying to create a quality rainbow trout fishery. Not that it isn't good already.

After Crane Prairie, Gold may be one of the buggiest lakes in the state. There are nearly constant hatches providing myriad opportunities to present nymphs, emergers, dries and spinner patterns. The lake has strong ant, caddis, damsel, mayfly, midge and mosquito hatches. Correct size, color and action matches are critical when fish key in on a particular insect. Fish preferences change frequently so be prepared with a well-equipped fly box and don't hesitate to experiment with leader length and retrieves. Gold lake fish display split personalities, favoring motionless dries, but

otherwise like actively moving wet flies. Fly sizes tend to be small, with 12-14's common for dries, 8-12's for nymphs and 6-8's on leech and streamer patterns.

There is a nice Forest Service campground with several lake front campsites, restrooms, recycling station and boat ramp on the west end of the lake. A faint trail leads most of the way around the lake, petering out in a boggy area on the east shore. There is some stream fishing opportunity in the Salt Creek outflow a short distance below the lake, but watch OSFR for special closures. Well-marked trails that double as cross-country ski routes in winter lead to the nearby Marilyn and Rosary lakes, Gold Lake Sno-Park and Willamette Pass Ski Area.

From Eugene, travel 70 miles East on State Highway 58, then 2 miles up Forest Road 500. The signed turn-off is about 1 mile west of Willamette Pass Ski Area.

From Bend, travel 80 miles south to Willamette Pass via Century Drive or U.S. Highway 97, connecting with Highway 58. Travel west past Willamette Pass Ski Area, then 2 miles up FSR 500.

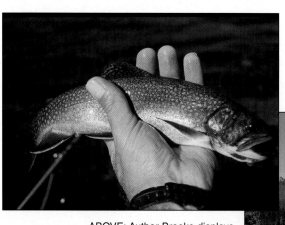

ABOVE: Author Brooke displays his brook. Gold Lake brookies are plentiful, and there is no limit on size or number per day.
RIGHT: Some sort of watercraft is helpful in locating fish.
Photos by Brooke Snavely

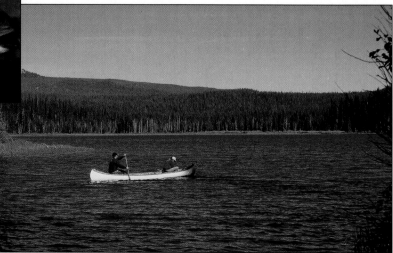

LAKE IN THE DUNES

Size:	4 lakes: 25 acres total
Depth:	easily waded
Main Catch:	rainbow & brown trout
Best Methods:	catch-and-release fly fishing only
Season:	March 1–Oct. 15
Best Time:	consistant throughout fishing season; best in morning
Tips:	private trout fishing operation only, pay-to-fish

Imagine the amazing experience of standing at 4,000 feet elevation in the middle of a remote alkali and sagebrush desert, a harsh

RIGHT: Peter Bowers shows off a thick bodied rainbow from Lake in the Dunes
Photo by Peter Bowers

BELOW: Catching trophy fish is what makes these manmade lakes so special.
Photo by Loren Irving

Private Fly Fishing

You book it – you are the only party there!

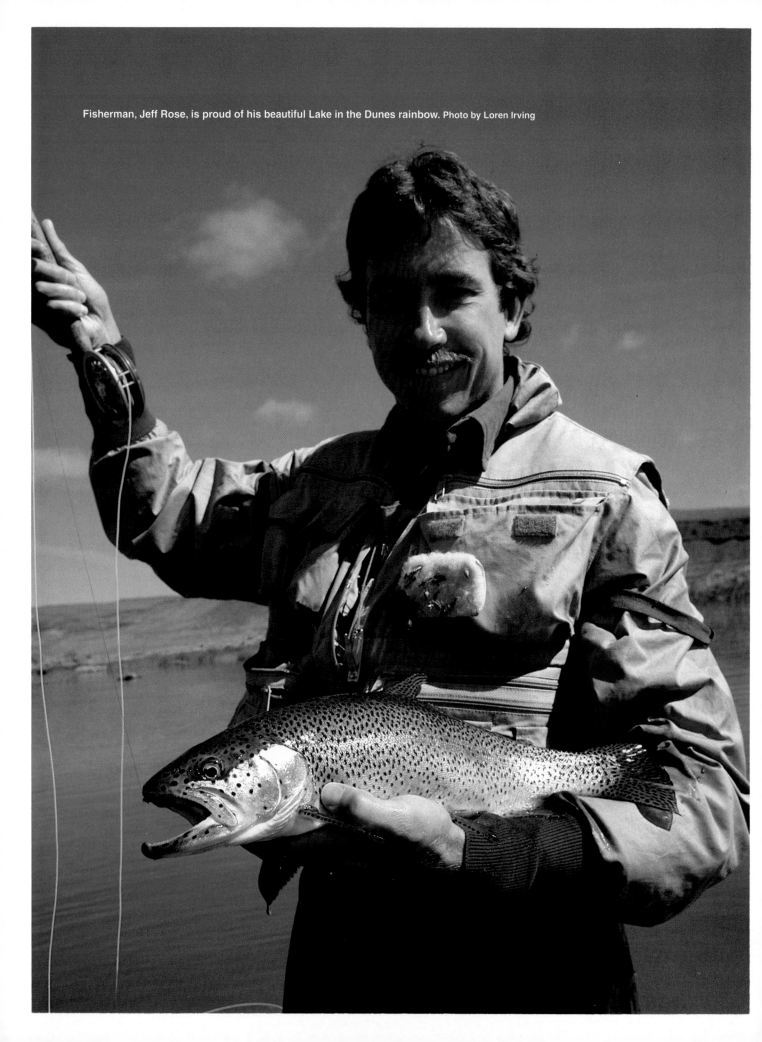

Fisherman, Jeff Rose, is proud of his beautiful Lake in the Dunes rainbow. Photo by Loren Irving environment of extreme temperatures and landscape and having at your feet four lakes filled not merely with your average trout but with leviathans of two trout species. Lake in the Dunes is a unique venture for those rare souls willing to drive to the middle of nowhere and pay to catch lunker salmonids, only to gently release them.

Lake in the Dunes is one of the finest private trout fishing operations in the state, offering pay-to-fish, catch-and-release fly fishing with barbless hooks. The operation is not a profit-making venture; fees just cover expenses. These small, fertile, manmade desert lakes are located near Summer Lake off State Highway 31, about 107 miles south-southeast of Bend.

Formed by a series of dikes, the lakes are fed by springs providing more than 2 million gallons of water daily at a constant 56°F temperature, ideal trout growing conditions. The pure, crystal clear water and the shallow nature of the lakes make catching these trophy fish a real challenge. Combined, the lakes cover 25 acres on the 480-acre ranch. The bulk of the ranch is managed as wetlands for wildlife. Bird watchers and photographers often rent the ranch solely for these opportunities, particularly in the spring.

Naturally reproducing rainbow trout dominate the lakes and average 12 to 16 inches, with some from 16 to 20 inches and a few up to 10 pounds. Fewer in number, brown trout average 12 to 15 inches, with the largest over 20 inches in length.

Presentation and fly size are the most important factors to consider while angling here. These fish are wary; you can see them, and they can see you. You must be stealthy. Fly selection will depend on the time of year. The lakes support a large variety of insects, so productive patterns will change as the day progresses. Mayflies predominate, and there is an abundance of damselflies.

The rainbow trout can usually be caught on small dries, often Callibaetis, Baetis, and midge imitations. Be prepared to fish both dries and nymphs. The browns will take pretty much the same flies as the rainbow, with a possible preference for small emergers and small mayfly dries. Midge imitations to size 20 or smaller may be necessary. Adams, Comparadun, Elk Hair Caddis, Olive Dun, Callibaetis, and Deer Hair Spider patterns would complete an adequate selection of dry flies. Prince Nymphs, damsel and Chironomid imitations, Hare's Ears, Montana and black AP Nymphs, Pheasant Tails, and Woolly Buggers round out a generous nymph assortment. Fishing success is pretty consistent throughout the March 1 through October 15 season.

Fishing is often best in the morning, due to periodically heavy afternoon winds. Since most of the lakes are shallow enough to be easily waded, floating devices are not need-ed. Grasses and cattails line the banks, and the bottoms are mostly smooth sand with some aquatic weeds. Additional structures, including manmade islands, are being added as time goes by.

A rustic log cabin is available on the property which will accommodate up to five people. There is a loft; a small, fully equipped kitchen; electricity, and an indoor bathroom with shower. It is possible to camp on the property with permission. The town of Summer Lake, 7 miles away, has a motel, gas, a restaurant, and a store. Nearby BLM land provides an opportunity for primitive camping.

Another trophy fish … the trout seem to thrive on the many insects available and also on a substantial population of freshwater shrimp in the lakes. Photo by Peter Bowers

Reservations for Lake in the Dunes are exclusively for your party. The booking contact is The Patient Angler Fly Shop in Bend. Prices for the 2001 season are as follows: weekends: 1–5 persons, $300 a day; week-days: 4–5 persons, $250 a day; weekdays: 1–3 persons, $180 a day.

Cabin rental is included in the daily rates. Guides are available through the booking agent for an extra fee, but are really not necessary. Directions to Lake in the Dunes are given when you make your reservation.

LAKE IN THE DUNES

Well Head

LAKE #3

LAKE #1

Canal

Kids Cabin Out House

Cabin

LAKE #4

ROAD

LAKE #2

Well Head

Gate FENCE

BACK COUNTRY LAKES

For anglers wishing to explore an area with more remote fish-filled lakes than can be experienced in a lifetime, Central Oregon is a dream-come-true. Magnificent scenery, old growth forests, sparkling clear, uncrowded water, and no motor vehicles, the hike-in lakes offer all this and fish. Most of the following lakes are in roadless wilderness areas; there are a few to which anglers can drive.

All angling techniques will work on these lakes. The fish have little fishing pressure and are not "educated in the ways of anglers," but they are wary of predators and can be spooked. Still-fishing bait, casting and trolling small lures, such as Rooster Tails or Thomas lures, are effective methods. Early in the season, the fish are aggressive and hungry (and so are the mosquitoes). Bait is popular early in the season, and flies are often best late in the season, especially for brookies, but any of these techniques can work year-round. Anglers should try wind drifting bait along the bottom, especially in mid-summer when fish are deep. Grasshoppers, worms, and Power Bait are all good choices. Fly fishing can, at times, be outstanding, either by matching the hatch or using old standbys, such as ant imitations, damsel nymph imitations, Woolly Buggers, Hare's Ears, and Tied-down Caddis. For brook trout, bucktail streamers are excellent. Ultra-light spinning gear with a bubble and fly is also effective. Light equipment is best for both packing in and catching small fish. Anglers should use small hooks, small lures, and light leaders.

Most, but certainly not all, of the back country lakes are similar in nature: shallow, snow-fed, with fairly stable water levels, short growing season, and very long winters. Fish in these lakes tend to be small; it takes a lot longer for them to get big. Excellent water quality contributes to both the beauty of the lakes and lower productivity. Most of the lakes are short on cover for the fish, and many are prone to winterkill. The natural beauty of these areas is, without a doubt, their most outstanding characteristic.

Trailhead permits are required in selected National Forests and wilderness areas including many trails in the Deschutes National Forest as well as the Mount Jefferson Wilderness (MJW), Three Sisters Wilderness (TSW), and the Mount Washington Wilderness (MWW). The trailpark permits are sold at ranger stations, Forest Service offices, and many local sports shops. Contact the local ranger district for further information.

Some areas of the wilderness are "being loved to death," and use of these areas is discouraged. Of the lakes described in this section of the book, Green Lakes and Matthieu Lakes have been identified by the Forest Service as high-use areas. Better experiences of solitude exist at other locations. Use no-trace techniques while in the wilderness; pamphlets on the subject are available free from the Forest Service. Wilderness and National Forest maps can be purchased at Forest Service offices. The most recent MJW map was published in 1991, the TSW map in 1994. Forest policy currently is to show only destina-

Trio Lakes (located near Waldo Lake) as seen from the air.
Photo by Geoff Hill

tion names on signs in the wilderness, without distances and trail numbers. Therefore, hikers and anglers should carry maps.

Forest Service campgrounds listed with descriptions of the lakes have campsites and outhouses, most have tables, and some have drinking water. Nearly all of the lakes have primitive campsites on their banks, and camping is always allowed on Forest Service land not otherwise posted. Stay limit outside of campgrounds is 30 days and within Forest Service Recreation Sites, 14 days.

Most of these lakes have, in the past, been stocked annually; however, due to lack of funding, helicopter stocking is now done during odd years only. The Confederated Tribes of Warm Springs stock sporadically. Lakes outside of wilderness areas are stocked by truck. Limited planting of pack-in lakes is accomplished using llama and human backs, mainly at lakes within 1 or 2 miles of roads. The more remote lakes have to depend on natural reproduction and weather conditions conducive to survival.

In the following descriptions, the species normally stocked in each lake are designated as follows: **BT** = brook trout; **CT** = cutthroat trout; **RB** = rainbow trout. Small numbers of other species left over from discontinued plantings may also be present in the lakes. Check with local ODFW offices for information on fish survival in unstocked and unlisted lakes. Also, check to be sure the lake is "fishable." Some may be too brushy to fish without a float tube or raft.

Locations of each lake are indicated by notations similar to 25/6/9, an abbreviation of the legal nomenclature for Township 25/Range 6/Section 9. Water depths listed are the maximum for each lake.

Be sure to check the current Oregon Sport Fishing Regulations before fishing.

CRESCENT LAKE AREA

Crescent Lake lies 75 miles southeast of Eugene just off State Highway 58 about 10 miles east of Willamette Pass. At the small community of Crescent Lake Junction, Forest Route 60 heads south and reaches the lake in 2 miles then runs along the west and south shores for about 5 miles to its junction with Forest Route 6015. Forest Route 6015 then follows the eastern shore back to Highway 58 just east of the lake.

Coming from Chemult, Crescent Lake is 18 miles northwest of the junction of Highway 58 and U.S. Highway 97. A shortcut from Bend is available by turning west onto County Route 61 from Highway 97 at the town of Crescent and following Route 61 to its junction with Highway 58 in 12 miles. It is then 3 miles west to Crescent Lake Junction on Highway 58.

Developed Forest Service campgrounds with various facilities are situated around Crescent Lake as well as a resort, store, and other services *(see Crescent Lake on pages 88-89 for more details)*. The Oregon Cascades Recreation Area (OCRA) is not a wilderness but is an area designated for non-motorized, mechanized use, which allows the operation of mountain bikes (unlike in the wilderness areas). The remainder of the lakes in the Crescent Lake area are within the Diamond Peak Wilderness (DPW). Permits are required for entry and are self-issued at trailheads.

Darlene Lake - BT, 5,950 feet elevation, 11 acres, 47 feet deep. Location 25/6/7, OCRA.

Take Forest Route 60 along Crescent Lake's west shore and park at the Windy Lakes Trailhead about .75 mile south of Tandy Bay Campground. Take Windy Lakes Trail 50 for 4 miles to the junction with Trail 46, then take Trail 46 1 mile east to Suzanne Lake. Darlene is 1 mile east of Suzanne on the south side of the trail.

Farrell Lake - BT, 5,580 feet elevation, 4 acres, 11 feet deep. Location 24//5 1/2//23, DPW.

From Forest Route 60 along the west shore of Crescent Lake turn onto Forest Route 6010, .25 mile south of Tandy Bay Campground, and drive west toward Summit Lake. Park at the Meek Lake/Snell Lake Trailhead in 4 miles and take Trail 43 north toward Snell Lake. Farrell Lake is about .5 mile in and about .1 mile bushwhack east of the trail. A small Forest Service campground with few amenities is available at Summit Lake, another 3 miles west of the Meek Lake/Snell Lake Trailhead on Forest Route 6010.

Fawn Lake - BT, 5,680 feet elevation, 43 acres, 27 feet deep. Location 24/6/4, DPW.

The trail to Fawn Lake originates at the boat trailer parking lot in Crescent Lake Campground on the northernmost point of Crescent Lake, just off Forest Route 60. It's 2.7 miles northwest on Trail 44A to Fawn Lake.

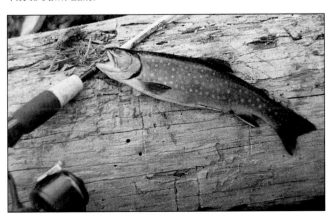

Brook trout are the most common species found in the high, back country lakes. Photo by Ed Dooney

Meek Lake - BT, CT, 5,580 feet elevation, 11 acres, 38 feet deep. Location 24/5/26, OCRA.

Follow directions to Farrell Lake, parking at the Meek Lake/Snell Lake Trailhead. Meek Lake is less than .5 mile to the south along Trail 43.1.

Oldenberg Lake - BT, 5,200 feet elevation, 28 acres, 29 feet deep. Location 25/6/10, OCRA.

From Forest Route 60 along the west shore of Crescent Lake continue on around to the south shore past the entrance to Spring Campground. About .25 mile past Spring park at the Oldenberg Lake Trailhead. Oldenberg is about a 4-mile hike to the south along Trail 45.

Snell Lake - BT, 5,555 feet elevation, 9 acres, 17 feet deep. Location 24//5 1/2//23, DPW.

See directions to Farrell Lake. Snell is a short distance north of Farrell on the east side of Trail 43.

Summit Lake - Stocked BT, RB, and kokanee (as food) for the self-sustaining mackinaw, 5,550 feet elevation, 470 acres, 63 feet deep. Location 24//5 1/2//28, OCRA.

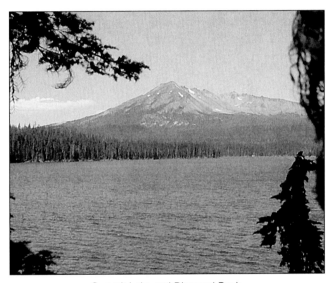

Summit Lake and Diamond Peak.
Photo by Franklin Carson, Oakridge Ranger Station

A large drive-in lake along Forest Route 6010 west of Crescent Lake and bordered on the west shore by spur road 700. From Route 60 along the west shore of Crescent Lake take Forest Route 6010, .25 mile south of Tandy Bay Campground, west about 5 miles to Summit Lake. Route 6010 continues along the west bank of Summit Lake. In addition to road access, Trail 46 runs for a short distance along the east shore, and the Pacific Crest Trail (PCT) touches the south shore. The trailhead for 46 is on the northeast point of Summit Lake on Route 6010. Summit Lake Campground is on the northwest corner of the lake.

Suzanne Lake - BT, 6,000 feet elevation, 10 acres, 47 feet deep. Location 25/6/7, OCRA.

Take route 60 along Crescent Lake's west shore and park at the Windy Lakes Trailhead about .75 mile south of Tandy Bay Campground. Take Windy Lakes Trail 50 for 4 miles to the junction with Trail 46, then hike Trail 46 1 mile east to Suzanne Lake.

Windy Lake, East - BT, 6,190 feet, 14 acres, 14 feet deep. Location 25//5 1/2//12, OCRA.
Windy Lake, North - BT, 6,190 feet, 5 acres, 27 feet deep. Location 25// 5 1/2//1, OCRA.
Windy Lake, South - BT, CT, 6,000 feet, 11 acres, 28 feet deep. Location 25//5 1/2//12, OCRA.
Windy Lake, West - BT, 6,000 feet, 16 acres, 18 feet deep. Location 25//5 1/2//12, OCRA.

The Windy Lakes are a group of four lakes at the end of the trail. The South lake usually has the best fishing. Two access routes exist, one approach is to continue on past Meek Lake (described previously) 4.5 miles on Trail 43.1.

The second possibility is to park at the Windy Lakes Trailhead about .75 mile south of Tandy Bay Campground on the west shore of Crescent Lake and take Windy Lakes Trail 50 for 4 miles to the northernmost of the group of lakes. The south lake is nearly 1 mile south of North Windy Lake.

WILLAMETTE PASS

Willamette Pass is on State Highway 58 about 70 miles southeast of Eugene, just west of Odell Lake. From Chemult, Willamette Pass is 21 miles northwest of the junction of Highway 58 and U.S. Highway 97. A shortcut from Bend is available by turning west off Highway 97 onto County Route 61 at Crescent and following Route 61 to its junction with Highway 58 in 12 miles. It is then about 8 miles west to the Pass.

Developed Forest Service campgrounds in this area are available at Odell Lake, Gold Lake, Waldo Lake, and Crescent Lake.

Gold Lake - All natural reproduction, BT, RB, 4,800 feet elevation, 104 acres, 25 feet deep. Location 22/6/30, Willamette National Forest.

A drive-in lake with excellent camping and open to fly angling only. No motors are allowed. Three miles west of Willamette Pass on State Highway 58, take Forest Service spur road 500 north off Highway 58. It's about 2 miles into Gold Lake. See page 94.

Maiden Lake - BT, 6,360 feet elevation, 6 acres, 23 feet deep. Location 23/6/1, Crescent Ranger District (CRD), Deschutes National Forest.

The most popular route into Maiden Lake is from the Pacific Crest Trail (PCT) north of Willamette Pass. Park at the PCT trailhead on the north side of Willamette Pass. Travel 2.5 miles into Rosary Lakes then continue on to the junction with Trail 41. A 2-mile hike to the east on Trail 41 brings you to Maiden Lake.

It's a shorter hike to Maiden Lake from the Davis Lake area. From the Eugene area Davis Lake is reached by taking Highway 58 east over Willamette Pass. About 3 miles past Crescent Lake Junction turn left onto County Route 61. In another 3 miles turn left onto Forest

Route 46 toward Davis Lake. The turn toward West Davis Campground is in another 3 miles onto Forest Route 4660. Continue on Route 4660 past the turn toward the campground, following signs to the Maiden Lake Trail for another 2 miles. At the junction with Forest Route 4664 turn right. In a very short distance on 4664, spur road 100 heads west (left). The trailhead is at the end of this spur road in a little over 1 mile, and it's about a 3-mile hike into the lake.

From Bend take U.S. Highway 97 south about 18 miles to the turn to Fall River on County Route 42. Follow 42 west to its junction with County Route 46, about 26 miles. A left onto 46 will bring you to the turn toward West Davis Lake Campground and the Maiden Lake Trailhead in about 14 miles. Continue on Forest Route 4660 following signs to Maiden Lake Trail for a total of about 5 miles to the junction with 4664, turning right. In a very short distance on 4664, spur road 100 heads west (left). The trailhead is at the end of this spur road in a little over 1 mile. From this vantage point Maiden Lake is a 3-mile hike to the west on Trail 41.

Rosary Lake, Lower - BT, RB, CT, 5,710 feet elevation, 42 acres, 50 feet deep. Location 23/6/3, CRD, Deschutes National Forest.
Rosary Lake, Middle - BT, 5,830 feet elevation, 9 acres, 31 feet deep. Location 23/6/3, CRD, Deschutes National Forest.
Rosary Lake, Upper - BT, 5,835 feet elevation, 8 acres, 21 feet deep. Location 23/6/3, CRD, Deschutes National Forest.

From Willamette Pass on State Highway 58, take the PCT northeast reaching Lower Rosary Lakes in 2.5 miles. See directions to Maiden Lake for more details.

WALDO LAKE AREA

Developed Forest Service campgrounds are available at Waldo Lake.

Bobby Lake - BT, RB, 5,420 feet elevation, 86 acres, 71 feet deep. Location 22/6/14, Crescent Ranger District, Deschutes National Forest.

The shortest hike in is from the west. Turn off State Highway 58, 3.5 miles west of Willamette Pass Summit onto Forest Route 5897 toward Waldo Lake. A 5.5 mile drive brings you to Trail 3663 and a small parking area on the right hand side of the road. The trailhead to Bobby is right across the road from Betty Lake Trailhead which has a very large parking area. Bobby is 2 miles east on Trail 3663.

Bobby can also be reached from the east by taking Forest Route 4652 west off Route 46, the Cascade Lakes Highway. The turn is just across the highway from the entrance to North Davis Creek Campground. About 3.5 miles down 4652 take spur road 400 which ends at the trailhead in about .5 mile. It is then a 4.5 mile hike into the lake.

Charlton Lake - BT, 5,700 feet elevation, 100 acres, 74 feet deep. Location 21/6/14, Bend Ranger District (BRD), Deschutes National Forest.

Charlton is a short hike along the Pacific Crest Trail (PCT) from off Forest Route 4290. Turn off State Highway 58, 3.5 miles west of Willamette Pass Summit onto Forest Route 5897 toward Waldo Lake. Continue north on Route 5897 about 12 miles to the junction with Route 4290. The PCT trailhead is 1 mile east on 4290. Charlton is .25 mile to the south on the PCT. Charlton can also be accessed from the east by taking the turn onto Forest Route 4290 from the Cascade Lakes Highway (Route 46) just 3 miles south of Rock Creek Campground on Crane Prairie Reservoir. From the east the PCT is a 10-mile drive on 4290.

Hidden Lake - BT, 6,200 feet elevation, 13 acres, 35 feet. Location 21/6/26, BRD, Deschutes National Forest.

Off the beaten path, Hidden Lake is 1.5 miles due south of Charleton Lake, on the west slope of Gerdine Butte. See directions to Charlton Lake. From Charlton, either continue on the PCT to its junction with Trail 21 west of Hidden Lake and about 1 mile south of Charlton or take Trail 19 for 1 mile south of Charlton Lake to connect with Trail 21 east of Hidden Lake. Hidden Lake is between these two trail junctions, approximately .5 mile south of Trail 21. No official trial leads to the lake, and it is difficult to find; most people end up at Found Lake instead. Take a good topo map of the area and a compass.

Johnny Lake - BT, 5,400 feet elevation, 20 acres, 21 feet deep. Location 21/7/29, BRD, Deschutes National Forest.

Five air miles due east of Waldo Lake, Johnny can be reached either from the east off Forest Route 46 (the Cascade Lakes Highway) or from Waldo Lake. From the east, take Forest Route 4290 west at the junction of Route 46 and Route 42, 2 miles south of Crane Prairie Reservoir. In about 4 miles, turn south onto spur road 200 which dead-ends in about 1 mile at the trailhead to Johnny Lake. Trail 99 reaches Johnny in about .5 mile. From the Waldo Lake area, turn east on Route 4290 near the north end of Waldo and drive about 7 miles east to spur road 200.

Lily Lake - BT, 5,700 feet elevation, 13 acres, 44 feet. Location 21/6/12, BRD, Deschutes National Forest.

Lily Lake is easily reached from the PCT east of Waldo Lake. Turn off State Highway 58, 3.5 miles west of Willamette Pass Summit onto Forest Route 5897 toward Waldo Lake. Continue north on Route 5897 about 12 miles to the junction with Route 4290. The PCT trailhead is 1 mile east on 4290. Lily Lake can also be

Charlton Lake (front), a short hike along the Pacific Crest Trail, lies a short distance east of Waldo Lake. Photo by Geoff Hill

accessed from the east by taking the turn onto Forest Route 4290 from the Cascade Lakes Highway (Route 46) just 3 miles south of Rock Creek Campground on Crane Prairie Reservoir. From the east, the PCT is a 10-mile drive on 4290. Hike the PCT north for 1.5 miles to the junction with Trail 19. Lily Lake is less than .5 mile east on the north side of Trail 19.

CULTUS LAKE AREA

Most of the following lakes are in the Three Sisters Wilderness (TSW). Developed Forest Service campgrounds are located on Cultus Lake and Little Cultus Lake.

To reach Cultus Lake take the turn to Sunriver (County/Forest Route 40) off U.S. Highway 97, 15 miles south of Bend and 15 miles north of LaPine. Twenty-two miles west of Sunriver, Route 40 reaches a junction with Route 46. Turn left (south) here and in a little over 1 mile turn right onto Forest Route 4635 toward Cultus Lake Resort and Cultus Lake. It's about 3 miles into Cultus Lake.

For access from the Eugene area take State Highway 58 over Willamette Pass continuing on to Crescent Lake Junction. Three miles past Crescent Lake Junction turn left toward Crescent on County Route 61. In approximately 4 miles turn left (north) onto Forest Route 46 toward Davis Lake. It's about 32 miles up the Cascade Lakes Highway (Route 46) to the turn into Cultus Lake.

To find Little Cultus Lake, about 1.5 miles in toward Cultus Lake on Route 4635, turn left onto Route 4630, following signs to Little Cultus Lake and Irish and Taylor Lakes. The east end of Little Cultus Lake is reached in about 3 miles at the junction with spur road 640 to Deer Lake. Turn left at this junction to reach Little Cultus Campground in less than .5 mile.

Big Finger Lake - BT, 5,400 feet elevation, 5 acres, 15 feet deep. Location 19/7/33, TSW, 3 air miles north of Cultus Lake.

Take the turn to Deer Lake on spur 640 off Forest Route 4630 into Little Cultus Lake. Drive in as far as you can to a dead-end and the beginning of Trail 6 to West Cultus Lake Campground. Trail 6 reaches to West Cultus Lake Campground, which has a boat dock and outhouses, in 1.4 miles. From the campground take Trail 6 northeast for about .5 mile to the junction with Trail 16 to Winopee Lake. In .4 mile toward Winopee Lake, Trail 9 heads to Teddy Lakes, Trail 16 continues to Winopee Lake. At the junction with Trail 33 in 4.1 miles, just past Winopee Lake, take Trail 33 east to Snowshoe Lake. Big Finger is .25 mile east of Snowshoe, with no official trail leading to it. It may be a smart idea to bring a good topo map and your bushwhacking gear.

Blowdown Lake - BT, 5,500 feet elevation, 4 acres, 8 feet deep. Location 20/7/31//36, Bend Ranger District (BRD), Deschutes National Forest.

From Little Cultus Lake Campground continue on spur road 600 past the lake about 4 miles. There is no sign and no maintained trail into Blowdown. The primitive trail is exactly 1 mile east of the Pacific Crest Trail (PCT) trailhead. The lake is accessed by a brief adventure through the brush, .25 mile south of the road. Good campsites are available at Irish and Taylor Lakes 1 mile west on spur 600.

Brahma Lake - BT, 5,500 feet elevation, 12 acres, 12 feet deep. Location 20/6/13, TSW, 3 air miles due west of Cultus Lake.

From Little Cultus Lake Campground continue on spur road 600 past the lake about 5 miles to the trailhead for the PCT. Brahma Lake is 2 miles north on the west side of the PCT.

Deer Lake - CT, 4,900 feet elevation, 70 acres, 20 feet deep. Location 20/7/21, BRD, Deschutes National Forest.

You can drive right to Deer Lake from the road into Little Cultus Lake. Where Forest Route 4630 touches the east end of Little Cultus Lake take spur road 640 north about 2 miles to Deer Lake. There are a few primitive campsites on the lake.

Dennis Lake - BT, 6,100 feet elevation, 12 acres, 42 feet deep. Location 20/6/12, TSW.

From Little Cultus Lake Campground continue on spur road 600 past Little Cultus about 5 miles to the trailhead for the PCT. Hike north along the PCT 4.2 miles to Blaze Lake. One-quarter mile beyond Blaze you cross a spring creek. At this point Dennis Lake is

.25 mile to the northwest and a steep 400 feet above the PCT. There is no official trail to the lake so take a good USGS topo map. Dennis has good bank fishing.

Hanks Lake, East - CT, 5,500 feet elevation, 10 acres, 27 feet deep. Location 20/7/30, TSW.

Hanks Lake, Middle - RB, 5,500 feet elevation, 15 acres, 30 feet deep. Location 20/7/30, TSW.

Hanks Lake, West - BT, 5,500 feet elevation, 15 acres, 13 feet deep.

The Many Lakes Trailhead to Hanks Lakes is 1.5 miles east of the PCT, about 3.5 miles west of Little Cultus Lake on spur road 600. Trail 15 heads north from the trailhead and reaches the west shore of Middle Hanks Lake in less than .5 mile. West Hanks is just to the west of Middle Hanks, and East Hanks is southeast of Middle Hanks.

Irish Lake - BT, 5,550 feet elevation, 28 acres, 16 feet deep. Location 20/6/25, TSW.

Irish Lake is a drive-in lake located along spur road 600 about 5 miles west of Little Cultus Lake and just east of the PCT trailhead. Irish Lake is on the north side of the road, the PCT follows the west shore of the lake. Taylor Lake is on the south side of the road just before Irish. Motors are prohibited on both lakes.

Kershaw Lake - BT, 5,500 feet elevation, 4 acres, 13 feet deep. Location 20/7/30, TSW.

The Many Lakes Trailhead, 1.5 miles east of the PCT and about 3.5 miles west of Little Cultus Lake on spur road 600, leads to Kershaw Lake. Many Lakes Trail 15 heads north and reaches the west shore of Middle Hanks Lake in less than .5 mile. To find Kershaw Lake continue on about another .5 mile north until you cross a depression with a small creek connecting a series of ponds. Kershaw Lake is east of the trail, a short bushwack just past this creek. Total distance from the road is not more than 1 mile.

Lemish Lake - BT, 5,200 feet elevation, 14 acres, 13 feet deep. Location 21/7/5, BRD, Deschutes National Forest.

The trailhead to Lemish Lake is about 1 mile west of Little Cultus Lake on spur road 600 on the south side of the road. It's about a .5-mile hike in.

Raft Lake - BT, 4,900 feet elevation, 10 acres, 27 feet deep. Location 20/7/29, TSW.

You'll need the USGS topo map for this one. About .5 mile west of the Lemish Lake Trailhead on spur 600, about 1.5 miles west of Little Cultus Lake, Raft Lake is .5 mile cross-country to the north. There is no official trail, and there are many other small lakes in the same area that you may find instead of Raft Lake.

Red Slide Lake - RB, 5,500 feet elevation, 2 acres, 18 feet deep. Location 20/6/24, TSW. This can be a tough one to find; bring the topo maps.

From Little Cultus Lake Campground continue on spur road 600 past the lake about 5 miles to the trailhead for the PCT. Brahma Lake is 2 miles north on the west side of the PCT, and Red Slide is about .25 mile south of Brahma. There is no official trail in to Red Slide and you may find any of the numerous other lakes instead.

Snowshoe Lake, Lower - BT, 5,100 feet elevation, 18 acres, 15 feet deep. Location 19/7/33, TSW.

Snowshoe Lake, Middle - BT, 5,150 feet elevation, 3 acres, 13 feet deep. Location 19/7/33, TSW.

Snowshoe Lake, Upper - BT, 5,150 feet elevation, 30 acres, 8 feet deep. Location 19/7/29, TSW.

Off Forest Route 4630 into Little Cultus Lake take the turn to Deer Lake on spur 640. Drive in as far as you can to a dead-end and the beginning of Trail 6 to West Cultus Lake Campground. Trail 6 reaches to West Cultus Lake Campground, which has a boat dock and outhouses, in 1.4 miles. From the campground take Trail 6 northeast for about .5 mile to the junction with Trail 16 to Winopee Lake. In .4 mile toward Winopee Lake, Trail 9 heads to Teddy Lakes, and Trail 16 continues to Winopee Lake. At the junction with Trail 33 in 4.1 miles, just past Winopee Lake, take Trail 33 east to Snowshoe Lake. Lower Snowshoe Lake is on the east side of Trail 33. Middle Snowshoe is .25 mile west of the northern end of Lower Snowshoe. Continuing north on Trail 33 from Middle Snowshoe will bring you to Upper Snowshoe in .5 mile.

Strider Lake - RB, 5,000 feet elevation, 3 acres, 22 feet deep. Location 20/7/29, TSW.

Strider Lake is in the same ballpark as Raft Lake on the north side of the 600 spur road west of Little Cultus Lake. About .75 mile past the Lemish Lake Trailhead, Strider is a .5 mile bush-pusher north.

Teddy Lake, North - BT, RB, 4,900 feet elevation, 30 acres, 28 feet deep. Located in 20/7/10, TSW.

Teddy Lake, South - BT, 4,900 feet elevation, 17 acres, 10 feet deep. Location 20/7/10, TSW.

On the way to Little Cultus Lake take the turn to Deer Lake on spur 640 off Forest Route 4630. Drive in as far as you can to a dead-end and the beginning of Trail 6 to West Cultus Lake. Trail 6 reaches West Cultus Lake Campground in 1.4 miles. From the campground take Trail 6 northeast for about .5 mile to the junction

with Trail 16 to Winopee Lake. In .4 mile toward Winopee Lake, Trail 9 heads to Teddy Lakes, Trail 16 continues to Winopee Lake. South Teddy Lake is not much more than 1 mile north of West Cultus Campground on the west side of Trail 9. North Teddy is .25 mile northeast of South Teddy.

Timmy Lake - RB, 5,500 feet elevation, 3 acres, 15 feet deep. Location 20/6/24, TSW.

Continue past Little Cultus Lake about 4 miles on spur road 600 to the PCT trailhead on the west side of Irish Lake. Timmy Lake is about 2 miles north on the PCT and about .25 mile east of the trail, just south of Red Slide Lake. There is no maintained trail in and the lake is difficult to spot because of its location on the top of a rise. Timmy is easy to fish from shore.

Winopee Lake - BT, RB, 4,950 feet elevation, 40 acres, 43 feet deep. Location 19/7/33, TSW.

From the east end of Little Cultus Lake take the turn to Deer Lake on spur 640 off Forest Route 4630. Drive in as far as you can to a dead-end and the beginning of Trail 6 to West Cultus Lake. Trail 6 reaches West Cultus Lake Campground, which has a boat dock and outhouses, in 1.4 miles. From the campground take Trail 6 northeast about a .5 mile to the junction with Trail 16 to Winopee Lake. Winopee is about 3 miles north.

SISTERS AREA

Most of the following lakes are within the Mount Jefferson Wilderness (MJW), but several have road access.

Booth Lake - BT, 5,050 feet elevation, 8 acres, 34 feet deep. Location 13/8/7, MJW.

To reach Booth Lake take U.S. Highway 20 to the Santiam Pass Summit either from Bend to the east or from the Albany area in the Willamette Valley to the west. The Santiam Pass/Pacific Crest Trail (PCT) parking lot is on the north side of the highway about .5 mile east of Hoodoo Ski Bowl. There is ample parking space, including room for horse trailers. Booth Lake is easily reached by first hiking a short distance from the parking area on the PCT, then continuing about 2 miles on Trail 4014 to Square Lake. Continue another 1.4 miles to Booth Lake on the Old Summit Trail. Booth is on the west side of the trail. The nearest developed campgrounds are at Lost Lake to the west or Suttle Lake to the east on Highway 20.

Cabot Lake - CT, 4,550 feet elevation, 6 acres, 22 feet deep. Location 1/8/34, MJW.

Take U.S. Highway 20 either from Bend to the east or from the Albany area in the Willamette Valley to the west. Seven miles east of the Santiam Pass Summit, 1 mile east of Suttle Lake, and about 13 miles west of Sisters, turn north onto Forest Route 12 from U.S. Highway 20. Drive north 5 miles on Route 12 then take Forest Route 1230 for 9 miles to its end at the trailhead. A 2-mile hike on Trail 4003 gets you to Cabot Lake. The nearest developed Forest Service Recreation Site is Abbot Creek Campground just off Forest Route 12.

Cache Lake - BT, CT, 4,350 feet elevation, 8 acres, 9 feet deep. Location 13/8/33, Sisters Ranger District (SRD), Deschutes National Forest.

The namesake of the Cache Lake Basin collection of lakes,

Cache Lake, itself, is a drive-in experience. Take U.S. Highway 20 either from Bend to the east or from the Albany area in the Willamette Valley to the west. Seven miles east of the Santiam Pass Summit, 1.5 miles east of Suttle Lake, and about 13 miles west of Sisters, turn south onto Forest Route 2066 off U.S. Highway 20. Stay on 2066 for about 2 miles then take Forest Route 2068 another 3 miles to the junction with spur road 600. Cache Lake is a short distance down the spur on the south side of the road. Primitive campsites are located on the lake. Motors are not allowed. The closest developed campground is at Scout Lake. To reach Scout Lake, take the Suttle Lake turn-off Highway 20 at the east end of Suttle Lake. Continue on this road about 1 mile to a fork, then take the left fork to reach Scout Lake in less than 1 mile.

Carl Lake - CT, 5,450 feet elevation, 30 acres, 51 feet deep. Location 11/8/28, MJW.

Take U.S. Highway 20 either from Bend to the east or from the Albany area in the Willamette Valley to the west. Seven miles east of the Santiam Pass Summit, 1 mile east of Suttle Lake, and about 13 miles west of Sisters, turn north onto Forest Route 12 from U.S. Highway 20. Drive north 5 miles on Route 12 then take Forest Route 1230 for 9 miles to its end at the trailhead. A 2-mile hike on Trail 4003 gets you to Cabot Lake, another 2.6 miles and the trail reaches Carl Lake. The nearest developed Forest Service Recreation Site is Abbot Creek Campground just off Forest Route 12.

Link Lake - CT, 4,350 feet elevation, 13 acres, 20 feet deep. Location 13/8/32, SRD, Deschutes National Forest.

One of several good lakes in the Cache Lake Basin, Link Lake is reached from Highway 20, 2 miles west of Suttle Lake, by turning south onto Forest Route 2076 at Corbett Sno-Park. Link Lake is about .1 mile off the west side of the road in 2 miles. A fire road leads into the lake. The nearest developed campgrounds are at Suttle Lake. No motors are allowed on Link Lake.

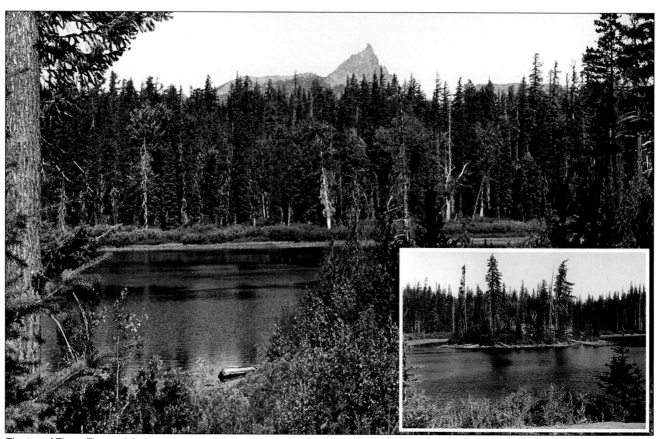

The top of Three-Fingered Jack can be seen from a slight rise on the southern shoreline of Island Lake. INSET: The island for which the lake is named lies near the western shore. This picturesque lake, subject to winterkill, is along the trail to Link Lake. Photos by Don Burgderfer

HIKING TRAIL

UNPAVED ROAD

PAVED ROAD

CARL LAKE

CABOT LAKE

4003

1230

PACIFIC CREST TRAIL

WASCO LAKE

65

1234

Three Fingered Jack

MARTIN LAKE

BOOTH LAKE

ROUND LAKE

SQUARE LAKE   4012

4014

LONG LAKE

1210

12

SANTIAM HIGHWAY

2076

SUTTLE LAKE

ISLAND LAKE

2068

LINK LAKE

MEADOW LAKE

CACHE LAKE

N

Martin Lake - RB, 5,150 feet elevation, 8 acres, 20 feet deep. Location 13//7 1/2//12, MJW.

A bit of a bushwhack, the route to Martin Lake begins at the Square Lake Trail, north of Highway 20 at the Santiam Pass/PCT parking lot, .5 mile east of Hoodoo Ski Bowl. Continue past Square Lake on Trail 4014 to Booth Lake, about 3.3 miles. In another .25 mile, follow a small creek due west and uphill about .5 mile and 400 vertical feet to Martin Lake. Developed campgrounds are at Lost Lake to the west and Suttle Lake to the east on Highway 20.

Meadow Lake - BT, 4,550 feet elevation, 16 acres, 20 feet deep. Location 4/8/5, SRD, Deschutes National Forest.

One of several good lakes in the Cache Lake Basin. Follow directions to Link Lake then continue 1 mile farther on Forest Route 2076. Meadow Lake is .25 mile west of the road. A fire road gives foot access to the lake. Only electric motors are allowed on the lake.

Round Lake - CT, 4,250 feet elevation, 22 acres, 41 feet deep. Location 13/8/16, SRD, Deschutes National Forest.

You can drive to this one. Take Forest Route 12 north off U.S. Highway 20, 1.5 miles east of Suttle Lake. Turn left onto Route 1210 in 1 mile, reaching Round Lake Campground in 4 miles. A

church camp is located on the west shore. Motors are prohibited. Round Lake can also be reached by foot from the west by following directions to Square Lake and then continuing on Trail 4012, 2 miles farther east to Round Lake.

Square Lake - BT, 4,750 feet elevation, 55 acres, 43 feet deep. Location 13/8/19, MJW.

Follow directions to Round Lake, continuing on past Round Lake on spur road 600 about .5 mile to its end at a trailhead. Square Lake is then 2 miles west on Trail 4012. Square Lake can also be reached from U.S. Highway 20 at the Santiam Pass/PCT trailhead. From Highway 20, Square Lake is 1.1 miles off the highway on Trail 4014.

Wasco Lake - CT, 5,150 feet elevation, 20 acres, 25 feet deep. Location 12/8/20, MJW.

Travel one mile east of Suttle Lake on U.S. Highway 20, then take Forest Route 12 north for 5 miles, then Route 1230 for 2 miles west, then Route 1234 for about 5 miles to its end. Jack Lake Campground and Trail 4014 are at the end of the road. Wasco Lake is 2.3 miles up the trail.

MCKENZIE PASS AREA

A primitive Forest Service campground (no drinking water) is located at Lava Camp Lake. Both of the following lakes are in the Three Sisters Wilderness (TSW). The Matthieu Lakes are designated as a high use area. From Central Oregon, drive to Sisters via U.S. Highway 20 then take State Highway 242 toward McKenzie Pass from the west end of the town of Sisters. It's about 16 miles west to the top of the pass. From the Eugene area travel State Highway 126 east to its junction with Highway 242 to McKenzie Pass then about 21 miles to the pass summit.

Matthieu Lake, South - BT, 5,850 feet elevation, 6 acres, 15 feet deep. Location 15/8/28, TSW.

From Sisters, head toward McKenzie Pass on State Highway 242. About 15 miles west of Sisters, .5 mile east of Dee Wright Observatory, take the turn toward Lava Camp Lake and the Pacific Crest Trail (PCT) trailhead. It's about 3 miles to South Matthiew Lake.

Yapoah Lake - RB, 5,520 feet elevation, 10 acres, 25 feet deep. Location 15/8/34, TSW.

Follow directions to Matthieu Lake. A short distance southeast of South Matthieu take Trail 4068 east for a little less than 1 mile. You'll need radar (or more likely, good eyes) to find the unmarked and unmaintained trail that goes into Yapoah. Look for a flat area after a short downhill section 1 mile in. The lake is .25 mile south of the trail. Yapoah is easy to fish from shore.

A rubber raft takes this angler to where the
big brook trout are on this back country lake.
Photo by Ed Park

WARM SPRINGS RESERVATION

Only lakes mentioned here are open to the public. Regulations for public use of the Warm Springs Reservation are outlined in "The Confederated Tribes of the Warm Springs Reservation of Oregon Fishing Permits and Regulations" brochure. A Warm Springs Permit is required to fish Area 1.

Area 1 - High Cascade Mountain Lakes

The High Cascade Mountain Lakes angling area of the reservation consists of seven lakes along the western border of the reservation. Among these is a chain of five high lakes with Trout Lake the farthest east and Island, Dark, Long, and Olallie lakes in a row along an unmaintained trail to the south. The other two lakes listed below are nearby. Only Olallie and Trout lake have road access. Tribal fishing permits are required of all anglers. Only anglers are allowed to camp overnight on the reservation and only at Trout Lake Campground.

Regulations on the reservation are as follows:
Fishing season is open from the last Saturday of April weekend through October 31.
Daily Bag Limit, 15 trout, no minimum size.
No motor propelled craft allowed.
All motorbike, ATV, and snowmobile riding are prohibited.
No woodcutting or gathering allowed.
Dogs must be kept on leash.
No horses allowed.
Overnight camping at Trout Lake only.

Boulder Lake - BT, RB, 4,780 feet elevation, 50 acres, 29 feet deep.
Boulder Lake is .5 mile southeast of Trout Lake on the western edge of the reservation. The trail begins about .25 mile east of Trout Lake Campground. Boulder Lake has about 2 miles of brushy shoreline with very large boulders covering most of the lake's bottom.

Dark Lake - BT, RB, 4,690 feet elevation, 22 acres, 52 feet deep.
Dark Lake is accessible only by trail from Olallie or Trout Lake. Dark Lake is 1.5 miles west of Trout Lake Campground and is the middle lake in the chain, just west of Island Lake. Dark Lake is the deepest lake in the chain, surrounded by steep, high talus slopes on the west and south shores. There is little shoal area to fish.

Harvey Lake - BT, 5,400 feet elevation, 27 acres, 40 feet deep.
Harvey Lake is a lightly fished hike-in lake in a gorgeous setting accessible by trail only. Harvey is reached by a 1.5-mile hike south from Breitenbush Campground on Breitenbush Lake. High, steep talus slopes surround this beautiful lake. An inlet waterfall from Lake Hilda and outlet waterfall into Shitike Creek frosts the cake. There is limited shoal area.

From the Salem area, take State Highway 22 about 50 miles east to Detroit. From Detroit, follow Forest Route 46 up the North Fork of the Breitenbush River about 20 miles to Forest Route 42, following signs to Breitenbush Lake for about another 9 miles.

From Central Oregon, take U.S. Highway 97 to U.S. Highway 20 toward Sisters and Santiam Pass. Continue on 20 to its junction with Highway 22 at the Santiam Pass Summit. It is then 31 miles to Detroit.

Island Lake - BT, 4,650 feet elevation, 26 acres, 10 feet deep.
With most of its acreage covered by 3 feet or less water, Island Lake is the shallowest lake in the chain. A 1-acre island located in the center of the lake gives it its name.

Island Lake is accessible only by unimproved trail from Olallie or Trout Lake. Island Lake is the next lake west of Trout Lake, a 1-mile hike by trail. Island can also be reached from Olallie Lake, as can all the lakes in the chain, but the shortest hike is from Trout Lake. Island Lake is best to fish from a floating device. Motors are prohibited.

Long Lake - BT, 4,850 feet elevation, 40 acres, 34 feet deep.
The fourth lake west from Trout Lake, Long Lake is just .4 mile east of Olallie Lake. The shortest hiking distance is from Peninsula Campground on Olallie Lake. A trail around the south end of Olallie connects with Trail 730 to Long Lake in .6 mile. It is then .4 mile on Trail 730 to Long Lake.

Trout Lake - RB, BT, 4,600 feet elevation, 23 acres, 28 feet deep.
Some natural reproduction occurs among the species in Trout Lake. Farthest east in the chain of five lakes, Trout Lake is a drive-in site with a primitive campground. To reach Trout Lake, take U.S. Highway 26 from Portland heading southeast, or from Madras driving northwest. From Highway 26, 6.5 miles north of Warm Springs on Highway 26, take Road p-600 west. Drive 4.5 miles west on this good gravel road to road b-210. It is then a 13-mile drive on b-210 to Trout Lake.

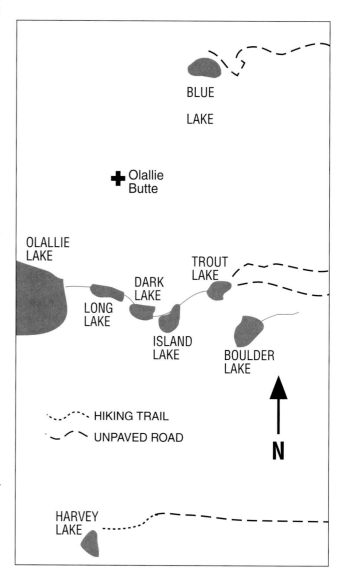

Area 6 - McQuinn Strip

No Tribal Permit is required to fish these lakes. Forest Service campgrounds are available at Breitenbush Lake, Monon Lake, and Olallie Lake.

Breitenbush Lake - BT, 5,500 feet elevation, 60 acres, 30 feet deep.

Breitenbush is a drive-in lake 105 miles southeast of Portland. Take Highway 26 southeast from Portland to the cutoff onto Forest Route 42 about 10 miles south of the junction of Highway 35 and 26. Stay on Route 42 for about 30 miles to its junction with Forest Route 4220, following signs to Olallie Lake. Olallie Lake is roughly 45 miles from Highway 26. Continue on past Olallie to Breitenbush Lake, another 4 miles south. Breitenbush has good shoal areas. A Forest Service campground is located on the lake. Motors are prohibited.

From the Salem area, take State Highway 22 about 50 miles east to Detroit. From Detroit, follow Forest Route 46 up the North Fork of the Breitenbush River about 20 miles to Forest Route 42, following signs to Breitenbush Lake for about another 9 miles.

From Central Oregon, take U.S. Highway 97 to U.S. Highway 20 toward Sisters and Santiam Pass. Continue on 20 to its junction with Highway 22 at the Santiam Pass Summit. It is then 31 miles to Detroit.

Brook Lake - BT, 4,700 feet elevation, 4 acres, 8 feet deep.

Brook Lake is located 3 miles north of Olallie Lake. See Breitenbush Lake for directions to Olallie Lake. Drive to Olallie Meadow Campground, 4 miles north of Olallie Lake on Forest Route 4220. A trail leads from the campground to a series of three lakes, of which Brook Lake is the first, the farthest west of the group. Brook Lake is .5 mile southeast of Olallie Meadow Campground. The lake's brushy shoreline is best fished from a floating device.

Gibson Lake - BT, 5,800 feet elevation, 6 acres, 14 feet deep.

A hike-in lake where overnight camping is allowed, Gibson Lake is .5 mile north of Breitenbush Lake. The trail to the lake starts across from the entrance to the Breitenbush Lake Campground. See directions to Breitenbush Lake.

Jude Lake - BT, 4,550 feet elevation, 2 acres, 14 feet deep.

Jude Lake is just east of Brook Lake and is the middle lake in the row of three. Jude Lake also has very brushy shores. See directions to Brook Lake.

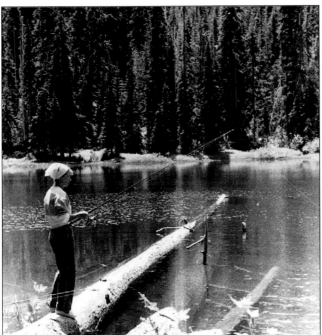

Vicki Hill enjoys the solitude of this high mountain lake. It was worth the difficult, steep climb in. Photo by Geoff Hill

Monon Lake - CT, BT, 5,000 feet elevation, 91 acres, 39 feet deep.

Monon is a drive-in lake .25 mile south of Olallie Lake on the same road, Forest Route 4220. Monon Lake Campground, a developed Forest Service facility, has a boat ramp.

Nep-te-pa Lake - BT, 5,000 feet elevation, 2 acres, 25 feet deep.

Located between the south end of Olallie Lake and the north end of Monon Lake, Nep-te-pa Lake is reached by a .5-mile hike south from Peninsula Campground on Olallie Lake.

Olallie Lake - BT, RB, 4,900 feet elevation, 240 acres, 48 feet deep.

Olallie Lake is the most popular and the farthest west of a chain of five lakes, which ends with Trout Lake to the east. See directions to Breitenbush Lake. Motors are prohibited on the lake. There are four Forest Service campgrounds on the lake, plus Olallie Lake Resort.

Russ Lake - BT, 4,700 feet elevation, 5 acres, 8 feet deep.

Russ Lake is the farthest east of the three lakes east of Olallie Meadows Campground and is considered to have the best fishing of the three. It is about .75 mile east of the campground. See directions to Brook Lake.

Spoon Lake - BT, 5,800 feet, 2 acres, shallow.

Spoon Lake is no longer stocked and is prone to winterkill. Spoon Lake is located along the west side of Skyline Road (Forest Route 4220) just north of Gibson Lake. A small population of brook trout struggles to survive here.

JOHN DAY RIVER

Length:	280 miles
Depth:	fluctuates seasonally
Main Catch:	smallmouth bass, steelhead, trout
Best Methods:	bank, boat, fly-fish
Season:	check OSFR
Best Time:	April-Sept for bass, Oct-Mar. for steelhead
Tips:	many sections accessible only by boat

The John Day River is a world class smallmouth bass fishery, a fine steelhead river, a decent trout fishery in its upper reaches, and a wonderfully scenic area to boot. Flowing nearly 300 miles from its sources in the Strawberry and Blue mountains to its confluence with the Columbia River, the John Day offers towering canyons, colorful rock formations, challenging boating, funky little towns, good visitor and camping facilities, and outstanding fishing. Catches of more than 100 bass a day have been documented, and the fishing is improving with habitat restoration and a growing catch-and-release ethic. Intriguing names, such as "Hoogie Doogie Mountain," "Picture Gorge," "Spray," and "Twickenham," add to the allure of the area.

Eighty smallmouth bass were planted in the John Day River at Service Creek in 1971. Later that year smallmouth fry were scattered over a 50-mile stretch. Today, smallmouth dominate the lower 200 miles of river, in numbers estimated up to 1,000 per mile. Bass average 12 inches, about 1 pound apiece, but get much larger. The author caught and released a 6-pound, 20-1/2-inch smallmouth his first day on the river while researching this article. The John Day appears capable of producing the next state record smallmouth bass. Medium diving crankbaits are best March-May for big spawners that feed before the more numerous, smaller bass wake up. Crawdad imitating plastic lures fished slowly along the bottom work well in backwaters as the water warms. Non-stop action is likely late summer when low water levels concentrate bass in pools, eddies and riffles where they compete for anything thrown their way. When bass are very aggressive, try removing the front hooks from crankbaits to limit physical damage and to expedite release. Live bait is also good but tends to make the fish difficult to release. Fly fishing with streamers can produce outstanding results. Bass limits are 5 fish per day, no more than 1 over 16 inches. Smallmouth bass between 12 and 16 inches must be released un-harmed. Bass fishing is permitted year-round in the mainstem from the mouth to the North Fork at Kimberly. Upstream, the bass season coincides with trout and steelhead seasons. Check the OSFR.

The John Day has one of the strongest wild inland steelhead runs in the state, varying from as few as 5,000 fish in poor years up to 40,000 in good years. John Day steelhead average 5-7 pounds with a few larger, multiple salt fish. Biologists theorize the John Day's shallow spawning habitat favors smaller, one salt steelhead. Like the Deschutes, the John Day gets its share of stray wild and hatchery fish, primarily near the confluence with the Columbia up to Tumwater Falls. About 25% of steelhead caught are fin-clipped. The majority of keepable hatchery steelhead are caught below Clarno, all others must be released, but that doesn't spoil the fun of trying for the turbo charged trout. Steelhead generally show at the mouth in late August or early September. The fish push up the river in October and November with cooler temperatures and higher flows at the end of irrigation season. They move through the basin all winter, spawning in the upper reaches of the mainstem, north and middle forks January through March.

Brooke Snavely with a 5-pound smallmouth caught while researching this editorial … what a job!
Photo by Steve Fleming

Techniques to try include drifting worms with pencil lead sinkers, corkies and slinkies, spoons, spinners and plugs in the deep holes. Jig fishing with bobbers is still untried here but could be the next great method. Fishing for steelhead is permitted Jan. 1-March 31 and June 16-Dec. 31 from the mouth up to Tumwater Falls. Steelheading is legal all year from Tumwater Falls to the North Fork. Above North Fork check the OSFR for varying seasons and restrictions on steelhead fishing in the mainstem, north and middle forks. The limit is 2 steelhead per day, 20 per season. Non-adipose clipped steelhead must be released unharmed.

Native redside and planted rainbow trout are available in the upper mainstem, especially in shaded, brushy areas with in-stream structure, such as downed trees and current breaking boulders. Hunters often encounter the best trout fishing of the year in October

John Day River Area Map

Public Access Points	River Mile
Rock Creek	22
Hay Canyon	30
Cottonwood Bridge	40
Clarno	110
Twickenham	145
Service Creek	157
Spray	170
Kimberly	184

Tips for Floating the John Day

Floaters should take a sturdy craft, plan their trip carefully, and know where river hazards are located. Guided trips for fishing on the John Day are readily available for anglers who don't have the proper boats and gear or the skills to negotiate this wilderness waterway. Bear in mind that water levels can fluctuate wildly between flood stage and drought, and that early season waters are cold enough to cause hypothermia after an accidental dunking.

Canoe, Driftboat, or Raft? The upper stretch is more suited to canoes and driftboats, while the lower section is most commonly floated in rubber rafts. Remember that open canoes, johnboats, and similar craft may swamp (fill with water) even in small rapids. Scout all whitewater from shore if you are uncertain about how to make the run correctly and line or portage if you are unsure of your ability to get through safely. It's a good idea to always wear your life jacket while floating or lining, just in case. Also be aware that motors are not permitted from Clarno downstream (and may be impractical upstream during periods of low water).

on the south, middle and north forks. Hatchery trout are planted in parts of the north, middle and south forks. Worms, salmon eggs and roe are legal and effective in most forks during high flows. Check to be sure. As water levels drop, flies and spinners are better. Most forks have midge, caddis and mayfly hatches. Trout season is the Saturday of the Memorial Day weekend to October 31. Limit is 2 trout per day. Trout over 20 inches are considered steelhead. There is no limit on the number or size of brook trout that may be kept. Bull trout are present in the headwaters and must be released unharmed.

The John Day River has a run of spring chinook salmon averaging 15-25 pounds, but it is closed to sport fishing at this time. The run averages 3,000 fish per year. The salmon arrive in spring, hold through summer and spawn in September in the upper reaches. They are rarely caught but if so, must be released. Fisheries managers hope that habitat improvement projects increase salmon numbers.

MAINSTEM

From the mouth up to impassable Tumwater Falls the lower 9 miles is slack water, primarily a plug trolling fishery for steelhead when they are present; bass, crappie and catfish year-round on lures and bait. Le Page Park is a complete boating/camping facility just off I-84 with additional camping and restrooms at Philippi Park accessible by boat a few miles upstream. Motorized boats are prohibited above Tumwater Falls to Clarno from May 1-October 31.

From Tumwater Falls upstream to Twickenham shore access is limited to bridge crossings, boat ramps and widely scattered parcels of public land. Floating in drift boats, canoes, kayaks and rafts is by far the most effective and enjoyable method to fish the lower river. Rafting skills are required to maneuver through class 2 - 4 rapids, which change difficulty at different flows. Adequate supplies must be carried for long drifts, weather extremes and primitive camping conditions. Popular fishing drifts are from Service Creek to Twickenham (12 miles), Twickenham to Clarno Rapids (35 miles), and from Cottonwood Bridge on Highway 206 to Rock Creek (18 miles). Longer, multiple night float trips are common.

Recommended flow levels for white-water thrill seekers is 2,000 to 6,000 CFS, with peak flows occurring April through June. Minimum flows for rafts are 1,500 CFS. Canoes, drift boats and smaller craft can get by in 500 CFS flows. Bass fishing is best when flows are stable or falling. Steelhead require higher water levels to migrate but won't bite in turbid conditions. The John Day is unregulated by dams but subject to irrigation withdrawals and responds rapidly to precipitation or snowmelt. For river flow information call the U.S. Dept. of Commerce, River Service Center at (503) 261-9246. Their website can be found online at http://www.oregon.wr.usgs.gov. Shuttle informatin may be obtained from Wheeler County Visitor Information: P.O. Box 122, Fossil, OR 97830, (541) 763-2355.

The BLM requires no trace camping in all boat-in campsites along the river. This includes packing out all trash, human waste and no campfires during fire season. Use elevated fire pans, propane or white gas stoves. Keep flames away from dry grass and vegetation. The river canyon is extremely susceptible to fast moving range fires.

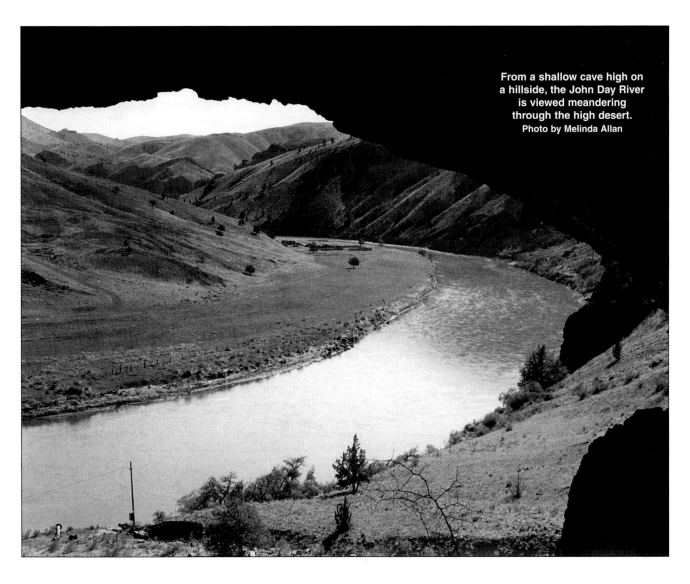

From a shallow cave high on a hillside, the John Day River is viewed meandering through the high desert.
Photo by Melinda Allan

Burn only wood from home, driftwood or charcoal. Do not cut live or dead vegetation. Pack out ash. Leave no fire rings. Smoking is permitted only while in a boat on the river. Group size is limited to 16 people to reduce impacts to campgrounds. It's okay to urinate on the ground away from the river but solid human waste must be carried out in porta-potty style containers and dumped at disposal stations at Clarno and Cottonwood takeouts. Check with the BLM in Prineville (541) 416-6700 for additional boating, camping and river use information.

There is good bank access to bass and steelhead water above Service Creek along Highway 19 through Spray, Picture Gorge, the John Day Fossil Beds National Monument, Kimberly and Dayville. Boat ramps are available at the North Fork confluence in Kimberly; at Balogna Creek; at milepost 99; at the ODOT gravel pile above Balm Creek; in Spray and at Muleshoe Creek BLM campground above Service Creek. Bass are present a short distance above Dayville. Highway 26 parallels the river through Mt. Vernon, John Day to Prairie City. County and forest roads follow the mainstem to its source near Lookout Mountain. Steelhead are available during winter up to Indian Creek. Wild trout are present from Mount Vernon upstream to the headwaters. Much of the upper mainstem above Dayville is bordered by private ranch land. Ask permission first or try Clyde Holiday State Park east of Mount Vernon. There is an RV Park in John Day, campgrounds south of Prairie City on county road 62, and forest camps in the nearby Malhuer and Whitman National Forests. Hotels, gas, services and supplies are available in Spray, Kimberly, Dayville, Mt. Vernon, John Day and Prairie City.

NORTH FORK

The North Fork heads in the Elkhorn Mountains west of Baker, flowing about 115 miles WSW to the mainstem at Kimberly. Bass are present up to Wall Creek, small stretches are stocked with rainbow trout, otherwise it's primarily a steelhead stream with bull trout in the headwaters. The best steelheading is November through April from Kimberly to the Highway 395 bridge. Paved then gravel roads follow the river upstream from Kimberly through Monument to Birch Creek. River miles 28 to 39 are roadless, best accessed by boats drifted from Camas Creek near Dale. A gravel road runs downstream from Dale to Potamus Creek.

Paved and gravel forest roads 55 and 5506 follow the North Fork about 11 miles above Dale. Above that, trail 5506 follows the river to its headwaters in the John Day Wilderness. Fishing is discouraged in the headwaters, as it is primarily salmon and steelhead rearing habitat with bull trout in deep holes. All must be released. Legal rainbow trout are stocked in the North Fork from Dale upstream 5 miles to Texas Bar Creek, and in Camas Creek. Campgrounds are available east of Dale at Tollbridge, Trough Creek, Gold Dredge and Oriental Creek. Primitive camping is allowed along the river downstream from Dale to Potamus Creek. Lone Pine campground is 1.5 miles NE of Kimberly toward the town of Monument.

MIDDLE FORK

The Middle Fork flows 75 miles west from Austin Junction, joining the North Fork at river mile 31 above Monument. More riffle than pool on its run through a shallow rimrock canyon, it offers good steelhead and rainbow trout fishing and road access for all but the lower 9 miles. Trout are planted as fingerlings, growing to 9-14 inches. Steelheading is best February-March up to the Highway 395 steelhead deadline east of Ritter. Developed camping is available at the Middle Fork Campground, about 6 miles NW of Highway 26 and at Dixie Campground, about 12 miles east of Prairie City.

SOUTH FORK

The South Fork flows about 60 miles north from Snow Mountain through Izee to join the mainstem at Dayville. The river plunges and pools in the upper reaches but meanders slowly the majority of its run. It has smallmouth in the lower reaches, planted and wild trout higher up. Occasionally unimproved roads follow almost its entire length. There is a lot of private property. Some of the best access and fishing is in the Murderer's Creek Wildlife Management Unit about 15 miles south of Dayville. The ODFW recently brought more land in the area into public ownership and is busy improving riparian habitat which should improve the fishing. Black Canyon Creek flowing in from a wilderness area by the same name can also be productive. Primitive camping is allowed in the Black Canyon Wilderness and Ochoco National Forest to the west and Malheur National Forests to the east and south.

Vehicle access is available at the John Day Pool where the river enters the Columbia River 30 miles east of The Dalles. Upstream access is drastically limited by private land.

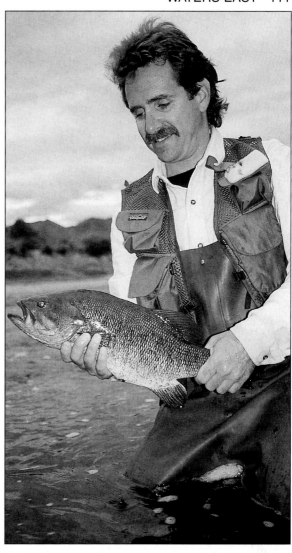

This angler shows off another reason the John Day River has a reputation for being a world class smallmouth bass fishery.
Photo by Brian O'Keefe

Road access is available at Rock Creek off State Route 19, at Cottonwood Bridge on State Route 206, at Clarno on State Highway 218, at Bridge Creek off U.S. Highway 26, and at Twickenham off State Highway 207.

State Highway 19 parallels the river from Service Creek all the way upstream past Kimberly to the junction with U.S. Highway 26 west of Dayville. At Kimberly, the North Fork comes in from the northeast, its headwaters in the Umatilla Forest.

East of Kimberly, County Route 20 parallels much of the Middle Fork into the Malheur National Forest. From its junction with Highway 19, Highway 26 runs along the mainstem upstream through Dayville to the junction with Forest Route 14 at Prairie City.

At Dayville the South Fork comes in and is paralleled by roads its entire length into the Ochoco National Forest south of Izee. Forest Routes follow the mainstem from Prairie City to its headwaters in the Ochoco National Forest.

CHICKAHOMINY RESERVOIR

Size:	491 acres
Depth:	10' average; 28' max.
Main Catch:	rainbow trout
Best Method:	flies, bait, lures
Season:	entire year; check OSFR
Best Time:	early spring at ice-out
Tips:	fishing good at ice-out

Chickahominy isn't much for scenery — surrounded by miles of rolling sage and few trees — but what most anglers come to this desert reservoir for is under the water: fast-growing rainbow trout, lots of them. ODFW plants 100,000 3-inch fingerlings per year here. Dining on a rich diet of scuds, midges, water boatmen and leeches, Chickahominy trout grow an average of 8 inches their first year. Carryovers reach an average of 16 inches their second year, push 20 inches by the third, and if they avoid fish hooks longer than that, become hulking 6-10 pound brutes. Add to that consistently good catch rates, and here is a place anglers travel long distances to fish and willingly forgo the scenery.

Chickahominy is open to fishing year round and produces well three of the four seasons, the heat of summer being slowest. Ice fishing is popular and productive in winters cold enough to produce ice strong enough to support people. Typically that happens in January and February, if at all.

Most ice fishing is done with bait such as worms, Velveeta cheese and salmon eggs on size 14-18 hooks. Also try small crappie jigs and Swedish Pimples on 2- and 4-lb. line tipped with bait. Start by fishing near the bottom and reel up in two foot increments until fish are located. If nothing happens, move 25-50 feet, drill another hole and start over.

Fishing can be very good at ice-out, throughout spring and early summer. The fish are hungry and on the prowl in the shallows, around edges and drop-offs. This is when fly fishers casting red and black leeches and Prince nymphs on sink tip lines catch a lot of big trout from shore. Slow, bottom-creeping retrieves are best. Lightly weighted offerings of roe, nightcrawlers and Power Bait begin producing for bait fishers. Bays and inlets are the favored spots; the theory being there is some gravel amidst the bottom muck where the trout try unsuccessfully to spawn. Beware of truck-sucking mud holes on the dirt access roads around the reservoir in wet conditions. Many four wheel drives have sunk beyond their axles only to be rescued by tow trucks from Burns. Big towing bill.

Boat anglers avoid the mess by launching at the paved ramp near the dam and heading for the popular "narrows" where power lines cross the lake. This area is only about 10 feet deep, but frequently produces on trolled Thomas spoons, by casting Rooster Tail spinners, bait fishing with worms, or by fast

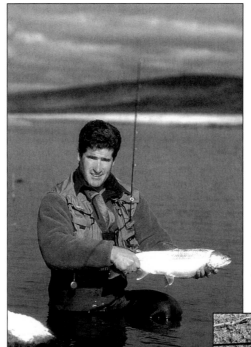

LEFT & BELOW:
These beautiful rainbows are the reason anglers travel the distance to Chickahominy Reservoir.
Top photo by Brian O'Keefe
Photo below by Steve Zink

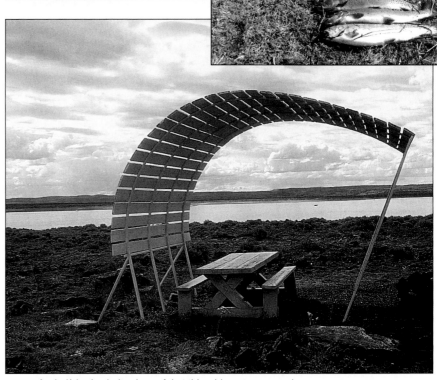

A wind/shade shelter is useful at this wide open reservoir. Photo by Brooke Snavely

stripping Muddler minnows. When it's good, Chickahominy is one of those lakes where all techniques work.

Fishing success tends to drop off in the heat of summer (July–August temperatures frequently near 100°F), due to increased recreational boat traffic and algae blooms, although determined anglers should try in the deepest water near the dam and watch for evening rises to abundant midge hatches in the coves. Fishing revives in late September, October and November with trout

going on fall feeding binges. Locals tell stories of 50 fish days.

The standard 5 fish per day limit is in effect, with only 1 over 20 inches. There are 28 developed BLM campsites with drinking water and restrooms costing $6.00 per day (2001), a no-fee picnic area with shaded tables, and lots of primitive lake shore camping accessed by marginal roads.

Chickahominy is located 100 miles east of Bend and 30 miles west of Burns on U.S. Highway 20.

FISH LAKE (2)
(Harney County)

Size:	16 acres
Depth:	average 15'; max. 30',
Main Catch:	rainbow
Best Methods:	bait, lures, flies
Season:	access limited by snow
Best Time:	summer, fall
Tips:	no motors allowed

Located 7,371 feet up the western flank of Steens Mountain, this is the highest of a dozen "Fish Lakes" in Oregon and quite possibly the prettiest. This 16-acre alpine gem is surrounded by stands of aspens and grassy meadows filled with wildflowers. It offers productive fishing for 8-12-inch stocked rainbow trout and a self-sustaining population of wild brook trout averaging 9-13 inches with trophies to 3 lbs.

No motors are allowed, making it ideal for rubber rafts, canoes and float tubes. Lacking motorized propulsion, wind drifting bait from boats is the most popular fishing technique. Many anglers bounce offerings of worms, salmon eggs and Power Bait off the bottom as they drift in whatever direction the wind takes them. Canoeists and row boaters do well casting and trolling Mepps and Panther-Martin spinners and Thomas spoons. Float tubers encounter success fishing dry flies in the shallows mornings and evenings, and with deeper sinking lines and

Grassy meadows and stands of aspens surround this high alpine, 16-acre lake. Fall is often the best time for fly fishing from the bank or with a floating device such as a canoe or float tube. Motors are not allowed.
Photos by Brooke Snavely

streamer/leech patterns during bright daylight hours. Fly fishing is often excellent in the fall. Bank fishing is most effective from the north and south shorelines.

The deepest spot, 31 feet, is basically dead center of the lake. Underwater springs on the east end near the campground and the outlet to Lake Creek on the west end can attract fish at times.

Catch limits are 5 fish per day, minimum 8 inches, 1 over 20 inches. No motors are allowed. The water is fairly cold most of the year, limiting all but the bravest swimmers to wading in the shallows. There is an attractive 23-space BLM campground and picnic area on the east end of the lake with drinking water and restrooms. Camping fees are $6.00 per night (in 2001) up to 14

days with sites available on a first-come, first-serve basis. Overflow camping is available at Jackman Park 2 miles up the road.

Check with the BLM before making the 80-mile drive south of Burns. Snow usually blocks the road to the lake through the first of June, sometimes later after heavy winters. Also be aware that the lake is exposed to strong winds that can last for days and sudden, dangerous but spectacular thunderstorms.

Other nearby activities include hiking, wildlife watching, sight seeing from the 9,773-foot summit of Steens Mountain..

From Burns, take State Highway 205 for 60 miles to Frenchglen; travel 20 miles east on Steens Mountain Back Country Byway to Fish Lake.

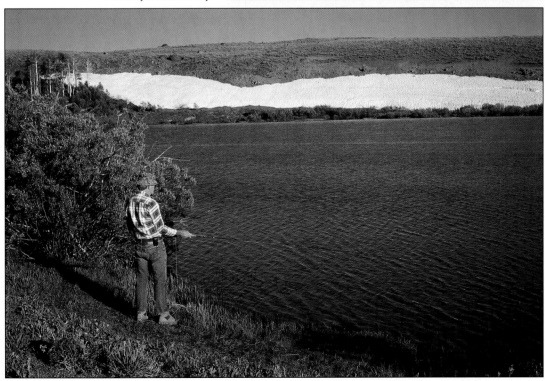

DONNER UND BLITZEN RIVER

Size:	Main stem: 65 miles
Depth:	5' average; 10' max.
Main Catch:	native redband rainbow
Best Method:	flies, lures
Season:	entire year; check OSFR
Best Time:	summer & fall
Tips:	The fish go nuts for grasshoppers in September & October.

Fishing on the Donner Und Blitzen River is a bush-wacking, rock-hopping, snake-dodging, native-trout-catching experience. Named for dramatic thunderstorms, the Donner Und Blitzen (German for thunder and lightning) is a Designated Wild and Scenic River that drains the west slope of Steens Mountain, flows north through the Malheur Wildlife Refuge, emptying into Malheur Lake. Only the upper half of the river above Bridge Creek is open to fishing, and most anglers concentrate on the upper third above Page Springs. This is rugged, remote, but surprisingly lush high desert country that requires a lot of walking to reach the best fishing areas.

Native redband rainbow trout are the main attraction. Mature redbands have striking red

ABOVE: Excellent camping facilities can be found at the Page Springs Recreation Site.

TOP: Designated as a Wild and Scenic River, the Donner Und Blitzen River drains the west slope of Steens Mountain and flows north, emptying into the Malheur Lake.

Photos by Brooke Snavely

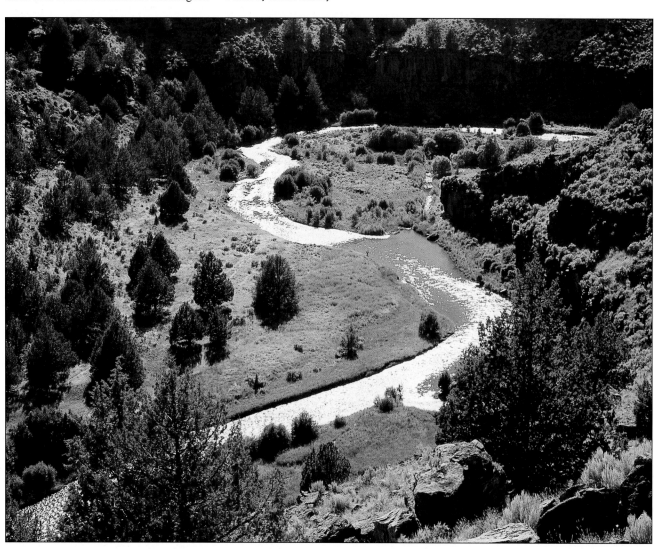

slashes; juveniles strings of ruby-colored par marks along their lateral lines. Tolerant of desert temperatures and fluctuating water flows, redbands feed hard in the short summer and fall growing season, fueling consistent action bordering on fantastic when conditions are right. The average Blitzen redband trout is 8 to 12 inches, with good numbers of 16- to 18-inchers and enough 24-30-inch trophies to keep anglers coming back year after year. Considered for special protection, the future of Blitzen redband rainbow is bright. In some reaches, fish populations have doubled where livestock grazing has been restricted, allowing streamside vegetation to regenerate. Fish passage issues around water diversion projects that block spawning migrations are also being addressed. A 2-fish harvest limit, only 1 over 20 inches, no bait and flies and lures only, and catch-and-release fishing only from November 1 through late May. Anglers are encouraged to release all trout in this river system which is managed as a trophy trout fishery.

In spring and early summer, the Blitzen and its five major tributaries: Bridge, Fish, Indian and Mud Creeks and the Little Blitzen River flow high, cloudy and cold with snowmelt from Steens Mountain. The best early season fishing is with spinners and streamers in the lower, warmer sections in the Malheur Wildlife Refuge. Fishing is permitted in the refuge downstream from Page Springs to the confluence of the Blitzen and Bridge Creek, including East Canal and Mud

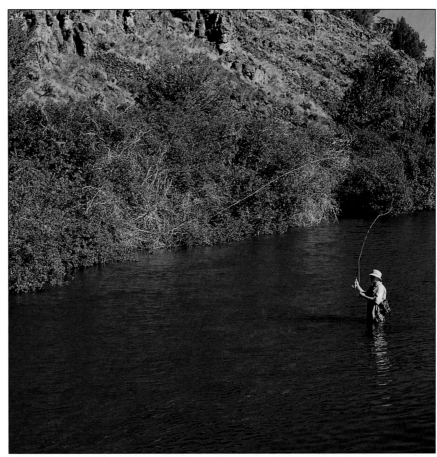

Rugged and remote, this river often requires a lot of walking to reach the best fishing areas. Above, a fly fisherman works the overhanging brush. Photo by Brooke Snavely

Creek. Anglers can only fish the aforementioned waters and walk designated access routes. Some areas are closed to protect sensitive birds, plants and mammals. No boats or floating devices of any kind are allowed on the refuge except on Krumbo Reservoir, a few miles north. Back casting space is limited, due to thick vegetation, favoring casting with spinners or roll and arrow casting with flies. Long rods to poke through brush and a willingness to bush-wack are mandatory in the refuge; big fish are the reward.

The river above Page Springs to Blitzen Crossing becomes fishable as runoff slows and temperatures rise in July and August, spurring a variety of insect hatches and good fly fishing. Here the river bounces, riffles and pools through undercut banks, lined with junipers and cottonwood trees, bushes, tall grass and rimrock basalt. Watch for rattlesnakes in the tall grass. Beating the grass with a stick or rod and staying in the water are ways to avoid fanged encounters. Wading is easy in shorts, old tennis shoes or wading boots and a welcome relief from summer heat. A #14 Royal Wulff is a good dry searching pattern. Adams, Comparadun, Elk Hair Caddis, Hopper, Humpy and Renegade are other effective dry flies. If no surface takers, probe in the shade of overhanging trees and undercut banks with Prince, Pheasant Tail or Hare's Ear nymphs and Woolly Worm, Muddler, Sculpin and Rainbow pattern streamers. There is enough pressure from Page Springs upstream two miles to the second dam to make the fish selective. Anglers willing to travel farther up the canyon and into the tributaries will find uneducated fish. Some anglers camp overnight on long hikes up the canyons. Afternoon and evening are usually best but fish bite periodically throughout the day.

The fish go nuts for grasshoppers in September and October. Plus, there is a noticeable upstream movement of large fish in search of springs and cool tributaries. Some of the creeks are so small that a person can step across them, and often there is no room to cast. The fish actually seem to like skated flies that drag on the water or swim upstream on the retrieve. 1/16- and 1/32-ounce chartreuse spinners work well in the small tributaries. There is a good fall feeding frenzy before winter's chill puts an end to sizeable insects. There is probably good midge fishing during winter but few people try.

Excellent camping facilities await those who make the 63-mile trek south of Burns on Highway 205. Page Springs and Steens South BLM campgrounds feature large, shaded sites with pit toilets and drinking water for $6.00 per night (in 2001). RV hookups, trailer rentals and some camping and fishing supplies are available at Camper Corral near Page Springs.

The nearby town of Frenchglen has two restaurants, a hotel, gas and groceries. Steens Mountain Backcountry Byway, Malheur Wildlife Refuge, and numerous pioneer settlements offer fascinating history, wildlife and sight-seeing opportunities.

MANN LAKE

Size: 276 acres
Depth: 6' average; 14' max.
Main Catch: Lahontan cutthroat
Best Method: flies, lures
Season: entire year; check OSFR
Best Time: spring, fall
Tips: Fly fishing may be difficult due to high winds. Boats, canoes, & float tubes are useful.

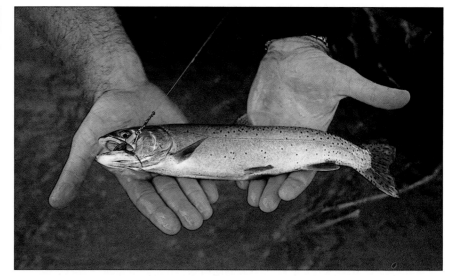

For anglers who like challenges, Mann Lake is a must. Literally in the middle of nowhere, with spectacular scenery, primitive camping facilities, extreme weather and terrific fishing, this lake has a lot to offer, but is not for everyone.

Mann Lake is the only place in Oregon where anglers can fish for Lahontan cutthroat trout. A candidate for endangered species listing, Lahontans are highly evolved desert trout that survive temperature and water quality extremes that preclude most other fish. With characteristic red slashes under their jaws and the same healthy appetite as west slope cutthroat, Lahontans are easy to fool and sporting to catch. Twenty fish days are common, particularly in spring and fall. Fishing for them is legal here, because the lake is stocked with a "naturalized" strain, raised in a hatchery, released as fingerlings to feed and grow, but unable to reproduce due to lack of spawning habitat.

Mann Lake is open year-round. Because of its remote location, it gets very little pressure during the winter, though ice fishing can be good with crappie jigs, bead headed flies and small spoons, jigged straight up and down. No bait is permitted. The fish feed ravenously at ice-out (March-April) by rooting around in the shallows for scuds, leeches and aquatic insects.

Casting with flies and lures from shore or wading produces excellent results. The lake is basically oval shaped with fish holding water within casting distance of almost all 2.6 miles of shoreline. Fly fishers do best with black and green Woolly Worms, Woolly Buggers, Damselflies and small black or grey Midges. Fishing two or three different dropper flies under a strike indicator is common when fish are shallow. Spin fishers catch plenty casting chartreuse-colored Mepps, brown Panther Martin spinners, and two-tone Thomas spoons. Hint #1: bring a spinning rod. Strong wind often makes fly fishing impossible, but spin fishers can make tremendous down wind casts that cover a lot of water. Hint #2: Green is the best color.

Mann is an excellent float tube, canoe, rubber raft and small boat lake. Motors are allowed. Flat-line trolling is good early in the year. Boat anglers merely add split shot

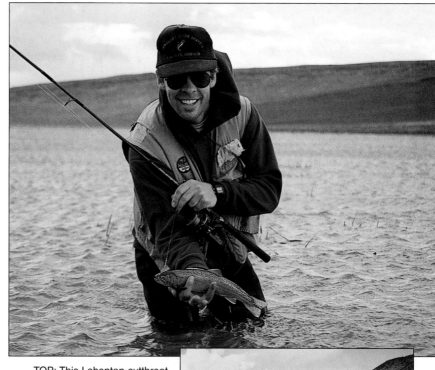

TOP: This Lahontan cutthroat caught with a green spinner displays the characteristic red slashes under the jaw.
Photo by Brooke Snavely

CENTER: Cutthroat trout is the main species caught in Mann Lake.
Photo courtesy of Brooke Snavely

BOTTOM: There is an amazing variety of bird, animal, and plant life in this remote setting
Photo by Brooke Snavely

Aside from challenging fishing, this remote high desert lake offers remarkable scenery during any season of the year. Photo by Brian O'Keefe

or use heavier flies or lures when fish move into deep water, all of 14 feet. There are two improved gravel ramps and easy launching for car-toppers and tubes anywhere along the gradual shoreline.

Fishing stalls in the heat of summer with thick algae blooms, courtesy of the many cattle that fertilize the watershed. But it comes back strong by late summer and fall, fueled by terrestrial insects, such as grasshoppers and ants, that fall or get blown into the lake, producing the best dry fly fishing of the year. The same spinners and spoons continue producing.

Catch-and-release is encouraged at Mann Lake. Barbless flies and lures are a good idea although not required. The limit is 2 fish per day, minimum 16 inches. The fish are muddy tasting. Most anglers release their fish.

As far as human comforts are concerned, there are none. The no-fee campgrounds are primitive with no developed sites. There are vault toilets and newly graveled access roads but not much else. No trees, no wind breaks, no drinking water. If you want it, you bring it. The closest store, restaurant and services are 50 miles south in Fields. They do a booming flat repair business there, as the gravel roads in this area are vicious on tires. Mann Lake veterans frequently carry two spares. Campers should use tents designed to withstand strong wind and dust and be prepared for noisy nights. Many people bring ear plugs to deaden the sound of the wind. It is almost easier to camp in a car, truck or RV.

The rewards for roughing it at Mann Lake are sublime. Besides the great fishing, the scenery is staggering. A 9,773-foot Steens Mountain towers over the wide-open landscape. While mostly dry and hot, there is an amazing variety of bird, animal and plant life

near water. Crumbling homesteads hint at rich pioneer and Native American history.

With nothing to do other than fish, watch wildlife and the weather, most Mann Lake visitors quickly fall into the patterns of the old west. Retire at dusk, wake up at dawn, fish all day and look forward to bathing when they get back home.

Mann Lake is located 87 miles southeast of Burns. From Burns take State Highway 78 southeast approximately 65 miles. Turn south on the Field/Denio Road (Harney County #201) and travel 22 miles to the lake.

Waters of South Central Oregon

Many fine fishing opportunities exist in South Central Oregon.
The next several pages cover popular waters from Howard Prairie to Gerber Reservoir,
including the Klamath Falls area.

Area of Map

N

To LaPine Bend

To Roseburg
Lemolo Lake
Miller Lake
To LaPine Bend
Chemult
31
Silver Lake
Diamond Lake
Diamond Lake
Mt. Bailey
Mt. Thielsen
230
138
97
To Lakeview
Thompson Reservoir
Crater Lake
Mt. Scott
Klamath Marsh
62
WILLIAMSON RIVER
To Grants Pass
Fort Klamath
WOOD R.
SYCAN RIVER
Chiloquin
Agency L.
Wild Billy Lake
To Medford Grants Pass
Mt. McLoughlin
Fourmile Lake
SPRAGUE RIVER
Sprague River
Beatty
140
Bly
140
Upper Klamath Lake
Lake In the Woods
Fish Lake
Aspen Lake
To Lakeview
5
Klamath Falls
Dairy
Ashland
Hyatt Res.
Howard Prairie Res
Keno
70
66
John Boyle Res.
Bonanza
Gerber Reservoir
39
KLAMATH RIVER
To Weed Redding

NOTE: MAP NOT TO SCALE

KLAMATH RIVER

Length:	40 miles (in Oregon)
Depth:	varies by stretch
Main Catch:	rainbow trout, bass
Best Method:	flies, lures, bait
Season:	regulations are complex; check OSFR
Best Time:	spring, fall

Only 18 of the Klamath River's 40 miles in Oregon are free flowing trout water. Dams back up the other 22 miles for power generation, irrigation and industrial uses. Most angling effort is focused on the free flowing sections, which are productive rainbow trout waters. Bass fishing is poor due to poor water quality.

The first mile of the river flowing out of Upper Klamath Lake into Lake Ewauna is known as the Link River, because it links the two lakes. A pretty little canyon just minutes west of downtown Klamath Falls, the Link River has resident rainbow averaging 10-16 inches and migratory trout to 5 lbs. Bait is best in spring, with lure and fly action in summer and fall. Access is via the Link River Trail from Lakeshore Boulevard to the north and Favell Museum on Main Street to the south. Veterans Park in down-

town Klamath Falls offers good bank access and paved boat ramp at the upper end of Lake Ewauna. Fishing on the Link River and Lake Ewauna is open the entire year. Limits are 1 trout and 5 bass per day.

Lake Ewauna extends 16 miles downstream before Keno dam releases the highly productive 6-mile-long "Keno reach" which flows into J.C. Boyle Reservoir. This is deep pocket water flowing through a steep canyon. Off color water and irregular streambed make wading treacherous. Try boulder hopping instead. Weighted Woolly Buggers, Leeches, Zonker and minnow pattern

ABOVE: A peek at the river from Highway 66. Photo by Geoff Hill

LEFT: Todd Ostenson with an 18-inch rainbow.
Photo courtesy of Trophy Waters Flyfishing Shop

streamers are best presented on sink tip lines. Heavier Rooster Tail spinners and sinking Rapalas are effective lures. No bait is allowed. Trout average 13-17 inches in this stretch, with many over 20 inches. Access is from Highway 66. Park on the highway shoulder and hike down, or walk downstream from the Keno dam recreation area. This stretch is not boatable. The Keno reach is open Jan. 1-June 15 and Oct. 1-Dec 31. Warm water temperature and high fish mortality rates prompt the summer closure. Limit is 1 fish.

The Klamath runs cooler, clearer but shallower below J.C. Boyle Reservoir to the powerhouse. This 5-mile stretch is better dry fly water for trout averaging 8-12 inches. The Klamath River road provides good access throughout this reach. Make sure to take the lower of the two roads, otherwise access is cut off by a sluice carrying water to the Boyle powerhouse. Fishing from Boyle Dam to the California border is allowed the entire year. Tackle is restricted to artificial flies and lures. Limit is 1 fish. Catch-and-release is required June 16 to Sept. 30.

Below the generating station, the Klamath regains its size, as do the fish, averaging 12-15 inches. There are also more of them, making this the best quantity and quality stretch. Flows in the lower 9 miles fluctuate according to power demands. Call 1-800-547-1501 for flow reports. Fishing is best at low flows, usually morning and evening. But the fish are accustomed to changing water levels and usually resume feeding after flows stabilize. Try stoneflies in spring, caddisflies summer and fall and spinners throughout the season. Access to this area is by the Klamath River Road past the powerhouse. The road gets very rough beyond the whitewater boat launch.

Pacific Power & Light operates a comfortable campground with showers at Keno Recreation Area near Keno. BLM offers the Topsy Campground at J.C. Boyle Reservoir, a boat launch below the powerhouse and two primitive riverside camps on either side of the Oregon-California border.

Keno is located 12 miles west of Klamath Falls on State Highway 66; 45 miles east of Ashland on State Highway 66; 153 miles south of Bend on U.S. Highway 97 & State Highway 66.

CLOCKWISE (from top):
Brian O;'Keefe with a dandy rainbow.
Brian with a huge 11-pound native Klamath River rainbow.
Brian O'Keefe photos
The Keno Dam, Klamath River.
The Keno reach of the Klamath River.
Photos by Brooke Snavely

WOOD RIVER

Size:	30 miles
Depth:	15' average; 5' max.
Main Catch:	rainbow & brown trout
Best Methods:	flies, lures
Season:	last Saturday in April to Oct. 31
Best Time:	Aug.-Oct.
Tips:	catch-and-release only; boat required to fish effectively

The Wood River is a wide, meandering meadow stream full of twists and turns with undercut banks and cold, clear water. Photo by Brooke Snavely.

The Wood River is often lumped together with the Williamson in conversations about fishing in the Klamath basin. They are similar but do not fish the same. Trout migrate up the Wood like they do the Williamson to escape warm lake conditions and to spawn. The migrations occur about the same times (June-October), the fish can be very large (5+ pounds) and access is difficult due to extensive private property holdings. But there the similarities end. The Wood is a 30-foot wide meandering meadow stream with undercut banks, downed trees, and breathtakingly cold, crystal clear waters. It has a grasshopper season, which makes fools of the biggest fish. And it is strictly catch-and-release throughout the season, the last Saturday in April through October 31.

From its source at Jackson F. Kimball State Park, the Wood River flows south through pastureland about 15 miles as the crow flies to Agency Lake. Actual river length is closer to 20 or 30 miles factoring in all the river's sinuous twists and turns. A boat is required to fish it effectively. Most drifts are from bridge to bridge or from the lower most bridge crossing (Weed Road) to the mouth, the most popular drift. Some bridges have very low clearance, requiring a short portage, favoring small boats like canoes, kayaks, float tubes and personal pontoon boats. Weed Road features a steep dirt ramp where drift boats can launch. Except for the bridge crossings, anglers must stay in their boats, as virtually all the shorelines are private property. The Wood River has no whitewater but flows deceptively fast through an irregular channel with occasional snags and twisting currents.

There is limited shore fishing access at the headwaters at Jackson F. Kimball State Park, though the fish are small and the mosquitoes ravenous. A few miles downstream, the Wood River Day Use Area off Sun Mountain Road features a quarter-mile of bank access with two handicap fishing platforms and nice trails. It is possible to launch car toppers and tubes here, but there is no ramp. The next shore access is many miles downstream at the Weed Road Bridge. The lower 1.5 miles were recently brought into public ownership. This area is accessible on foot or bike from the Modoc Point Highway. Most anglers launch at Petric Park on Agency Lake, then motor or paddle 1.5 miles to the mouth of the Wood.

Most fishing on the Wood occurs at the mouth where it flows into Agency Lake and the lower 3 miles along Wood River Ranch which is now managed by the BLM. Large green, black and brown leech pattern flies with the tails trimmed to discourage short strikes fished just below the surface will fool rainbows. Upstream there's a better chance at brown trout with mouse pattern flies cast onto the far shore, pulled into the water with a splash, then fast stripped back to the boat, especially after sunset. Rainbows and browns rise willingly to grasshopper imitations drifted along undercut banks in late summer. There are other insect hatches but few rival the grasshopper surface action in August and September. Leeches and streamers are the best all around patterns for fly fishers. Spin fishers can present flies with plastic bubbles or cast and retrieve spinners, spoons and crankbaits through likely holding areas.

Lodging is available in Fort Klamath, at fishing lodges on the Wood River and in Chiloquin. Nearby campgrounds include Jackson F. Kimball State Park, Fort Klamath RV Park, and Agency Lake Resort on Agency Lake. Nearby points of interest include Crater Lake National Park, historic Fort Klamath, and the Klamath State Fish Hatchery.

From Bend, travel 115 miles south on U.S. Highway 97 to Chiloquin then west 15 miles to Fort Klamath. From Klamath Falls, travel 25 miles north to Chiloquin, then west 15 miles to Fort Klamath.

WILLIAMSON RIVER

Size:	86 miles
Depth:	6' average; 50' max.
Main Catch:	wild rainbows, browns
Best Methods:	flies, lures
Season:	regulations complex; check OSFR
Best Time:	June-Oct.
Tips:	big fish generally from Klamath Lake upstream to Kent Canyon

The Williamson is probably the best river in Oregon for a chance at 5- to 15-pound rainbow and brown trout. The monster trout migrate from Upper Klamath Lake June through October in search of comfort and spawning habitat. Like steelhead, the big fish are wary and hard to catch. They come up out of the lake covered with cocopods, a kind of fresh water lice. Fresh fish announce their presence by jumping and rolling in an effort to shake the parasites. There are smaller resident and juvenile trout that would probably be considered big fish in other streams.

The best big fish opportunities are from Klamath Lake upstream about 15 miles to Kent Canyon. Within this stretch, most of the fishing is concentrated from the U.S. Highway 97 bridge to Chiloquin.

Below this reach the river turns to slack water and is better suited to trolling from boats motored up from the lake. Access is difficult with most of the riverbanks in private ownership. The minimal public land around Collier State Park is heavily fished, and the big migratory trout don't get that far upstream until September or October. There is a public park off the south Chiloquin access road where small trailered boats can launch, although the ramp is steep and four-wheel drives are advisable. Shore anglers can wade a short distance downstream from the Chiloquin put-in but constant pressure educates fish in the area. Beat the access and pressure problems by hiring a guide who has permission to fish private property, or stay at resorts with river frontage.

A drift downstream from Chiloquin takes a boat angler through shallow riffles that

ABOVE: Although many of the riverbanks are in private ownership, access by wading is still available, especially through guides with permission to fish private property or at a resort with river frontage.
Photo by Brian O'Keefe

RIGHT: There are so many good fishing spots it can take all day to float the Williamson.
Photo by Geoff Hill

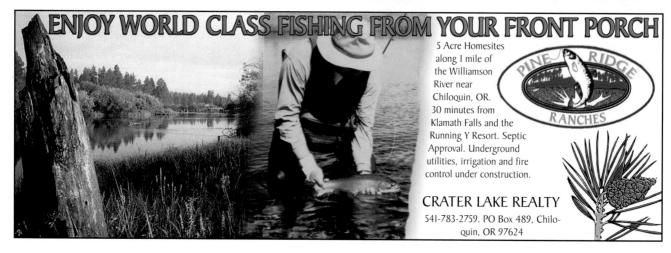

spill over rock ledges into deep pools, along brushy banks and through deeply slotted channels. Good boat handling skills are required to prevent hanging up in shallow spots, let alone spotting fish-holding water before disturbing it. A drift boat with a fishing guide at the oars pointing out places to cast and flies to try is the best way to learn. Many do-it-yourselfers float the river in canoes, kayaks and float tubes, though tubers may have to stand up in places. There are so many good fishing spots it can take all day to float the 5 miles from Chiloquin to the River Bend Motel and Waterwheel RV Park take-outs on either side of the Highway 97 bridge. Both charge a take-out fee. Most drifts are timed to end after dark, giving anglers a shot at evening hatches. Shuttle and guide services can be arranged through the Williamson River Anglers.

The Williamson offers a variety of hatches that fluctuates madly from day to day. The *Hexagenia limbata* (Yellow Mayfly) is noteworthy, eliciting surface strikes from even the most reluctant lunkers and presents good nymphing opportunities. Look for them in July in slower water where bank side vegetation allows adult mayflies to congregate. Other dry and emerger patterns to have on hand are Blue Wing Olive, caddis, stoneflies, Pale Morning Duns and Red Quill. Use leeches, Seal Buggers and streamers most of the time. The migratory trout are accustomed to feeding on big nymphs and baitfish in the lake, and that preference continues in the river. Big wet flies far and away produce the most fish. Fish them all on at least 14-foot leaders, 6X tippets for dries, 4X for wets when the light is low and be prepared to make 60-foot casts. Practice casting before hitting the river.

The upper Williamson begins as a spring roughly 25 miles northeast of Chiloquin in the Winema National Forest, flows north then west through mostly private land into the Klamath National Wildlife Refuge where access is closed during sensitive bird nesting seasons. Check with the refuge headquarters

The Williamson River is known for its large trout, as evidenced by this nice 6-pound rainbow, as well as its scenic surroundings.
Photo by Geoff Hill; inset photo by Brian O'Keefe

before trying this area. From the marsh, the river acquires a root beer brown color that is mostly strained out near Kirk, where the river flows underground before re-emerging a short distance downstream. Until Spring Creek joins it at Collier State Park, the upper Williamson is a small stream sporting mostly small brook and some decent rainbow trout. It can be good fishing in places, barren in others and difficult to access because of all the private land. A map of the Winema National Forest is a must, as is a copy of the Oregon fishing regulations.

From the mouth upstream to the Modoc Point Bridge Road, the Williamson is open to all angling methods late May through October 31 with a 1 fish limit. From Modoc Point Bridge upstream to Chiloquin Bridge, no fishing from boats under power, same season but catch-and-release is required for trout after August 1 and tackle is restricted to artificial flies and lures. From Chiloquin Bridge upstream to Kirk Bridge no fishing is allowed from floating devices in addition to the previous restrictions, essentially eliminating public access below Collier State Park. However, there is no limit on size or number of brook trout. Finally, from Kirk Bridge upstream to the headwaters the river is open to the harvest of 2 rainbows, and any number of brookies late April through October 31. Designed to protect spawning runs, these progressively restrictive regulations are subject to change so check before going.

Services and accommodations are available around Chiloquin, where there are highway hotels, RV parks, cafes, fishing lodges, gas, groceries and supplies. Camping is available at Collier State Park and Williamson River Campground. A fair number of small planes land at the Chiloquin airstrip, disgorging passengers with rod cases.

The river is located 115 miles south of Bend or 25 miles north of Klamath Falls on U.S. Highway 97.

SPRAGUE RIVER

Size:	100 miles
Depth:	5' average; 10' max.
Main Catch:	trout, bass, catfish
Best Methods:	flies, lures, bait
Season:	late April-Oct 31
Best Time:	early summer, fall
Tips:	remote fishing as area relatively unknown to tourists

The Sprague is a major tributary of the Williamson River originating in the Gearhart Mountain area about 100 miles east of Chiloquin, about 30 miles west of Lakeview. The upper Sprague and its tributaries offer good fishing for wild rainbow, brook and bull trout. The mainstem has brown trout, largemouth bass and catfish. Near its confluence, the Sprague shares

RIGHT: Erwin Miller of Chiloquin proudly displays the mount of his 16-lb. rainbow caught on his lunch break in late October, 1993.

BELOW: The scenic Sprague River is home to some large trout which migrate from the Upper Klamath Lake and Williamson River.

Photos by Geoff Hill

some of the Williamson's big rainbow trout that migrate from Upper Klamath Lake. The Sprague River is relatively unknown to tourists but lacks nothing in the way of scenery, fishing and camping opportunities. For those who enjoy outback style fishing experiences this area is well worth exploring.

The Sprague heads in the Gearhart Mountain Wilderness, an area of stunning vistas, dense forests, steep ridges and cold creeks that peaks out at 8,300 feet above sea level. The upper 10 miles of the North Fork are Designated Wild and Scenic and home to good populations of wild brook, rainbow and bull trout. Bull trout must be released unharmed. Anglers are allowed to keep 2 trout per day, minimum 8 inches, only 1 over 20 inches. There are no size restrictions or harvest limits on brook trout. In fact, harvest of brook trout probably helps the native bull trout, which are nearing threatened and endangered status.

All techniques, including bait in one section, are permitted. Bait works wonderfully well on brookies and can provide a positive experience for beginning anglers. Spinners, dry flies and nymphs are also effective. Forest roads 19, 3411 and 3372 parallel much of the Wild and Scenic section and cross it several places, affording easy access with short hikes getting anglers away from pressured areas. The South Fork is good for small brook up high and brown trout in the lower reaches and is accessible from State Highway 140 and Forest Highway 34. Always check OSFR.

The slower flowing mainstem is an underutilized warm water fishery, offering miles of bass, catfish and brown trout habitat. Shore fishing is limited to sidings along highways 858 and 140, bridge crossings, the Sprague River Day Use area east of Bly and permission from property owners. Most anglers target catfish with worms. Bass will take spinnerbaits, plastic worms and floating crankbaits. Brown trout go for mouse, grasshopper and streamer pattern flies. Floating the river in a canoe, kayak or pram would be the best way to access unexplored

Good populations of wild brook, rainbow and bull trout are found on the North Fork of the Sprague River. Photo by Todd Ostenson

waters. Get permission from property owners first. There are scads of rough fish in this section, some of which are protected (shortnosed and Klamath suckers, blue and tui chubs) and must be released.

Access improves and springs cool the river just above Chiloquin where rainbow and brown trout to 3 lbs. share the water with bass and catfish. Bait, lures and flies will all work in this section. Access is via Chiloquin Ridge Road off Sprague River Road. Downstream from the dam near Chiloquin High School to the Williamson River, angling is restricted to artificial flies and lures and limited to 1 trout per day. Large trout migrate into the lower Sprague from Klamath Lake. They are catchable in late summer and fall on leeches, Woolly Buggers and spinners. Upstream from Chiloquin Dam, the Sprague River is open to fishing the last Saturday in April through October 31. Below the dam the season is from late May through October 31. Check the OSFR.

Other than small hotels in Chiloquin, it's all camping for overnight visitors to the Sprague River. Near the headwaters, Sandhill Crossing, Lee Thomas and Campbell Lake forest camps offer toilets, picnic tables and fire rings. None charge fees. If they are full, camping is permitted anywhere on National Forest land for up to 14 days. S'Ocholis private campground is 12 miles east of Chiloquin on Hwy. 858.

Points of interest include the Mitchell Monument, site of the only deaths on the continental United States during WWII. In May 1945, six people on a Sunday school picnic were killed when a Japanese balloon bomb exploded. Weyerhaeuser Co. maintains a picnic area and monument about 10 miles northeast of Bly on Hwy 34.

The Sprague River is accessible from Chiloquin from the west and Lakeview from the east. State highways 858 and 140 are the primary routes with numerous side roads. Winema and Fremont National Forest maps provide details.

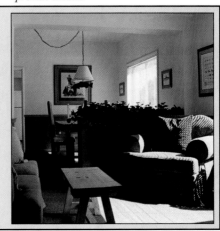

SYCAN RIVER

Length:	50 miles
Depth:	varies seasonally
Main Catch:	brook, brown, & rainbow trout
Best Methods:	flies & lures only
Season:	late April-Oct. 31;
Best Time:	spring, fall check OSFR
Tips:	light use due to rough roads

Flowing through a basalt canyon over large water carved boulders, the Sycan River is reminiscent of the Crooked River, only more forested and much more remote. A medium size tributary of the Sprague River, the Sycan heads in the northeastern corner of Klamath County, flows about 20 miles northwest into the Sycan Marsh, then 30 miles southwest before joining with the Sprague near Beatty. Divided by the marsh, the entire upper and much of the lower river are Designated Wild and Scenic. Most of the river flows through National Forest and private timberland that is open to the public. Rough roads explain the Sycan's light use, mostly by anglers in summer, hunters in fall and a brief shot of rafters during spring runoff.

The upper Sycan and its tributaries, such as Long and Coyote creeks, harbor mostly small brook trout that willingly rise to flies and chase lures. There are native redband rainbow trout to 14 inches and occasionally larger bull trout. Bull trout must be released unharmed. The trout limit is 2, one over 20 inches per day, but feel free to keep all brook trout regardless of size. ODFW wants brook trout eradicated, and what better way than to cook them over a campfire. Access the upper Sycan via Forest roads 28, 30 and 3239, which parallel and cross the river in several places. Developed campsites are available at Pike's Crossing and Rock Creek. There are nice dispersed campsites along the river available to those willing to hike, drift or drive unimproved roads. A word of caution to streamside campers: the drainage is actively logged and subject to flash flooding. Camp above the high water mark and keep an eye on the weather. Thunderstorms are common in summer. Rising river levels cause turbidity which can hurt the fishing.

Downstream from the privately owned Sycan Marsh, 10-to 18-inch brown trout are available to anglers willing to travel. The lower Sycan is warmer and by late summer shallow and weedy. Focus fishing efforts near springs where cool water concentrates game fish. Or try earlier in the year during higher flows for spawners migrating up from the Sprague. Undesirable and in some cases protected chubs, dace, suckers and sculpin are also present. Streamer pattern flies can be effective for browns. Traditional caddis, mayfly and midge patterns will take rainbow. There are no developed campsites along the lower river, but plenty of suitable areas accessible by secondary roads, foot, and horseback. Forest roads 44, 46 and 27 are primary routes. Don't go without maps of the Fremont and Winema National Forests.

From Klamath Falls travel about 40 miles northeast on State Highway 140 to Beatty. From Chiloquin, travel about 40 miles east on State Highways 858 and 140. From Lakeview, travel 45 miles west on State Highway 140. From Silver Lake, travel 35 miles south on Forest Road 28.

The remote Sycan River flows through a basalt canyon over large water carved boulders and is surrounded by National Forest and private timberland that is open to the public.
Photos by Brooke Snavely

WILD BILLY LAKE

Size:	200 acres
Depth:	21'
Main Catch:	rainbow trout
Best Method:	wet flies
Season:	ice-off to ice-up (typically mid-Feb. to mid-Dec.)
Best Times:	spring, fall
Tips:	private fee lake

FROM TOP: Outdoor writer Steve Probasco with a Kamloop trout. Photo by Ron Meek;

Randy Rosin with another beautiful Kamloop trout. Photo by Ron Thienes;

A big rainbow for Daren Henderson. Photo by Butch Price

Wild Billy Lake gets its name from two men named Bill; both got in fights in early pioneer times that resulted in deaths. Nowadays most of the fighting at Wild Billy Lake is between anglers and trout with casualties ranging from sore fish lips to wrist exhaustion. The rest is verbal disagreements over who caught the biggest fish. A pay-to-fish operation since 1996, Wild Billy is gaining a reputation as one of Oregon's premier private fly fishing lakes.

A natural lake in the Sprague River valley east of Chiloquin, Wild Billy is planted with four strains of rapidly growing rainbow trout: Lassen, Kamloop, steelhead hybrid and triploid. All regularly attain sizes over 10 pounds. Lake operators are excited about recently introduced triploids, which are sterilized female trout. The theory is sterile fish won't waste energy spawning, just live long lives eating and growing to obscene sizes, possibly as large as 18 pounds. The current lake record is estimated at 15 pounds with the average trout running 18 inches, weighing about 3 lbs.

The best action is with minnow imitating wet flies on sinking lines cast toward shore and stripped back to the boat. Large trout hit minnow patterns hard, frequently breaking 6- and 8-pound tippet if they happen to strike while an angler is stripping. If trout aren't visibly chasing minnows in the shallows, try fishing deeper with Woolly Buggers and leeches toward the middle of the lake. A creek inlet in the northwest corner, rocky bank along the southeast shoreline, and underwater ridges toward the middle of the lake are prime places to begin searching for submarine size trout.

There are damselfly, dragonfly, mayfly and midge hatches in warm weather, but the fish display only fleeting interest in them with the higher energy minnow food source so available. Most Wild Billy anglers forget about dry flies once they've experienced what minnow patterns can do. Eightly is the record for most fish caught in one day. One butterfingered angler lost 3 rods in a day to the hard-charging trout.

At least 5- or 6-weight rods are recommended with type II and III uniform sinking lines. 4X-6X tippets are necessary to give anglers a fighting chance on the bigger fish. Leader length doesn't seem to matter. It would be silly to fish without backing. A quality reel with smooth drag system certainly helps. Size 6 minnow/leech/streamer pattern flies in black, green, white and tan do a good job imitating the minnows. Best times are February through June, sometimes into July depending on algae blooms, and in October and November.

Operators maintain the quality of the fishery by limiting use to 3 days a week by a maximum of 24 people per week. All fish must be released. Only small gap barbless hooks are allowed. Even at the rate of $150 per day per angler (in 2001) the lake is booked months in advance. Cabins can be rented for an additional $40 per night. Camping is allowed at two sites. Drift boats are included in the fee, giving anglers a mobility advantage over float tubes, which work well for those who aren't in a rush to get around this medium size private lake. Fishing from shore can be effective.

Wild Billy Lake is about 25 miles east of Chiloquin via the Sprague River Road. Chiloquin is 115 miles south of Bend on U.S. Highway 97; 26 miles north of Klamath Falls on Highway 97. Contact Wild Billy Lake (541) 747-6896 for information, reservations and directions. Lodging and restaurants are within driving distance.

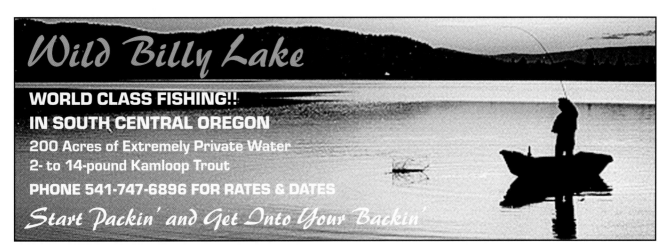

MILLER LAKE

Size:	565 acres
Depth:	148' max.
Main Catch:	brown trout; kokanee
Best Methods:	trolling; still-fishing; fly fishing near shore
Season:	entire year; check OSFR
Best Time:	just after ice-out; fall
Tips:	kokanee deep in mid-summer

Miller Lake, 8 miles west of Chemult as the raven flies, offers year-round fishing for kokanee, rainbow and brown trout. Even though there is nothing striking (except the fish) about the area, the outdoor experience is exceptionally pleasant. Miller Lake's wooded shoreline and 565 acres of inviting water is accessible yet secluded, 12 miles off U.S. Highway 97, Central Oregon's "freeway." Miller Lake lies at 5,616 feet elevation.

Overly successful natural reproduction of kokanee has caused size to decrease in recent years, the average fish currently about 8 inches in length, but they are abundant. Kokanee are caught by trolling, still-fishing with bait, or jigging a small lure. Since the lake's maximum depth is 148 feet, the kokanee can be quite deep by mid-summer.

Brown trout are stocked annually, and there are some good-sized ones prowling in here. Brown trout average from 20 inches in length up to 30-inch lunkers. Rainbow trout are no longer stocked, but some are still present in the lake. Both species of trout are angled for by trolling lures and flies. Troll slowly with a long line for brown trout. Fly fishing near shore and stream inlets in the evenings can be good. Brown trout are often more easily caught in the fall or very early or late in the day.

The east end of the lake is the most frequently fished section. Fishing from shore is not common, since most banks have a fairly steep drop off. The more shallow east end is one of the few spots fished from shore. The east end also supports most of the weedbeds. Many anglers fish from the boat dock near the campground. Water levels are quite stable. Cover for fish is mainly in the form of logs lying along the shoreline.

Winema National Forest's Digit Point Campground on the northwest shore of the lake offers excellent camping facilities: a boat ramp and dock, picnic area, a pressurized drinking water system, flush and vault toilets, trailer dump sites, a swimming area, a waterskiing area, and trailheads. A fee is charged to camp. Be ready for hoards of mosquitoes in this area.

The catch limit is 25 kokanee per day with no size restrictions, in addition to the trout limit of 5 per day with a 8-inch minimum, and of these no more than 1 over 20 inches. Boats are limited to a speed of 10 mph throughout most of the lake. Miller Lake is now open to angling 24 hours per day to take advantage of the abundant brown trout.

Trailheads from Digit Point lead into the Mount Thielsen Wilderness and around the lake. Another trail leading into the Wilderness takes off from Forest Route 9772, 1 mile from the campground. Many high lakes accessible from these trails offer decent fishing. During the winter, this is a popular recreation area for cross-country skiers and snowmobilers. A sno-park is located just off Highway 97 on Route 9772 into the lake. Ice fishermen are uncommon. The nearest services are in Chemult.

Miller Lake is 12 miles west of U.S. Highway 97 just north of Chemult. From the Eugene area take State Highway 58 over Willamette Pass all the way to it's junction with Highway 97. Turn south on Highway 97 and drive 8 miles to the turn onto Forest Route 9772 1 mile north of Chemult. Miller Lake is at the end of Route 9772, in 12 miles. From Bend drive south on Highway 97 about 74 miles to the turn onto Route 9772.

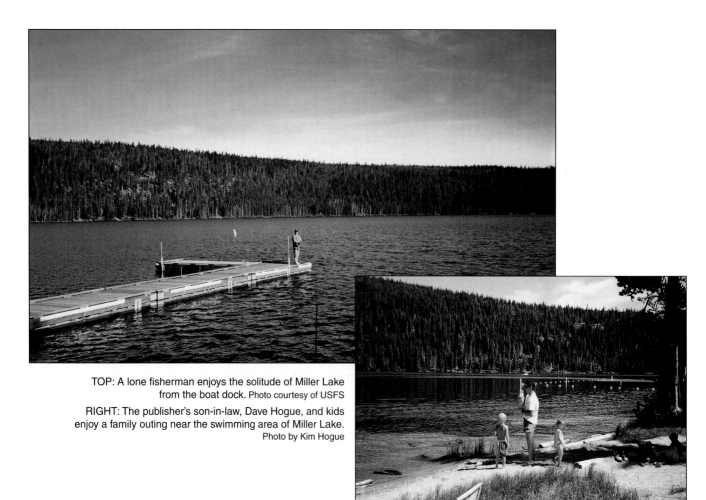

TOP: A lone fisherman enjoys the solitude of Miller Lake from the boat dock. Photo courtesy of USFS

RIGHT: The publisher's son-in-law, Dave Hogue, and kids enjoy a family outing near the swimming area of Miller Lake. Photo by Kim Hogue

DIAMOND LAKE

Size:	3,000 acres
Depth:	max. depth 52'
Main Catch:	hatchery rainbow trout; chub
Best Methods:	still fishing from a boat; fly fishing
Season:	last Saturday in April to Oct. 31; check OSFR
Best Time:	early spring to mid-June
Tips:	problems with chub

Diamond Lake's setting in the Umpqua National Forest, surrounded by Mount Thielsen, Mount Bailey, and the remains of Mount Mazama (Crater Lake), is a fishing, camping, and hiking mecca. Diamond Lake lies at an elevation of 5,182 feet, covers approximately 3,000 acres, and has a maximum depth of 52 feet. This rich body of water normally grows large fish fast, but currently suffers severe problems with chub.

Diamond Lake is 3.5 miles in length and 1.5 miles in width, with a total of 11.5 miles of gently sloped, tree-lined shore. Water levels fluctuate little, and there are many weedbeds. Silent Creek at the south end of the lake and Lake Creek at the northwest corner both form channels that extend about .25 mile into the body of the lake. Afternoon winds are common, as are afternoon thunderstorms in the summer.

The best time to catch trout on Diamond Lake is from very early spring through mid-June. Catching slows in July then picks up again in late September. Fifty-thousand legal size trout are planted each year at Diamond Lake, and of these, 15,000 are two-pounders. Fishing is improving and can still be good despite the chub. In years without chub competition, the fall would normally provide good fishing for spring-planted rainbow fingerlings grown to 9 to 10 inches in length.

The most often used method of catching fish here is still-fishing from a boat with Power Bait. Some fishers troll surface lures, such as FlatFish or artificial flies in early morning and evening. Bank fishing is primarily along the north and northwest shores. A few fishers use float tubes or wade in from shore. Always check the current OSFR before fishing.

A 10 mph boat speed limit is in effect during fishing season except in the middle of the lake from 9:00 am to 6:00 pm where waterskiers may cool off. Paved boat ramps are available at South Shore Picnic area, Thielsen View Campground and Diamond Lake Campground.

Three large Forest Service campgrounds are located on the lake: Thielsen View Campground on the west shore, Diamond Lake Campground on the east shore, and Broken Arrow Campground set back in the woods on the southeast corner of the lake. All three

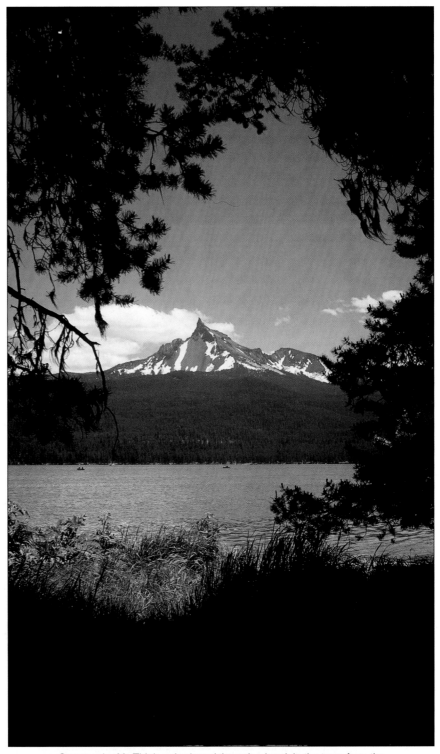

Spectacular Mt. Thielsen is viewed through a break in the trees from the west shore of Diamond Lake. Photo by George W. Linn

charge a fee and have pressurized water systems and units for the disabled. There are many other facilities on the lake, including a full-service resort, restaurants, convention center, stables, and an RV park. Other recreational opportunities include hiking trails and a paved bike path around lake. In the winter, snow-cat skiing, snowmobiling, cross-country skiing, ice-skating, snow-shoeing, and a snow-play hill with ski tow are available.

Diamond Lake is located 90 miles southwest of Bend. From Bend, take U.S. Highway 97, to State Highway 138 toward Roseburg, then take State Highway 230 and Forest Road 6592 into the south shore. At the next junction, Forest Road 4795, Broken Arrow Campground, South Shore Picnic Area, and Thielsen View Campground are to the left, and Diamond Lake Campground and the resort are straight on 4795.

LEMOLO LAKE

Size:	420 acres total
Depth:	max. depth 110'
Main Catch:	brown trout & kokanee
Best Methods:	casting & trolling lures; drifting bait
Season:	last Saturday in April to October 31
Best Time:	very early in the season; fall for kokanee
Tips:	90% of catch are brown trout

Lemolo Lake has the outstanding characteristics of being fed by the North Umpqua River and of being only 12 miles from Diamond Lake. It is known for the wild brown trout and kokanee lurking in its pale, jade-green waters. The reservoir covers 420 acres and is 110 feet deep at the dam. It has several shallower inlets and nice shoal areas.

Water levels at Lemolo rise from late April to Memorial Day in May and lower after Labor Day in September, but are quite stable in between. At low water, stumps can be hazardous to boaters. At higher water, waterskiing is a popular pastime, and winds are not as strong as at Diamond Lake. The North Umpqua River and Lake Creek form channels that meet in the middle of the reservoir, forming one deeper channel that runs clear down to the dam.

Ninety percent of the catch at Lemolo are brown trout, averaging 11 to 14 inches. Kokanee are the next most abundant species, with fish in the mature age class, averaging 10 to 14 inches. There are also a few brook trout and rainbow trout, averaging 8 to 12 inches. All fish in the lake are wild. Chub are abundant.

The best time of the year to catch brown trout is very early in the year when water levels and temperatures are both low and the fish are in the inlets, and in the fall when the larger brown trout return to the inlets to spawn. Kokanee are spread throughout the lake during most of the summer at mid-water depths and in the fall move into the Umpqua River to spawn. Catches of rainbow and brook trout are accidental.

Many methods of fishing are used at Lemolo, from mealworms and nightcrawlers right through Rapalas, wedding rings, and artificial flies. For the brown trout, casting and trolling lures, such as Bingo Bugs and Panther Martins, and drifting bait are popular methods. In mid-summer, the browns will be in deeper water by mid-day, in the morning and evening they will be closer to the surface. A few folks either wade-fish early in the year in the North Umpqua and Lake Creek arms, bank angle for the browns using Rapalas, or drift bait in these inlets. For kokanee, troll wedding rings and flashers. Always be sure to check the current OSFR before fishing.

There are six campgrounds on the lake. Lemolo Lake Resort, Poole Creek, Bunker Hill, Lake Creek, East Lemolo, and Inlet. All campgrounds charge a fee. Lemolo Lake Resort has full hook-ups, Poole Creek is developed with centralized water, paved roads, a boat ramp, group camp area, and a beach/swimming area. All the other campgrounds are primitive with outhouses and picnic tables. Lemolo Lake Resort has about anything one would ever need. One can also enjoy jetskiing, waterskiing, hiking, and mountain biking in the area, and in the winter snowmobiling and crosscountry skiing.

To get to Lemolo Lake travel State Highway 138 from either eastern or western Oregon. Take the turn onto Birds Point Road (road 2610) 6 miles north of Diamond Lake and 73 miles east of Roseburg. Lemolo Lake Resort is 5 miles in from highway 138. All other campgrounds are located around the 8 miles that circle the lake.

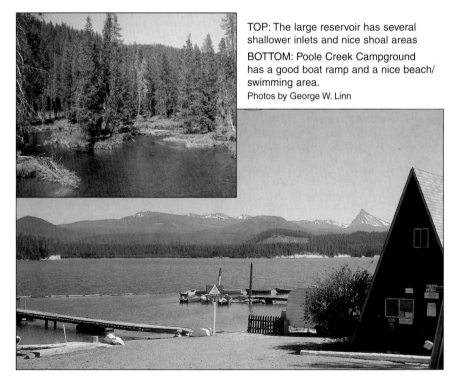

TOP: The large reservoir has several shallower inlets and nice shoal areas

BOTTOM: Poole Creek Campground has a good boat ramp and a nice beach/swimming area.

Photos by George W. Linn

UPPER KLAMATH LAKE

Size: 96 sq. miles
Depth: 7' average; 50' max.
Main Catch: rainbow, brown trout
Best Methods: flies, trolling, bait
Season: entire year; check OSFR
Best Time: summer & fall
Tips: Fishing is best at mouths of creeks; around springs & weedbeds; in deep water; & along steep, rocky shorelines.

Upper Klamath Lake's shallow, weedy, bug-infested, wind-swept water does not fit the trout lake stereotype. But appearances are deceiving. This is trophy trout water, challenging to fish, a pleasure to visit.

Upper Klamath is home to Klamath strain rainbow trout, arguably the fastest growing, largest rainbow trout in North America. The average size fish here is 5-7 pounds. Ten-pounders are common. A few fish over 20 pounds are taken every year. Their amazing size can be attributed to ample feed and the species' penchant for eating minnows, a behavior long credited to the big brown trout with whom they share the lake.

Locating these monsters in nearly 100 square miles of water is no easy feat, but can be done by breaking the lake down into sections, seasons and methods.

Fishing is best at the mouths of creeks, around springs and weedbeds, in deep water, near the outflow, and along steep, rocky shorelines. By concentrating on these areas, anglers eliminate 95% of the lake. The primary techniques are trolling with lures, still fishing with bait and fly fishing. When the water is cold in winter and spring, trolling the shorelines is the best way to find widely scattered fish. Long-line, weightless trolling is effective with minnow imitating lures like Freaks, F-S-T's, Little Cleos, Rebels and Rapalas. Depth is not nearly as important as distance behind the boat. Most fish are caught within 10 feet of the surface, regardless of season or tactics. Dead minnows are also trolled with and without attractor blades. Shore anglers occasionally score

with nightcrawler and marshmallow combinations fished with slip sinkers on slack line. Trolled and still-fished dead chubs attract bigger fish. Do not catch and kill chubs or suckers from the lake, as they are protected. Dead bait is available at bait shops throughout the area. Minnow imitating streamers and black, brown and olive Seal Buggers and leech patterns are best for fly fishing.

As the water warms in late spring and early summer, the fish gravitate to deeper holes and cooler water. This is the time to focus trolling, bait and fly fishing efforts in deep water, of which there isn't much, also near springs and creek channels. The deepest water in the lake is at the tip of Eagle Ridge, also between the ridge and Bare Island south to Squaw Point. The mouth of

Wocus Bay and the tip of Ball Point also have some deep spots. Fish also begin showing at the mouth of the Williamson River, Agency Lake strait, Thomas Creek, Pelican Bay and an area known as "Fish Banks" where the wildlife refuge projects into the main body of the lake. A lake map showing bottom contours and depthfinder is helpful. A boat and a willingness to move are essential to finding feeding fish. Lure, bait and fly patterns remain the same.

Fishing really gets good in summer as fish seek relief from the heat in cool water of creek mouths, around springs at Rocky Point, in deep channels and begin swimming up the creeks themselves. Big spawners migrate out of the lake in September and October. Pelican Bay is one of the best areas this time of year, with easy access to Crystal, Harriman, and

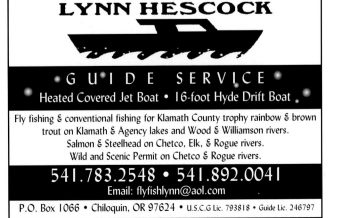

ABOVE: A fisherman hooks a beauty in the Rocky Point area of the lake.
Photo by Brian O'Keefe

LEFT: Handicap access is available at Putnam Point at the south end of the lake.
Photo by Brooke Snavely

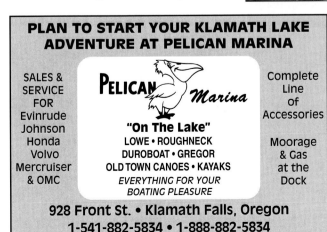

Recreation creeks. All methods remain effective, though fly fishing may have an advantage with fish paying more attention to bug hatches. Midges are the most common insect, with large caddis, mayfly, damsel and dragonflies offering seasonal variety. Wet or dry, fish all patterns on long leaders, at least 12 feet. Big fish are instinctively cautious. Tippet material should be 4-6-pound test, strong enough to land large fish, supple enough to let the fly move realistically. Use tapered leaders to keep suspended algae from hanging up on the line and ruining the presentation. Don't be thrown off by the lake's heavy algae growth. The fish use it for cover.

The limit is 1 trout per day, minimum 8 inches. Brown bullhead and perch are also available with no size restrictions or catch limits.

Upper Klamath is a spectacular bird watching, sight-seeing, boating, and camping area. At any time, upwards of 40 species of birds are present. Designated canoe trails give paddlers close-up views of water lilies, beavers and birds in the Klamath Wildlife Refuge. Regular afternoon winds make for great sailing. Numerous trails lead to many fine hike-in fishing lakes in the Sky Lakes and Mountain Lakes Wilderness areas. Picnicking, camping, and boat launches are available at public and private parks, marinas, campgrounds and resorts all around the lake. Moore Park on the lake's south shore in Klamath Falls is one of the prettiest waterfront parks anywhere. And be sure to watch the sunsets, especially when there are clouds to reflect the evening glow.

From Bend, travel 100 miles south on U.S. Highway 97 to Chiloquin, then west 20 miles to Fort Klamath to west shore or continue south along east shore to Klamath Falls for 26 miles.

From Medford: Travel 46 miles east on State Highway 140 to Rocky Point Jct., or continue south 24 miles along west shore to Klamath Falls.

From Ashland: Travel 64 miles east on State Highway 66 to Klamath Falls.

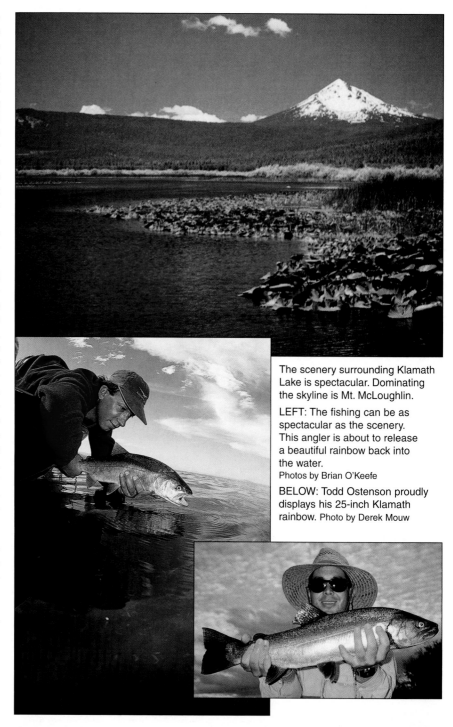

The scenery surrounding Klamath Lake is spectacular. Dominating the skyline is Mt. McLoughlin.

LEFT: The fishing can be as spectacular as the scenery. This angler is about to release a beautiful rainbow back into the water.
Photos by Brian O'Keefe

BELOW: Todd Ostenson proudly displays his 25-inch Klamath rainbow. Photo by Derek Mouw

AGENCY LAKE

Size:	14 sq. mi. (8,960 acres)
Depth:	10' max.
Main Catch:	rainbow & brown trout, perch
Best Methods:	shallow trolling with lures, flies, bait
Season:	entire year; check OSFR
Best Time:	May-Oct.
Tips:	probe the side channels

Agency Lake, named for the nearby Klamath Indian Agency, is basically part of the larger Upper Klamath Lake and fishes much the same. A broad, shallow, silty lake exposed to the wind and subject to dense algae blooms, water clarity is rarely more than 3 feet. None of this seems to bother the 5- to 15-pound brown and rainbow trout that migrate through on their way to and from spawning tributaries such as the Wood River and Seven Mile Canal. The lake's organically rich water grows trout fingerlings into 20-inchers in three years. Massive schools of yellow perch thrive in weedy, shallow areas, becoming available to anglers in mid-summer.

A boat is required to fish Agency Lake, as it is almost entirely surrounded by private lands. The 25-mile long shoreline consists mostly of man-made levies laced with canals and pumps designed to drain farmland. The steep sloped dirt levies are the dominant structure in the lake with outflow from canals and pumps creating fish attracting currents. In spring when farmers drain their fields, it's a good idea to cast lures and flies around the pumps where fish may feed.

The inlet of the Wood River and the straits draining the lake are two more hot spots. Long line surface trolling around the mouth of the Wood can be effective with Canadian Wonder spoons, shallow running crankbaits, dead minnows or nightcrawlers. Still fishing can be good along levies and weed lines where submerged brush or overhanging trees may hold fish. Fly fishers favor leech and minnow type flies, both trolled and cast on floating and intermediate sinking lines, then stripped back with long, slow pulls. Beware of a deadline at the mouth of the Wood River denoting a change to catch and release, no-bait regulations and restricted seasons in the river itself.

Trout congregate in the mile-long narrow strait connecting Agency Lake to Upper Klamath as they pass through in search of comfortable water temperature, food and spawning habitat. Here again, shallow trolling with flies and lures is the best way to connect with roaming trout, though still fishing and casting can also produce. Be sure to probe the side channel created by dredging to build levies paralleling the natural strait. The side channel, also known as the inside channel, is deeper and frequently more productive.

Perch fishing is productive in July and August when schools congregate in Four Mile Canal. This 10-foot deep, tule-lined waterway is best fished with small jigs, worms without bobbers and perch meat. Agency perch average 10-12 inches and are considered very good eating. The perch fishery attracts many out-of-state anglers.

Free launch ramps are available at Petric and Henzel parks, county parks with restrooms. Agency Lake Resort charges a launch fee. All three ramps are accessible from the Modoc Point Road. Both lakes can whip up in a hurry in windy conditions, so keep an eye on the weather.

Regulations: 1 trout per day. No size limit or catch restrictions on perch.

From Bend travel 100 miles south on U.S. Highway 97 to Chiloquin, then west 5 miles on the South Chiloquin Road; turn north on the Modoc Point Road which fronts Agency Lake.

From Klamath Falls travel 30 miles north to Chiloquin on U.S. 97; from there follow the same directions to the lake.

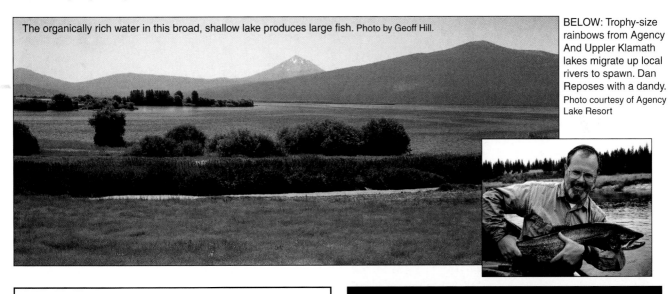

The organically rich water in this broad, shallow lake produces large fish. Photo by Geoff Hill.

BELOW: Trophy-size rainbows from Agency And Uppler Klamath lakes migrate up local rivers to spawn. Dan Reposes with a dandy. Photo courtesy of Agency Lake Resort

LAKE OF THE WOODS

Size: 1,146 acres
Depth: 27' avg.; 55' max.
Main Catch: kokanee, rainbow & brown trout, bass
Best Methods: trolling; casting lures
Season: entire year; check OSFR
Best Time: spring, fall
Tips: good ice fishing in winter

To Klamath Falls

Lake of the Woods Hwy

To Fish Lake
Medford

140

140

Lake of the Woods

Dead Indian Rd.

West Side Rd.

LAKE OF THE WOODS

N

▲ CAMPGROUND
◢ BOAT RAMP
— PAVED ROAD
S STILL FISHING
----- **T** TROLLING

The Lake of the Woods is a classic fish and ski family lake in a beautiful wooded setting on the east slope of the southern Oregon Cascade mountains at 4,949' elevation. A typical day finds anglers trolling at sunrise until about 10 a.m. when waterskiers take over. Then there's a raft and swimmer hatch in the shallows until about dinner time when the lake quiets down and anglers return to fish the evening bite. The timing works for all parties, including the fish.

Trolling with a set of flashers (Ford Fenders, Flashlights) and Wedding Ring spinner tipped with corn is the universal approach for kokanee, rainbow and brown trout. It is possible to catch fish without the heavy trolling blades, just a Dick Nite or Triple Teazer, with or without bait. Either way, the fish are available near the surface in the spring. Browns to 7 pounds are most likely this time of year, though they periodically surprise anglers expecting 9- to 12-inch kokanee and similarly sized rainbow trout throughout summer. The 11-lb., 4 oz. lake record rainbow was caught on a trolled Rapala in April of 1994, proving again that big trout like big baits.

Summer surface temperatures to 70°F push the trout down to the thermocline, typically 33 to 40 feet by late summer. Trollers add weight or fish with lead core line and concentrate on the deep water along the west shore, following the contours out into the north bay and back again. Good bait bank fishing and casting opportunities exist along all shores spring and fall, but mainly along the west shore in summer. Power Bait and worms are the best bait, with Rooster Tails and Panther-Martins the most effective lures for casting and retrieving. Largemouth bass like the west side docks, north and south end shallows, and downed trees in Rainbow Bay. Bass to 6 pounds go for plastic worms and spinner baits on light lines in this clear water. They will hit Jitterbugs and surface poppers in low light conditions. Perch, small catfish and carp are also caught on still fished baits.

Busy with school or work, most anglers

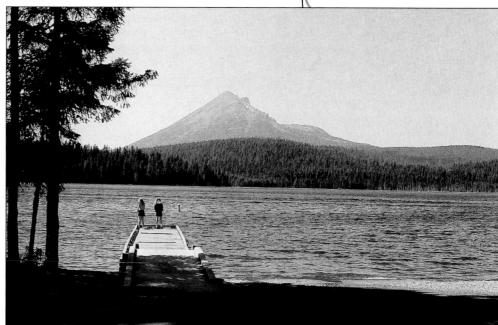

Anglers must share popular Lake of the Woods with waterskiers and other summer fun seekers; however, there is room for everyone on this large lake in the shadow of Mt. McLoughlin . Photo by Geoff Hill

miss the good fall bite when trout return to the surface to sip the last insects of the year with renewed vigor. Its about the only time fly casters do well on dry flies. Trolled streamer pattern flies can be very good on fly rods or spinning rods on light monofilament. Kokanee spawn in the east shore gravel. By the time they get there they are too dark for eating but offer great sport. Target them before they turn color with jigged Buzz Bombs and trolled lures in 30-40 feet of water. Bass become very aggressive, chasing lures far from their usual haunts. Ice fishing is good in winter. Limits are 25 kokanee per day; 5 trout per day, 1 over

20 inches; 5 bass per day, 1 over 15 inches; there is no limit on bullheads, perch or carp. Lake of the Woods is now open 24 hours a day to take advantage of the abundant brown trout.

There are three paved boat ramps, 130 Forest Service camp sites and the full service Lake of the Woods Resort, offering RV camping with hook ups, tent sites, store, restaurant, marina and boat rentals.

From Klamath Falls travel 35 miles west on State Highway 140; from Medford, take State Highway 62 north to Highway 140 then east 45 miles; from Ashland, travel 35 miles east on Dead Indian Road.

FISH LAKE

(Jackson County)

Size: 483 acres
Depth: 18' avg.; 31' max.
Main Catch: rainbow, brown
& brook trout
Best Methods: trolling with bait, flies
Season: entire year; check OSFR
Best Time: May-October
Tips: best to troll near
Doe Point & the dam.

Appropriately named, Fish Lake is one of the most consistent trout producing lakes in the southern Oregon Cascades. Located at 4,642' elevation near the summit of Highway 140, surrounded by old growth forests, this is a clean, cool pleasant body of water to fish in or just hang around.

The lake is stocked annually with about 20,000 legal size rainbow trout. Those that carryover reach 15-16 inches in two years, and if they survive a third, attain 20 inches or more. Four pounds is considered the standard for big fish, and every year dozens that size and larger are caught. The lake record is a 9.75-lb. rainbow, on display at Fish Lake Lodge. ODFW also plants 5,000, 8- to 10-inch steelhead in the lake. The steelhead grow to 22 inches, tend to be slimmer than the rainbows, but are considered by some anglers more active when hooked. Brook trout are not stocked, but some are caught every year as they apparently spawn in the lake. A few brown trout are present, along with an illegally introduced population of chubs.

Trolling is the most popular method to catch fish in Fish Lake. Ford Fenders followed by a gold Needlefish with a red tip, a streamer fly or a Wedding Ring spinner tipped with a worm are the norm. The best trolling spots are near Doe Point and close to the dam. A 10-mile per hour speed limit keeps boat noise to a minimum. Still fishing is good from boats and shore with worms, salmon eggs and Power Bait. One of the best still-fishing spots is around a small island across from the lodge that sports a small cross. The cross memorializes a 1950s drowning victim. Also try suspending bait near the bottom off points in the main lake and near the dam. Good bank fishing is available next to the Doe Point boat ramp. The deepest water is right down the middle of the lake. Some fly fishing occurs along the shorelines when fish are rising to ants, the biggest insect in this cold spring-fed lake. Better fly fishing is available in Little Butte Creek below the dam.

Ice fishing is possible most winters, though not many people try, with worms and salmon eggs on small hooks and light line. Savage strikes are likely in spring on orange Rooster Tails cast to fish cruising the receding ice. Bait is good as soon as the water is open and throughout the year. Trolling gives more action and shows lures to more fish that get a little lazy in the summer months. There is terrific, uncrowded fall fishing September through mid-November. The limit is 5 fish per day, including steelhead, minimum 8 inches.

A boat ramp and 41 tent/trailer sites are available at Doe Point and Fish Lake campgrounds. Fish Lake Resort offers a 45-space trailer park with hookups, cabins, boat rentals, boat launch and a rustic lodge with restaurant and supplies. Check out the resort's 10 years of photo albums showing proud anglers displaying their catch.

From Medford, travel 35 miles east on State Highway 140.

From Klamath Falls, travel 39 miles west on Highway 140.

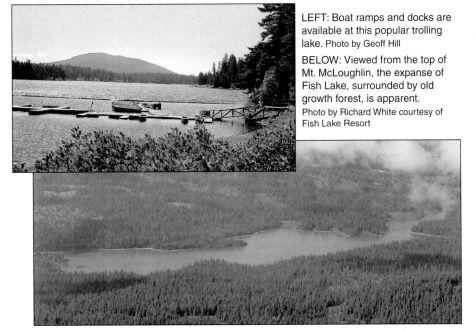

LEFT: Boat ramps and docks are available at this popular trolling lake. Photo by Geoff Hill

BELOW: Viewed from the top of Mt. McLoughlin, the expanse of Fish Lake, surrounded by old growth forest, is apparent.
Photo by Richard White courtesy of Fish Lake Resort

FISH LAKE

To Lake of the Woods
Klamath Falls

Fish Lake Campground
Doe Point Campground
Fish Lake Resort

To Medford

Lake of the Woods Hwy

CASCADE CANAL

N. FORK LITTLE BUTTE CR.

140

North Fork Campground

DAM

LAVA FIELD

N

▲ CAMPGROUND
◢ BOAT RAMP
— PAVED ROAD
- - - UNPAVED ROAD
········ HIKING TRAIL
S STILL FISHING
T TROLLING

FOURMILE LAKE

Size:	763 acres
Depth:	155' average; 75' max.
Main Catch:	kokanee, brown, brook & rainbow trout
Best Methods:	troll, still-fish, fly fishing
Season:	late April-Oct. 31
Best Time:	August
Tips:	primarily boat fishing lake

Scenically located at the base of Mt. McLoughlin, Fourmile Lake is a large, deep, cold trout lake with nice camping and good access to many nearby hike-in lakes. At 5,744' elevation on the crest of the Cascades, the lake is exposed to rapidly changing weather and can often whip into white caps in a hurry.

A natural lake artificially enlarged with a dam in 1922, the lake features submerged trees that provide good fish habitat but significant boating hazards. The lake is not four miles long as the name suggests (closer to 3 miles) but that doesn't diminish its popularity. The campgrounds are full most summer weekends.

Fourmile is primarily a boat fishing lake. The shorelines and shallows are littered with dead standing and fallen timber, making shore fishing difficult. Most anglers fish from boats along the edges of the submerged forests. It's kind of similar to Crane Prairie, except when boaters tie off to a tree, they may be in 50 or 60 feet of water. Effective trolling rigs for trout and kokanee consist of flashers; Wedding Ring spinners tipped with corn fished 20-40 feet deep. The best trolling area is off the trees along the north shoreline. Panther Martin and Rooster Tail spinners are also good trolling lures, and even better when cast to rising fish in and around the trees.

Fly fishers troll leech and crawdad pattern wet flies when nothing is rising, and switch to ants, dragonflies and damselflies when those hatches come off. The best still-fishing hole is on the southwest shore opposite the Swan Creek inlet. Here, anglers tie to trees and offer worms, salmon eggs and Power Bait close to the bottom. Anglers should be prepared with extra tackle, as snagging and losing equipment on the trees is likely. Four-pound test leaders are the norm in this very clear water.

Fourmile hosts an overabundance of small kokanee averaging 6-10 inches. The kokanee limit is 25. Ten- to 19-inch naturally reproducing brook trout are available in good numbers. Ten thousand rainbow trout are stocked annually. They run 10-22 inches. Browns average 10-14 inches, with larger specimens likely an experimental hybrid, unable to spawn, hopefully expending their energy eating the abundant kokanee.

Trout limits are 5 per day, 1 over 20 inches. ODFW is considering planting lake trout to control the kokanee and provide more variety for anglers. Motors are allowed. There is no boat speed limit though caution is advised with numerous deadheads.

Thirty developed campsites with hand pumps for water, handicap accessible vault toilets, gravel boat ramp and day use area are available on a first-come, first-serve basis on the lake's south end.

Other activities include climbing 9,495' Mt. McLoughlin, a strenuous but rewarding 7-hour round trip, horseback riding, wildflower and wildlife watching.

From Medford travel 37 miles east on State Highway 140, then north 11 miles on Forest Service Road 3650 to Fourmile Lake. From Klamath Falls travel 37 miles west on State Highway 140, then 11 miles north on Forest Service Road 3650.

Located at the base of Mt. McLoughlin, large, deep Fourmile Lake is primarily a boat fishing lake.
Photo by Brooke Snavely

HOWARD PRAIRIE

Size: 2,070 acres
Depth: 80'
Main Catch: rainbow trout, catfish
Best Methods: trolling, bait, flies
Season: late April-Oct. 31
Best Time: spring, fall
Tips: lake loaded with fish!

Howard Prairie is the most popular fishing lake in Southwest Oregon, with good reason. The lake is loaded with fish. Fishing is good here when it stinks everywhere else. And when fishing is good elsewhere, it's even better here. Limits are common. Add to that a beautiful location and excellent boating, camping and picnicking facilities and its obvious why Howard Prairie attracts more than one quarter million visitors annually.

An outstanding fishery since it was constructed as an irrigation reservoir in 1958, ODFW experimented with stocking rates for years, trying to produce a balance of quantity and quality size trout. They appear to have it dialed, stocking 350,000–400,000 3-inch fingerlings in May. By the following spring, the planters average 11-13 inches. Carryovers regularly stretch 15-22 inches. Bigger trout are possible. Abundant aquatic insect and minnow populations supply the food and give anglers plenty of things to imitate. The lake's three islands, varied shape and depth provide all kinds of fishing opportunities based on season and water levels.

Trout fishing is usually very good opening day (last Saturday in April) through midsummer, then again in the fall. The most popular techniques are trolling and still fishing with bait. Early and late in the season when the water is cold and fish are shallow, troll brass Needlefish or Triple Teazers on 4-pound test along the shorelines for quick limits. Add a piece of worm or corn to stimulate the bite. For larger trout, try small silver and gold Rapalas and dark colored F4 Flatfish to imitate the baitfish bigger trout feed on. As the water warms, add weight, flashers or use deeper diving lures to stay in touch with fish in the cooler depths. The most consistent trolling areas are the east and west shorelines south of Howard Prairie Resort toward the dam.

Still fishers do well with chartreuse and rainbow colored Power Bait, inflated worms, salmon eggs and marshmallows suspended 24 inches off the bottom on size 14 treble hooks. Red Rock Cove, Buck Island, the jetty at the resort and Doe and Fawn islands are perennial bait dunking hotspots. Start the season in 15 feet of water, going deeper as conditions dictate. Fly fishers do fine trolling and casting streamers, such as the Brown Bailey, towards shore and weed lines. Coves around the lake and the narrows up to Lily Glen are popular float tube areas.

CLOCKWISE: This reservoir has been an outstanding fishery since it was constructed in 1958.

Boat rentals, moorage, and paved boat ramps are available at the Howard Prairie Marina
Photos by Geoff Hill

Fishing is good all season.
Photo by Brooke Snavely

Trout fishing slows in the heat of summer, because the fish have so much to eat, but is still worth the effort. Brown bullhead catfish, 8- to 11-inch, pick up the slack, feeding heavily in the shallows, agreeable to worms and chicken gizzards providing good bank fishing on simple tackle. Limits are 5 trout per day, only 1 over 20 inches, no limit on catfish. Always check current OSFR.

Three Jackson County operated campgrounds (Klum Landing, Grizzly Creek and Willow Point) offer paved boat ramps, restrooms, picnicking and camping. Howard Prairie Resort on the west shore has boat rentals, moorage and storage, cabins, RV hook ups, 300 campsites, fishing supplies and advice. All facilities charge entry fees. Other activities include sailing, swimming, arrowhead hunting, bird and wildlife watching. Nearby Hyatt Lake has larger average size trout.

From Ashland travel 22 miles northeast on Dead Indian Road. From Klamath Falls travel 50 miles west via State Highway 66 and the Keno Access Road.

To Lake of the Woods

HOWARD PRAIRIE LAKE

N

Dead Indian Rd.

Keno Rd.

To Ashland

Hyatt Prairie Rd.

HOXIE CREEK

▲ CAMPGROUND
◢ BOAT RAMP
— PAVED ROAD
······ HIKING TRAIL
S STILL FISHING
T TROLLING

Grizzly Creek

Doe Island

Howard Prairie Resort

S

S

T

Buck Island

S

JENNY CREEK

To Hyatt Lake

Howard Prairie Dam Access Rd.

S

DAM

Pacific Crest National Scenic Trail

GERBER RESERVOIR

Size:	4,047 acres
Depth:	27' avg.; 65' max.
Main Catch:	crappie, perch, bass, trout
Best Methods:	small lures, bait
Season:	entire year
Best Time:	spring, fall
Tips:	hard to reach so very low fishing pressure.

Gerber Reservoir is probably the best publicly accessible panfish water in the Klamath basin. Gerber Reservoir produced the state record white crappie, a 4-lb., 12-oz., 18.5-inch beauty in 1967. The state record 4-lb., 18-inch black crappie came out of the Lost River downstream from Gerber in 1978. Yellow perch are available in abundance, along with largemouth bass and a few rainbow trout, remainders of a discontinued stocking program. Built for irrigation and flood control, Gerber features a variety of flooded timber, brush, inlets, coves, rocky shorelines, shoals and deep holding water. The habitat is so good and the reservoir large enough that most anglers haven't figured out where the fish go some of the year. A hard 50-mile drive east of Klamath Falls on narrow, bumpy roads, Gerber doesn't get much fishing pressure and has the potential to grow more state records.

The crappie bite starts in April or May when water temperatures reach 62° to 65°F, motivating the fish to spawn in shallow water with sand or gravel bottoms. 1/16 and 1/32 ounce maribou crappie jigs, small plastic grubs, worms and green peas catch mostly male crappies guarding the nests. The key is to approach quietly, not anchor on top of the nesting areas, drop the bait in with a long pole or cast from a distance and fish below a sensitive bobber. Creek inlets and shallow points around the island are perennial spawning areas. By mid-June, crappie move deeper, hanging around submerged trees close to the dam and near the eagle's nest on the Barnes Creek arm. Use light wire hooks that will bend if snagged or easily broken leader material.

In July and August when anglers complain the crappie disappear and switch to perch, crappie are probably suspended in open water off points and drop-offs, sometimes 15-30 feet deep. To locate them, try trolling soft bodied jigs and Beetle Spins, switching to vertical bait presentations when found. If fluctuating water levels permit, crappie move back into flooded brush and standing timber in the fall for another round of good fishing.

Perch follow similar patterns, but don't move as deep as crappie and prefer weeds over brush. Perch fishing is good most of the summer in 5- to 10-foot deep water with worms, leeches, perch meat, small jigs and lures. In areas where only small perch are caught, try a bit farther out and deeper for larger fish. Bigger plastic worms and spinner baits will catch bass in the same areas, especially around cover. Before trout stocking stopped, anglers used to troll the creek channels with good results. Now most trout fishing is limited to bank fishing in the narrows of Ben Hall Creek around the point to the dam. Miller Creek below the dam offers good stream trout fishing. Watch for rattlesnakes.

The BLM operates two nice day-use areas and campgrounds with restrooms, fish cleaning stations and gravel boat ramps on the west side of the lake. There is an improved boat ramp at Barnes Valley Creek on the east shore with fewer amenities.

From Klamath Falls, go 19 miles east on State Highway 140, then take County Road 70 about 17 miles to Bonanza and Lorella, then 8 miles NE up Gerber Reservoir Road.

From Lakeview, take Highway 140 west to Bly, follow Forest Route 375 and Forest Route 381 south for 10 miles to the lake.

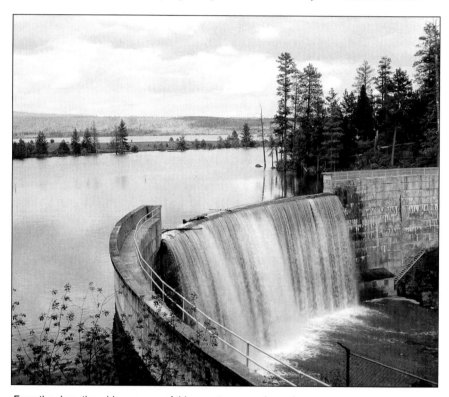

From the dam, the wide expanse of this remote reservoir can be seen. Photo by Brooke Snavely

Western Cascades Drainage Area

Many fine fishing opportunities exist along the highways crossing the Cascades. The next several pages cover popular waters along highways 22, 20, 126, and 58.

NOTE: MAP NOT TO SCALE

N

To Salem
Portland

LITTLE NORTH SANTIAM R.

Breitenbush Springs

BREITENBUSH R.

Mill City

46

NORTH SANTIAM RIVER

22

Detroit

Idanha

Detroit Reservoir

Mt. Jefferson

QUARTZVILLE CREEK

NORTH SANTIAM R.

Three Fingered Jack

Green Peter Reservoir

MIDDLE SANTIAM R.

22

Foster Reservoir

Hoodoo Ski Bowl

20

To Sisters

To Albany
Corvallis

Sweet Home

Cascadia

S. SANTIAM RIVER

20

Clear Lake

Big Lake

15

Mt. Washington

To Sisters

BLUE RIVER

Smith Reservoir

126

Blue River Reservoir

McKENZIE PASS

242

CLOSED IN WINTER

To Sisters

Rainbow

Belknap Springs

Vida

McKenzie Bridge

Three Sisters
Faith, Hope & Charity

To
Springfield
Eugene

McKENZIE RIVER

Blue River

McKENZIE R.

Cougar Reservoir

Broken Top

Fall Creek Reservoir

18

19

To
Springfield

FALL CREEK

Lookout Point Reservoir

N. FORK OF MIDDLE FORK WILLAMETTE R.

To
Eugene

Lowell

58

24

Mt. Bachelor

SALMON CREEK

Waldo Lake

Oakridge

Fish Hatchery

McCredie Springs

Gold Lake

Hills Creek Reservoir

SALT CREEK

58

21

Salt Creek Falls

Willamette Pass Ski Area & Visitors Info

MIDDLE FORK WILLAMETTE RIVER

Diamond Peak

To
Hwy 97
Chemult
Crater Lake

BREITENBUSH & OLALLIE LAKES

Breitenbush

Size: 60 acres
Depth: 30'
Main Catch: rainbow, brook trout
Best Methods: trolling flies, bait, lures
Season: entire year; check OSFR
Tips: fish feed on emerging insects mornings & evenings.

Olallie

Size: 240 acres
Depth: 48'
Main Catch: rainbow trout
Best Methods: flies, bait, lures
Season: entire year; check OSFR
Best Time: June-July
Tips: troll along the shoreline.

Breitenbush and Olallie are two of the largest lakes in the beautiful Olallie Lakes Scenic Area north of Mt. Jefferson. Of the two, Olallie is more developed and accessible, featuring a resort and four Forest Service fee campgrounds with very good fishing for planted trout. Breitenbush's remote setting lends itself to solitary camping and fishing for small wild brook and occasionally planted rainbow trout.

Olallie is stocked annually with about 15,000 legal-size rainbows and several hundred 4- to 10-pound brooders (640 in 1998), resulting in easy limits and an occasional whale before they are fished out or wise up. Power Bait and worms still fished from shore and boats catch lots of fish. Trolling along the shorelines from rowboats, rafts and float tubes with Spruce flies on a 2-lb. test leader can be very productive as the hatchery fish learn to

eat organic or starve. Casting or trolling Rooster Tails or Frog Flatfish work well, as does trolling worms behind Ford Fenders. No gas or electric motors are allowed. No swimming is permitted to protect the lake, which is a source of drinking water. Swimming is allowed in several nearby lakes.

Breitenbush Lake is four miles south over the rough Forest Service Road 4220 past Monon, Horseshoe, and Gibson lakes, all good camping and fishing spots.

Breitenbush has nice weed lines and shoal areas where fish feed on emerging insects mornings and evenings. In bright sunshine it may be necessary to fish deep with bait, lures and wet flies in the main body of the lake. Canoes, kayaks and float tubes allow anglers to keep up with cruising fish. A no-fee campground with picnic tables and a

gravel boat launch are the only amenities. Five fish limits, 1 over 20 inches, are in effect on all lakes in the Olallie Scenic Area.

Breitenbush Lake is in the McQuinn strip, a boundary area along the Warm Springs Indian Reservation. Any hiking or fishing expeditions to the east require a Warm Springs Tribal permit.

From Bend, Salem and Eugene go through Detroit, then north 24 miles on Forest Highway 46; east 7 miles on FS Road 4690; south 8 miles on 4220 to Olallie Lake. Turn off FS 46 at milepost 18 to reach Breitenbush Lake 8 miles up FS 4220.

From Portland take U.S. Highway 26 to FS Road 42, about 9 miles east of Government Camp. Ollallie is about 32 miles south on FS roads 42 and 4220. Breitenbush is 4 miles south on 4220.

ABOVE: In Breitenbush Lake, floating devices allow anglers to keep up with cruising fish.

LEFT: A variety of methods from bank fishing to trolling work for anglers at Olallie Lake.

BELOW: Denise Martin (left) is happy with her 5-pound Olallie rainbow. Lynn Killon (right) shows off her 7-pound rainbow.
Photos by Brook Snavely

NORTH SANTIAM RIVER

Size:	60 miles in length
Depth:	shallow above Detroit Reservoir; deeper below the dam
Main Catch:	trout; steelhead; salmon
Best Methods:	above reservoir: wade & bank fishing with flies, bait, & lures; below dam: boat & bank fishing
Season:	check current OSFR
Best Time:	winter steelhead: March–May; summer steelhead: April–Dec.; spring chinook: May–July
Tips:	multiple recreational use area; many parks

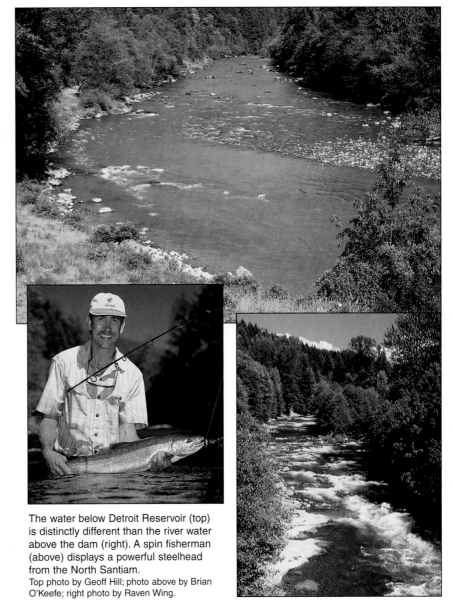

The water below Detroit Reservoir (top) is distinctly different than the river water above the dam (right). A spin fisherman (above) displays a powerful steelhead from the North Santiam.
Top photo by Geoff Hill; photo above by Brian O'Keefe; right photo by Raven Wing.

The North Santiam River is the slightly larger of the north and south forks of the Santiam River, both very productive trout, steelhead and salmon streams. The North Santiam begins its journey high in the Cascade mountains at Santiam Lake in the Mount Jefferson Wilderness Area and runs for 60 miles to its confluence with the South Santiam near the town of Jefferson.

Above Detroit Reservoir, the crystalline, green-blue water of the North Santiam forms a wild rocky and shallow little river, with a steep gradient and water levels which fluctuate with the seasons. Below Cliff Dam, levels are fairly stable year-round; the river calms down a bit and is now nearly opaque and light green in color as a result of fine clay from the reservoir. This is a popular drift, although there are some nasty rapids. Boat ramps are available, starting 5 miles below the dam.

Salmon and steelhead are present in the river below Big Cliff Dam. Winter steelhead fishing is at its peak from March through May, summer steelhead are in the river from April through December, and spring chinook from May through July. Many fly fishers successfully fish for steelhead on the North Santiam, as do bait and lure anglers. Plugs, spinners and spoons, bobbers and jigs, and drift fishing with corkies and bait are all successfully used methods. Most of the spring chinook fishing occurs between Stayton and Mill City. For salmon, most folks use bait, Kwikfish wrapped with a sardine, bobbers and bait, or floats and plugs. The best trout fishing is above Detroit Reservoir, especially with flies, although spinners, worms, and Power Bait are also effective. Trout in the North Santiam run up to 13 inches, steelhead 5 to 18 pounds with a few larger, and chinook 8 to 35 pounds.

With an endangered species listing for the Santiam's run of native winter steelhead expected in 1999, and special protections possible for spring chinook, fishing regulations in the river below Big Cliff Dam are likely to change to no-bait, mandatory catch-and-release with barbless flies and

lures. Seasonal closures are possible as well. To eliminate competition for the struggling native steelhead and salmon, ODFW may discontinue stocking non-native summer steelhead and catchable size trout, further reducing fishing opportunities in the lower river. The changes are controversial and likely to cause confusion for anglers who've fished here for generations. To escape the changes, fish the river above Detroit Reservoir where planted and wild trout should continue to be available to most angling methods. Check the current OSFR before wetting a line.

Wade and bank fishing is the rule above the reservoir. Boat and bank anglers have access to the river at the many parks below Big Cliff Dam. Various government agencies offer campgrounds along the North Santiam. Beginning farthest upstream and ending a few miles below Mill City they are: Marion Forks, Riverside, Whispering Falls, campgrounds on Detroit Reservoir (South Shore,

Hoover, and Detroit Lake State Park), Niagra, Minto Park, Fisherman's Bend, and North Santiam. Several day-use areas with picnic sites and boat ramps are located below the reservoir.

Hiking, boating, and water sports on the reservoir, picnicking, drift trips, and, in the winter, snowmobiling and skiing round out the recreational opportunities along the North Santiam River.

State Highway 22 follows the North Santiam from Stayton to within 8 miles of its headwaters. West of Stayton, a maze of county roads access the river at the Stayton-Scio Bridge, Hess Road, and the Jefferson-Scio Bridge.

From Salem take Highway 22 east to meet the North Santiam at Stayton. From Bend and Sisters, take U.S. Highway 20 west to the junction with Highway 22 at Santiam Junction. Highway 22 first crosses the river about 7 miles from Santiam Junction.

DETROIT LAKE

Size:	3,000 acres
Depth:	varies according to downstream water & power needs
Main Catch:	rainbow trout; kokanee; land-locked chinook salmon
Best Methods:	still fishing with bait; trolling
Season:	entire year; check OSFR
Best Time:	April–May for rainbow; fall for kokanee
Tips:	most heavily stocked body of water in Oregon

ABOVE: Piety Island is located at the eastern end of Detroit Reservoir and can become a peninsula at low water times in the fall. BELOW: The wide expanse of the reservoir can be appreciated when viewed from the dam. Photos by Geoff Hill

Detroit Reservoir is the most heavily stocked body of water in Oregon. Sixty-five-thousand rainbow trout, kokanee, and landlocked chinook salmon are planted every year. Detroit offers year-round fishing, in addition to camping, waterskiing, sailing, picnicking, hiking, and mountain biking. At full pool, Detroit Reservoir covers over 3,000 acres. The reservoir's water level drops from Memorial Day in May on, but is most rapid from Labor Day in September through December. Boaters, beware of stumps at low water, and Piety Island becomes a peninsula.

Not much fishing is done here by wading; the shorelines are fairly steep. Fishing from shore is best in the Santiam, Breitenbush, and French Creek arms. Channels formed by the North Santiam and Breitenbush rivers come together on the south side of Piety Island to form the main Santiam channel. Winds can get very gusty in the afternoons; most boaters move to the arms to avoid whitecaps.

Rainbow trout here average 10 to 12 inches, and kokanee up to 14 inches. Chinook average 9 to 16 inches. Brown bullhead are also available in good numbers, mainly in the shallows near Detroit. Most anglers still-fish with bait from boats or troll hardware. Fishing for rainbow is best in April and May, as is chinook fishing. Kokanee fishing begins around September 1. Anglers should try around Piety Island and in the Hoover Arm for trout. These hatchery trout will take about

To Salem
(45 miles)

Big Cliff Dam
& Powerhouse

DETROIT LAKE
Elevation 2,022'

N

**BIG
CLIFF
LAKE**

Detroit Dam
& Powerhouse

FISHING OFF DAM

NO BOATING

CUMLEY CREEK

KINNEY CREEK

FRENCH CREEK

BREITENBUSH RIVER

Detroit
Ranger
Station

Detroit Lake
State Park

Detroit

*SHALLOW WATER
DANGER AREA*

Mongold

Piety
Boat Camp

To BEND
(75 miles)

Hoover

South Shore

N. SANTIAM RIVER

Blowout Road

BOX CANYON CREEK

BLOWOUT CREEK

△ DAY USE AREA

▲ CAMPGROUND

◄ BOAT RAMP

■ POINT OF INTEREST/VIEWPOINT

— PAVED ROAD

BANK FISHING

⑤ 5 MPH ZONE

T TROLLING AREA

anything. A common trolling rig is flashers with a rubber snubber, followed by a wedding ring and half-worm and kernel of corn. Kokanee are caught on the same set-up, at the mouth of Blowout Arm and in the Santiam Arm. Many folks also still-fish for trout with a half-worm and glob of Power Bait. The chinook are mainly in deeper water on the highway side of the reservoir. Catching the salmon will require a downrigger with flashers and a size 7 to 9 sinking Rapala. Check the current OSFR for season and catch limits.

Boat ramps are located at Mongold State Park (day-use only), Detroit Lake State Park, Kane's Marina, and Hoover and Southshore campgrounds. Campsites are available at Detroit Lake State Park, Upper Arm Campground, Hoover Campground, South Shore Campground, and on Piety Island. Additional accommodations are available at resorts on the lake and in the town of Detroit.

Detroit Reservoir is easily accessible from both the west and east from State Highway 22 which runs the length of its northern shore. Highway 22 extends from the Oregon coast highway (U.S. 101) and east to Salem, Detroit Reservoir, up along the North Santiam River, ending at its junc-tion with U.S Highway 20 at Santiam Junction on the crest of the Cascade mountains.

From Bend and Sisters, take U.S. Highway 20 west to Santiam Junction then State Highway 22, continuing west to Detroit Reservoir.

SOUTH SANTIAM RIVER

Size:	80 miles
Depth:	seasonal fluctuations
Main Catch:	summer steelhead; spring chinook
Best Methods:	shore fishing with flies, bait & lures; drift fishing
Season:	check current OSFR
Best Time:	summer steelhead: April–Dec.; spring chinook: May–July
Tips:	best trout fishing above Foster Dam

The South Santiam River begins high in the Willamette National Forest and flows about 80 miles to its confluence with the North Santiam near Jefferson. The South Santiam is the smaller of the north and south forks of the Santiam but is an equally productive stream for summer steelhead and spring chinook. Rushing through mixed conifer forests and dotted with forest service campgrounds in its upper stretches, the river's lower miles flow slowly through heavily populated areas.

Above Foster Dam, the South Santiam is a wild stream with associated seasonal fluctuations in water levels. It is lower and warmer than the North Santiam in mid-summer. Below the dam, water levels are stable from May to August. Like its North fork cousin, fish management and regulations are in a state of flux on the South Santiam. Managers are moving to protect endangered wild steelhead and salmon runs. Protective actions may include discontinuing planting of non-native trout, salmon and steelhead, harvest and tackle restrictions; even seasonal closures are possible. Check the current OSFR before fishing.

Fly fishers successfully fish for steelhead on the South Santiam, as do bait and lure anglers, although bait may soon be forbidden. Plugs, spinner and spoons, bobbers and jigs and drift fishing with corkies are all successfully used methods. Most steelhead angling takes place between Sweet Home and Foster Dam. Spring chinook fishing occurs below Foster Dam. Salmon anglers may soon be without their favorite methods: Kwikfish wrapped with sardines and bobbers and bait. Float fishing with unbaited jigs and casting plugs should continue to be legal. Trout fishing opportunities and techniques above Foster Dam are liable to change to catch and release with flies and lures to protect steelhead and salmon smolts, easily mistaken as trout. The south Santiam below Foster Reservoir is popular water for both drift boats and jet sleds. Boat ramps available at Wiley Creek Park, Sweet Home, Sanderson's Bridge, McDowell Creek and Lebanon Dam.

Campgrounds available on the South Santiam, beginning farthest upstream, include House Rock, Fernview, Yukwah, Trout Creek, Longbow, Cascadia State Park, those on Foster Reservoir, and at Gedney County Park.

U.S. Highway 20 follows the river closely from the confluence of the creeks that form the South Santiam, near House Rock Campground downstream to Foster Reservoir. Below Foster Reservoir, a tangle of county roads access the river in several spots, while the rest of the river is bordered by private property. Boat ramps are available at Foster Dam, Sweet Home, Gedney County Park, and Lebanon. U.S. Highway 20 is a slow, winding, two-lane mountain pass, not for those in a hurry. Many pullouts along the river and the wealth of campgrounds make access to the river easy.

From Albany, take U.S. Highway 20 east to Lebanon Park on the North Santiam. From Bend and Sisters, take U.S. Highway 20 west over Santiam Pass to the South Santiam just below House Rock Campground.

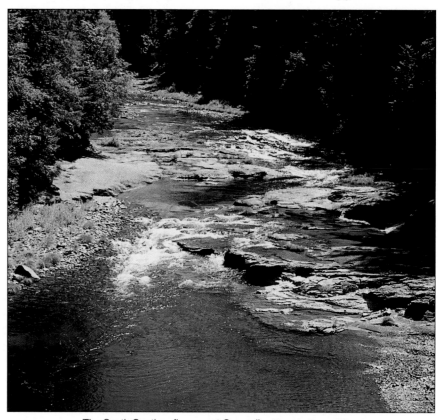

The South Santiam flows past Cascadia. Photo by Raven Wing

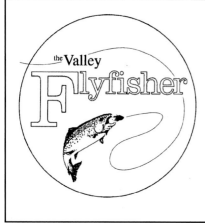

GREEN PETER RESERVOIR

Size:	3,720 acres; 10 mi. long
Depth:	max. depth 327'
Main Catch:	kokanee; rainbow trout
Best Methods:	trolling flashers
Season:	check current OSFR
Best Time:	spring & early summer

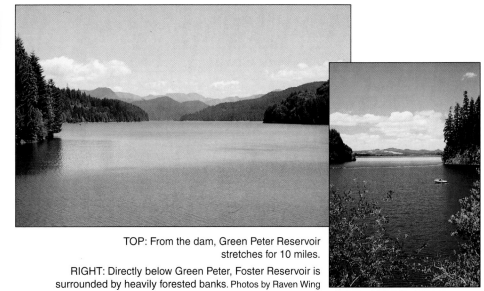

TOP: From the dam, Green Peter Reservoir stretches for 10 miles.

RIGHT: Directly below Green Peter, Foster Reservoir is surrounded by heavily forested banks. Photos by Raven Wing

Green Peter Reservoir is a flood control facility on the Middle Santiam River, just a few miles east of the town of Sweet Home. It is 10 miles long, covers 3,720 acres at full pool, and is 327 feet deep at the dam. Highest water levels occur in May and the lowest in December. The banks are heavily forested and fairly steep. The majority of angling here is for a self-sustaining population of kokanee, up to 12 inches in length. Most fishers troll flashers, such as Ford Fenders, while some use Buzz-Bombs or Nordic jigs from the bank on the southeast side of the dam or from the bridge on the Whitcomb Arm.

ODFW plants a few rainbow trout every April, and occasionally a native cutthroat or rainbow will be caught. Largemouth and smallmouth bass have been illegally introduced, and these might also turn up in the creel. Spring and early summer are the best times to fish for kokanee, and early spring for the stocked rainbow. Check the current Oregon Sport Fishing Regulations before fishing. Green Peter is also a popular water-skiing and jetskiing area.

Access to the reservoir is from a paved road that runs along the north side of the reservoir. Improved boat ramps are available at Thistle Creek Park and Whitcomb Creek Park, and small boats can be launched at a make-shift ramp on the southeast side of the dam. Thistle Creek Park is a day-use area with restrooms and a boat launch; Whitcomb Creek Park offers overnight camping, charges a fee, and has restrooms, drinking water, a picnic area and beach/swimming area, a boat launch, tent sites, and RV sites without hookups. Both are operated by Linn County Parks.

To get to Green Peter Reservoir, take the turn off U.S. Highway 20 toward Green Peter Reservoir, about 6 miles east of downtown Sweet Home. The dam is reached in 5 miles. Continue another 4.5 miles to Thistle Creek and an additional mile to Whitcomb Creek.

FOSTER RESERVOIR

Size:	1,220 acres
Depth:	max. depth 126'
Main Catch:	rainbow trout
Best Methods:	trolling lures; bank fishing along north shore
Season:	check current OSFR
Best Time:	April–June; October

Foster Reservoir lies directly below Green Peter Reservoir, covers 1,220 acres when full, and has a maximum depth of 126 feet. Its teal-blue water is surrounded by heavily forested banks, but they are less steep than at Green Peter, and bank fishing opportunities are much better. Foster is stocked heavily with rainbow trout; most caught will be 10 to 13 inches in length. An occasional kokanee, bass, bluegill, or crappie may also show up on your hook. Most rainbow are caught by trolling lures. Bank fishing opportunities are greatest along the north shore. Fishing is best from April through June and then again in October — check the current Oregon Sport Fishing Regulations for season and catch limits. Water levels at the reservoir are fairly stable, and this is a popular water-skiing and jet-skiing destination.

Several county recreation sites are located on Foster Reservoir: Shea Point, along U.S. Highway 20, is a rest stop and viewpoint; and Gedney Creek Park (boat launch) and Lewis Creek Park are both day-use areas located on the north shore. Sunnyside Park, which offers a boat launch, camp sites with electricity, and RV sites with and without hookups, is located on the Middle Santiam Arm below Green Peter Dam.

Foster Reservoir lies along U.S. Highway 20 just east of the town of Sweet Home. Sunnyside Park is accessed from U.S. Highway 20 by taking the turn to Green Peter Reservoir. The north shore and Lewis Creek Park and Gedney Creek Park can then be reached by a left-hand turn past Sunnyside Park, or by continuing toward Sweet Home on Highway 20 and taking the turn to cross Foster Dam to the north shore.

McKENZIE RIVER

Size:	89 miles
Depth:	varies
Main Catch:	rainbow, bull & cutthroat trout
Best Methods:	bait, lures, & fly fishing; drifting
Season:	check OSFR
Best Time:	June & July
Tips:	well-known for whitewater; lower 50 miles accessed mainly by boat

The McKenzie River is well-known for its whitewater and the McKenzie drift boat, developed specifically for its rapids. This is a river of many personalities, beginning as a tiny mountain creek, emerging from Clear Lake and ending 89 miles later as a large, slow river near its junction with the Willamette River. Bait, lures, and fly fishing are all used successfully to catch fish on the McKenzie. Anglers should check the current Oregon Sport Fishing Regulations; the regulations for this river are complex.

The uppermost McKenzie, from Clear Lake to Trailbridge Reservoir, is fished little and mainly holds small, wild brook, cutthroat, and bull trout. This stretch is most appreciated for its rushing water punctuated by waterfalls and complicated by lava flows. From Trailbridge down to Paradise Campground, the river holds decent-size native rainbow, bull trout, and cutthroat trout, but in this fast water, good holes are few and far between. The best fishing is in June and July. Rafters and kayaks can frequently be seen running this stretch.

The most heavily fished miles of the McKenzie are between Paradise Campground and Hayden Bridge in Springfield. Much of this is also premier drift water. It is heavily stocked with rainbow trout which average 12 to 16 inches, with occasional catches between 18 and 20 inches. The bigger fish are generally downstream. There are also good numbers of native rainbow, cutthroat, and bull trout. The bulk of the steelhead and salmon fishing occurs below Hayden Bridge.

The lower 50 miles of the river are accessed mainly by boat — bank access is limited by private land. There are dozens of

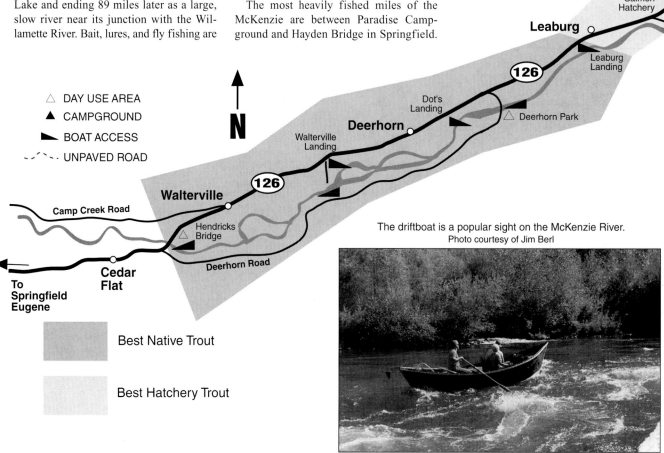

△ DAY USE AREA
▲ CAMPGROUND
▶ BOAT ACCESS
〰 UNPAVED ROAD

Best Native Trout

Best Hatchery Trout

The driftboat is a popular sight on the McKenzie River.
Photo courtesy of Jim Berl

The McKenzie River shows many faces, starting as a small creek and ending as a wide, rambling river. Oregon Tourism Commission photo

Angler's Code of Ethics

While enjoying the sport of fishing, please keep in mind this voluntary Angler's Code.

The Ethical Angler

1. Supports conservation efforts.
2. Practices catch and release where needed.
3. Doesn't pollute, and properly recycles and disposes of trash.
4. Practices safe angling and boating.
5. Obeys fishing and boating regulations.
6. Respects other anglers' rights.
7. Respects property owners' rights.
8. Shares fishing knowledge and skills.
9. Doesn't release bait into water.
10. Promotes ethical sport fishing.

boat ramps on the McKenzie, the highest at Olallie Campground and the lowest at Armitage Park in Eugene. The most popular drift section is between Blue River and the Leaburg Dam. Notice to boaters: the McKenzie requires expert boating skills in several areas, and the 1996 flood created new obstacles near mile post 44, below Delta Campground and at Boulder Creek Rapids, .4 mile below the Frissel–Carpenter Bridge.

A variety of parks and waysides, but few camping opportunities, is available to visitors in the lower 50 miles of the river, although other accommodations are offered. Good Forest Service campgrounds are available from Blue River upstream, along with several small resorts.

Many hiking trails are within the National Forest, including the McKenzie River Trail. Winter offers skiing and snowmobiling. Farther downstream, civilization offers many pleasant distractions from fishing.

State Highway 126, the McKenzie Scenic Byway, follows the river from the town of Springfield upstream to its origin at Clear Lake 4 miles south of the junction of State Highway 126 with the South Santiam Highway, U.S. Highway 20. From Sweet Home or Sisters take U.S. Highway 20 to the junction with State Highway 126, 4 miles west of the Santiam Junction. The headwaters are 4 miles south on Highway 126. From Eugene/Springfield, follow State Highway 126 along the McKenzie for 89 miles to Clear Lake.

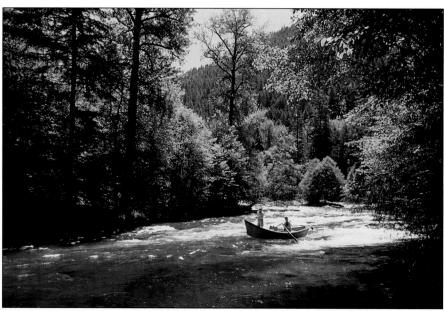

Anglers enjoy running the river and taking in the magnificent scenery, as well as the fishing.
Photo by Brian O'Keefe

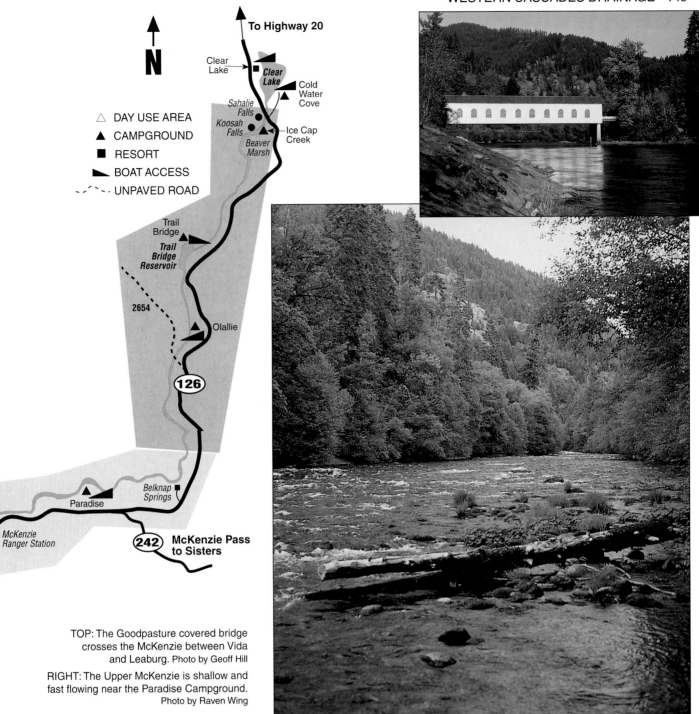

Map Legend

- △ DAY USE AREA
- ▲ CAMPGROUND
- ■ RESORT
- ◤ BOAT ACCESS
- ‑‑‑‑ UNPAVED ROAD

N

To Highway 20

Clear Lake
Clear Lake
Cold Water Cove
Sahalie Falls
Koosah Falls
Ice Cap Creek
Beaver Marsh

Trail Bridge
Trail Bridge Reservoir

2654

Olallie

126

Belknap Springs
Paradise

McKenzie Ranger Station

242 McKenzie Pass to Sisters

TOP: The Goodpasture covered bridge crosses the McKenzie between Vida and Leaburg. Photo by Geoff Hill

RIGHT: The Upper McKenzie is shallow and fast flowing near the Paradise Campground. Photo by Raven Wing

CLEAR LAKE

Size:	148 acres
Depth:	max. depth 175'
Main Catch:	hatchery rainbow trout; cutthroat; brook trout
Best Methods:	bait fishing from a boat or the bank
Season:	entire year; check OSFR
Best Time:	spring through July; fall for brook trout

The source of the famous McKenzie River, Clear Lake was formed when the river was dammed by a lava flow about 3,000 years ago. The forest that was standing in the valley can still be seen through 100 feet of the lake's crystal-clear water. Fed by ice-cold springs, the lake stays between 34°F and 38°F year-round and, because of the huge volume of water coming from the springs, never freezes over. The lake covers 148 acres, has a maximum depth of 175 feet, and water levels are stable. It is surrounded by the thick forests of the Cascade Crest.

The major catch here is hatchery rainbow trout. Thirty-three thousand legal-size rainbow trout are stocked each year. The average catch will be 9 to 11 inches in length. There are also a few small native cutthroat, of which the largest are 11 inches, and introduced brook trout of mostly 6 to 8 inches, with a few in the 13- to 14-inch range.

Overall fishing is best when the lake is first accessed in the spring through July, although fishing for the brook trout is best in the fall.

Bait is the most common fishing technique used — Power Bait and night crawlers still-fished from small boats. There is also much opportunity for bank fishing. Fish tend to stay scattered throughout the year-round fishing season. The catch limit is 5 trout per day, 8-inch minimum length, and of these no more than 1 over 20 inches, no limit or size restriction for brook trout. Always check the current OSFR before fishing. Motors are not permitted on the lake. Boat ramps are available at the resort and campground.

Coldwater Cove Campground, on the southeast shore of the lake, has 35 pay campsites, a hand pump for drinking water, a small boat launch, and it is completely paved. There is also a small beach, but swimming would be for Polar Bear Club members. Clear Lake Resort and picnic area, one mile north of the turn into the campground, is a pleasant area for relaxing. The resort is open year-round and offers accommodations, a restaurant, store, and boat rentals.

Other activities in the area include a variety of hiking trails, including the McKenzie River Trail, and trails around the lake, Koosah and Sahalie falls, additional fishing in the McKenzie River, Fish Lake and Carman, Smith and Trailbridge reservoirs, photography, white-water trips, mushrooming, and scenic drives.

Clear Lake is located on the McKenzie Scenic Byway, State Highway 126, 3 miles south of its junction with the South Santiam Highway, U.S. Highway 20. Clear Lake is 86 miles northeast of Eugene/Springfield, following Route 126. From Sweet Home or Sisters, take U.S. Highway 20 to the junction with State Highway 126, 4 miles west of Santiam Junction. The turn into Clear Lake Resort is 4 miles south on Highway 126, Coldwater Cove Campground is in 5 miles.

The north end of Clear Lake is much like a secluded cove (top photo). The large expanse of the lake (bottom photo) can be viewed looking south from the restaurant. This large, clear lake is fed by cold springs, thus the water temperature remains constant year-round. Photos by Geoff Hill

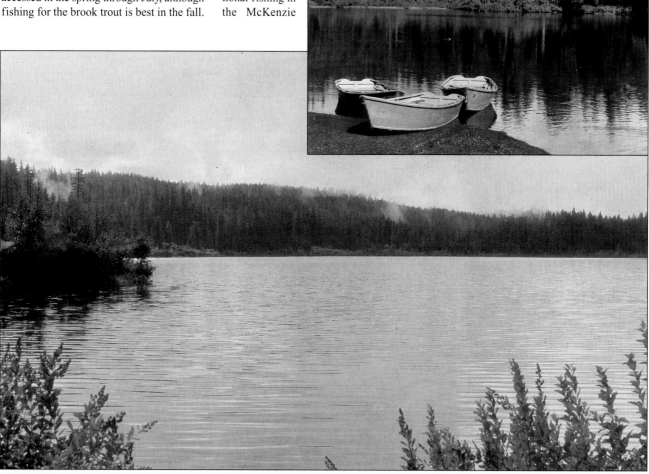

Carmen Diversion, Smith & Trail Bridge Reservoirs

Carmen, Smith and Trail Bridge reservoirs are three easily accessible lakes along Highways 20 and 126 in the Santiam Pass area. These are small, surprisingly scenic waters for being so close to highways, offering productive fishing for planted trout. They are good "day trip" fishing holes, with many anglers stopping for a few hours on their way over the pass. Camping is popular at two of the three.

Carmen Diversion Reservoir is the smallest of three hydropower impoundments that generate electricity for Eugene. Located 72 miles east of Eugene on State Highway 126, Carmen covers 30 acres with a maximum depth of 25 feet. Stocked regularly with legal-size rainbow trout, it produces limits for those who know the secret of 2-pound leader, Power Bait, worms and salmon eggs. The best fishing areas are near the boat ramp, along the dam, off the bridge that crosses the McKenize River inflow and from anchored and rowed boats. The standard 5 fish, 1 over 20-inch limit applies here and on Smith Reservoir. No camping is permitted at Carmen, but there is a Forest Service campground a short walk upstream at Koosah Falls.

Water from Carmen is diverted to **Smith Reservoir**, the largest and perhaps most scenic of the power project reservoirs located a few miles west up a one-lane, switchback road. Long, narrow and deep, Smith favors boats, though shore fishers have access at the dam and from a metal floating log boom. Casting without weight, slowly sinking worms, salmon eggs and Power Bait produces eager strikes from frequently planted hatchery trout. Larger fish are taken with bait and lures around the mouths of inflowing streams. Camping is available at Lake's End Campground, accessible by boat on the upper end of the reservoir.

Trail Bridge is the lowest elevation, most visible, accessible and developed of the three hydro project waters. It offers the best camping, shore fishing and boat access to 30,000 rainbow trout stocked annually in this 120-acre reservoir. Fishing is catch-and release for trout, restricted to flies and lures only. Boat fishers should try the McKenzie River channel at the upper end of the reservoir.

Endangered bull trout are present in all of these three reservoirs and must be released unharmed. All three reservoirs are subject to water level fluctuations, according to power demands.

TOP: Shore fishers have access to Smith Reservoir via a metal floating log boom.
BOTTOM: Scenic Carmen Reservoir covers 30 acres with a maximum depth of 25 feet. Photos by Brooke Snavely

COUGAR RESERVOIR

Size: 1,280 acres; 6 miles long
Depth: fluctuates
Main Catch: rainbow & bull trout
Best Methods: still fishing; trolling
Best Time: early & late in season
Season: check current OSFR
Tips: best access with boats

Cougar Reservoir, filled by the South Fork of the McKenzie River, is 6 miles in length and covers 1,280 acres. It is heavily stocked with rainbow trout, and catches average 10 to 12 inches in length. Large bull trout also inhabit Cougar, and it is required to release them unharmed.

Shorelines are quite steep, and most fishing is done from boats, although bank fishing is possible around the reservoir. Water levels fluctuate from highest in mid-May to lowest after Labor Day in September.

Winds can be strong, usually in the afternoon during the summer. Fishing tends to be best early and late in the season, in March and April and then again in October and November.

Anglers have luck fishing the many coves for concentrations of trout and make sure to check the current Oregon Sport Fishing Regulations before fishing.

Still-fishing with bait and trolling Ford Fenders and gold or silver lures are the most used fishing methods on this water.

There are three U.S.F.S. campgrounds at the reservoir (Slide Creek, Sunnyside, and French Creek) and Echo Park day-use area. Slide Creek offers tent sits, trailer parking (without utility connections), piped water, picnic area, boat ramp, and waterskiing. Sunnyside has tent sites and a boat ramp, but no water. French Pete Campground, with tent sites and water, is located at the end of the reservoir.

In addition, Delta Camp ground, located below the reservoir between the McKenzie and South McKenzie rivers, offers trailer parking (without hook-ups) and has water. all areas have sanitary facilities. A new fee system is in effect.

To reach Cougar Reservoir take the McKenzie Scenic Byway, State Highway 126, to Forest Route 19, about halfway between the tiny towns of Blue River to the west and McKenzie Bridge to the east. It is 3 miles to the reservoir on Route 19. Turn to cross the dam on Forest Route 1993 to reach Echo Day-Use Area in another 3 miles, or continue another 8 miles past the dam on Route 19 to Slide Creek Campground. Boat ramps are available at both sites.

View was taken from the dam looking south. Photo by Geoff Hill

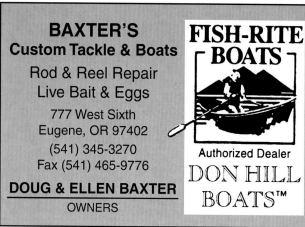

BLUE RIVER

Size: 11 miles long
Depth: varies; easily waded
Main Catch: rainbow trout; cutthroat
Best Methods: all methods
Season: check OSFR
Best Time: spring
Tips: hatchery trout not picky

A tiny, crystal-clear river with a tinge of turquoise, Blue River's entire existence is expended within 10 miles above Blue River Reservoir and a mile below. Little fishing is done below the reservoir due to private property. Above the reservoir, a gravel road follows the river for its entire length. At its largest point, the river is 10 to 20 feet in width, with varying depths, but never more than a few feet deep. It is lined with alder and surrounded by the timberland of the Willamette National Forest. There are many opportunities for primitive camping along the river. In addition, nearby Blue River

Reservoir has a good Forest Service campground and other facilities, and accommodations are available in the small towns of Blue River and McKenzie Bridge.

Eight thousand rainbow trout are stocked in the river above the reservoir every June. Catches will max out at 10 to 12 inches, and fishing is best right after stocking. There is also a good population of native cutthroat of 5 to 12 inches in length. All methods work on this little stream — the hatchery trout are not picky. Bait, small lures, and artificial flies will all work. Water levels are highest during spring run-off and lowest in late summer. Check the current OSFR for season and catch limits.

Besides fishing this little river, visitors can go boating, fishing, or picnicking on the reservoir, visit the nearby towns of Blue River and McKenzie Bridge, or fish nearby Cougar Reservoir or the McKenzie River.

To get to Blue River above the reservoir,

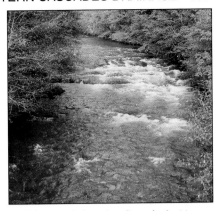

This crystal-clear river flows for just ten miles above Blue River Reservoir and one mile below. Photo by Geoff Hill

take State Highway 126, the McKenzie Scenic Byway, to the turn to Blue River Reservoir, about 3.5 miles east of the town of Blue River. Continue on Forest Route 15 past the reservoir and up along Blue River.

BLUE RIVER RESERVOIR

Size: 1,420 acres
Depth: varies; drops during summer
Main Catch: rainbow trout
Best Methods: all methods
Season: entire year; check OSFR
Best Time: April & May
Tips: best access with boats

Blue River Reservoir is a long, narrow body of water fed by Blue River. Its teal-blue waters cover 1,420 acres, and the shoreline is 6.5 miles long. Banks are quite steep and vegetation thick, so there is little access for bank fishing except down by the dam and at the inlets of Lookout Creek and Blue River. Water levels drop throughout the summer, and, at low pool, many stumps are exposed. This reservoir is more protected from wind than many, because it is so narrow.

Rainbow trout, mainly of catchable size, are stocked several times in the spring, and a few native rainbow and cutthroat trout enter Blue River Reservoir from the river above. The main catch is rainbow trout from 8 to 11 inches in length, with a few hold-overs to 14 inches. Most fishing is done from boats, and the best catch rates are in April and May, immediately after the stocking. All methods will catch these hatchery trout: bait still-fished from shore and boats and small lures and flies cast or trolled. Always check the current OSFR before wetting that line.

There are two boat ramps on the reservoir: the one at Saddle Dam where the road first reaches the reservoir is better at low water. The other ramp is at a shiny new boating facility on Lookout Creek, 3 miles past Saddle Dam on Forest Route 15. Just past Lookout Creek, a road crosses the inlet to the reservoir (Blue River) which leads to

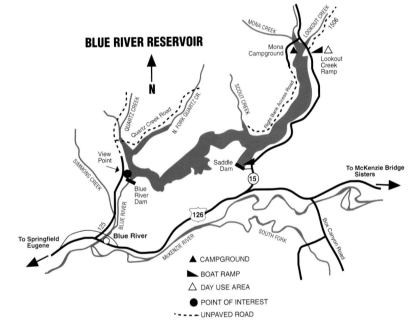

BLUE RIVER RESERVOIR

▲ CAMPGROUND
◣ BOAT RAMP
△ DAY USE AREA
● POINT OF INTEREST
·---- UNPAVED ROAD

Mona Campground, a nice facility with paved roads, group sites, drinking water, and fees. All campsites are right on the reservoir's shore.

Other forms of entertainment in the area include waterskiing when the water is warmest and highest, golf at nearby Tokatee, and fishing at a variety of nearby locations, including Blue River, the McKenzie River, and Cougar Reservoir *(see pages 146 & 152 for information). To get to Blue River Reservoir, see above.*

Steep banks line Blue River Reservoir, a long, narrow body of water on the west side of the Cascades. Photo by Raven Wing

WILLAMETTE RIVER
Middle & North Forks

Size:	Middle Fork: 40 mi. long
	North Fork: 15 mi. long
Depth:	varies
Main Catch:	Middle Fork: hatchery rainbow trout
	North Fork: wild rainbow, cutthroat & brook trout
Best Methods:	Middle Fork: bank fishing & drifting; North Fork: fly angling with barbless hooks only
Season:	check OSFR
Best Time:	throughout season
Tips:	both rivers easily accessible by car

The Middle Fork of the mighty Willamette River begins as a tiny mountain creek about 30 miles above Hills Creek Reservoir, south of Oakridge. The main catch above the reservoir is hatchery rainbow trout. Below Hills Creek Reservoir, the river flows for about 10 miles before being impounded in Lookout Point Reservoir. This stretch has wild rainbow and cutthroat trout and is a popular drift stretch, but has some nasty rapids. Boat ramps are available at Green Waters Park in Oakridge and Black Canyon Campground downstream. Below

The Middle Fork changes character frequently along its 40-mile length.
Photo by Raven Wing

The North Fork of the Middle Willamette is pictured about fifteen miles upstream. Photo by Raven Wing

Lookout Reservoir, the river is a hatchery salmon and steelhead game.

The North Fork of the Willamette River enters the Middle Fork just west of the town of Oakridge. Most of the North Fork is restricted to fly angling only. It harbors all wild fish which include rainbow, cutthroat, and brook trout. At its mouth, the river is about 40 feet wide, but within 15 miles upstream has become creek-size. Much of the North Fork is pocket water — anglers should look for fish-holding pools between the shallower sections.

Both the Middle and North Forks are beautiful, aqua-colored freestone rivers, surrounded by maple, alder, and fir trees. Many Forest Service campgrounds are scattered along the Middle Fork. Both rivers are easily accessible by car in many, but not all, areas. There are a number of hiking and mountain biking trails in the area.

One can get to the headwaters of the Middle Fork from Lemolo Lake by back roads heading toward Timpanogas Lake. The Middle Fork is more commonly accessed from State Highway 58 between Springfield and Oakridge and from Forest Route 21 above Hills Creek Reservoir, a few miles southeast of Oakridge (see directions to reservoir on page 155). From the reservoir, one can continue toward the headwaters on Forest Route 21.

To reach the North Fork, just west of Oakridge, take the turn to Westfir and the North Fork of the Willamette River. The excellent paved road which runs along the North Fork is designated as the "Aufderheide National Scenic Byway." Visitors may stop by the Oakridge Ranger Station for a tour brochure. The only Forest Service facility on the North Fork is Kiahanie Campground, 20 miles upriver, although coyote camps are scattered along the length of the river.

HILLS CREEK RESERVOIR

Size:	2,735 acres; 8 miles long
Depth:	fluctuates; fullest mid-May
Main Catch:	rainbow trout
Best Methods:	bait fishing from boats
Season:	entire year; check OSFR
Best Time:	spring & fall
Tips:	protected from afternoon summer winds

Hills Creek Reservoir is located on the Middle Fork of the Willamette River, a few miles from the town of Oakridge. The reservoir is 8 miles long and covers 2,735 acres. The 200,000 fingerling rainbow trout stocked here each spring reach 13 inches in one year, with the best catch rates in the spring and fall. Chinook salmon, cutthroat, bass, bluegill, and crappie also inhabit the reservoir in small numbers.

Bait fishing from boats is the most popular fishing method here, although some folks fish from the bridge at the south end of the reservoir and from the dam at the north end. Shorelines are steep and rocky. Water levels drop about 90 feet each year between August and February, while the reservoir is at its fullest by mid-May. There is one channel that runs through the middle of the reservoir. This reservoir is somewhat protected from afternoon summer winds.

Three boat ramps are located on the reservoir. Packard Creek Campground is best when water is low. The other two are located at CT Beach, a day-use area with a grassy "beach" area on the Hills Creek Arm, and at the south end of the reservoir where Forest Route 21 crosses the reservoir.

The easiest path to the reservoir is to take State Highway 58 toward Oakridge. The turn to Hills Creek Reservoir is onto Forest Route 21, a couple of miles east of Oakridge. The dam is 2 miles up the road.

Cross the dam on Forest Route 23 to reach CT Beach in 3 miles. Stay on Route 21 instead of turning onto the dam to reach Cline-Clark Picnic Area in about a mile, Packard Creek Campground in another 2.5 miles, and the south end of the reservoir in an additional 5.5 miles.

Hills Creek Reservoir is a large body of water, eight miles in length. Photos by Franklin L. Carson

INSET: This angler proudly displays his big bass. Photo courtesy of Bert's

WALDO LAKE

Size:	10 sq. miles
Depth:	420' max.
Main Catch:	brook trout
Best Methods:	trolling
Season:	entire year; check OSFR
Best Time:	June & October
Tips:	open year-round; fish very deep in summer; notorious for mosquitoes

A huge, crystalline, alpine gem, Waldo Lake contains some of the purest water in the world, chemically similar to manmade double-distilled. Small populations of brook trout, kokanee, and rainbow trout exist here, but in a lake this large it can be troublesome to find them. Waldo Lake covers 10 square miles and has a maximum depth of 420 feet. The cobalt blue water is so clear that the bottom can be seen through 100 feet of it. Waldo is the second largest and second deepest natural lake in Oregon, surpassed only by the Klamath/Agency Lake complex in size and Crater Lake in depth.

RIGHT: Waldo Lake, the second largest natural lake in Oregon, as viewed from the south end.
Photo by Don Burgderfer

BELOW: The cobalt blue water in Waldo Lake is so clear that the bottom can be seen through 100 feet of it.
Photo by Geoff Hill

Waldo Lake is now managed for natural reproduction of all species. Brook trout are the most abundant, averaging 10 to 13 inches with the largest up to 18 inches. Most are caught by trolling lures, spoons, and spinners or fly fishing in the shallower areas of the lake. Shoal areas are at the north and south ends of the lake near Shadow Bay and North Waldo Campgrounds. Another popular fishing spot is at "the brookie slide" on the west side of the lake. Trolling is generally the most productive method unless surface feeding fish are found, then bait and fly fishing work well. Fishing is best in June when the lake is first barely accessible and then again in October after the mosquitoes are gone. In the summer, the fish are deep, making catching them even more difficult.

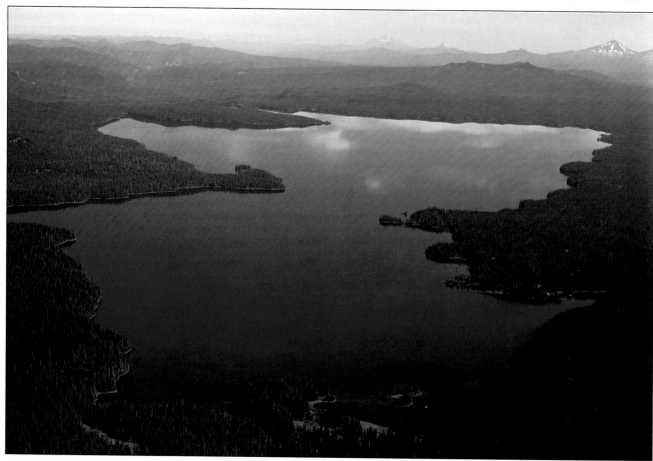

Stocking of rainbow trout ceased many years ago. There is a small amount of natural reproduction in the lake outlet, but rainbow trout are probably on their way out. The story about kokanee in the lake is similar, with a small remnant population naturally reproducing in the lake. The kokanee range up to 14 inches in length but are seldom seen. Waldo is essentially a brook trout fishery.

Waldo Lake has primarily a rocky shore with only a few beach areas and is surrounded by thick hemlock forest. Even though there are steep drop-offs offering numerous spots from which to bank fish, most angling is done from a boat. Fishing near the campgrounds, from the bank or a boat, is liable to be as good as anywhere else on the lake. If the wind comes up, one should beware if in a small boat. Water levels fluctuate very little. The shoals on the north end are rocky. The only weedbeds are very short and occur in very deep water.

Reliable afternoon winds at Waldo Lake create a great spot for sailboats and windsurfers. Unfortunately, Waldo is notorious for mosquitoes that mob its shores through the month of August. Waldo has some of the least crowded campgrounds in Oregon. Getting far out on the lake sometimes offers respite from the ruthless bloodsuckers. In addition to angling and swatting, Waldo has sandy beaches for sunbathing, picnic areas, hiking and mountain bike trails, and is often used by canoeists and kayakers.

High lakes accessible by trail offer more fishing. The Pacific Crest Trail comes as close as a mile to the east shore. A spider web of other trails circle the lake, lead into many nearby high lakes, and head into the Waldo Lake Wilderness.

Waldo Lake has excellent camping and boating facilities. The Willamette National Forest maintains three Forest Service campgrounds on the eastern shore, reached by 13 miles of paved road. North Waldo Campground is farthest north, Islet Campground a mile south, and Shadow Bay Campground is at the south end of the lake. All have pressurized water systems, day-use and swimming areas, flush toilets, and boat ramps, and charge a fee to camp. Many primitive campsites are scattered around the lake. The west shore is only accessible by boat or trail. Rhododendron Campground, on an island on the west side of the lake, has an out-house and three tent sites.

Waldo Lake's 22 miles of shoreline is flanked by the Waldo Lake Wilderness on the north, west, and south. The crest of the Cascade Mountains is only a few miles east. At an elevation of 5,414 feet, the recreation season is brief. Campground facilities are usually open July 1 into September and can be snowed-in the rest of the year. The nearest year-round services are at the resorts on Odell Lake or at Crescent Lake Junction, about 11 miles east on Highway 58.

Waldo Lake is open year-round but is not a popular ice fishing destination. The trout limit is 5 per day with an 8-inch minimum, and of these no more than 1 over 20 inches. Always check the current OSFR before fishing. There is a boat speed limit of 10 mph.

To get to Waldo Lake from the Eugene area take State Highway 58 about 50 miles east. The turn into Waldo on Forest Route 5897 is 3 miles west of Willamette Pass. From Bend follow directions to Odell Lake but continue approximately 3 miles past the west end to the turn onto Forest Route 5897.

▲ CAMPGROUND

◄ BOAT RAMP

PAVED ROAD

UNPAVED ROAD

HIKING TRAIL

FLY FISHING

Fly fishing is not nearly as difficult as it sometimes looks, but it does require some patience and practice. The rewards are immeasurable. Fool a fish with an artificial fly, which you may have tied, and you feel like the supreme fly angler. You'll get more pleasure fighting a fish on fly tackle than any other type of fishing gear. Fly fishing gear is, after all, the original ultra-light tackle.

Casting with any kind of fishing tackle requires some weight, otherwise the lure or fly goes nowhere. For instance, with spinning gear, you either pinch on splitshot or use a weighted lure to cast. With fly fishing gear, the line is the weight. Consequently, you have to repeatedly false cast (a back and forth action of the rod) until you have enough line out to reach the desired distance. You then complete the cast when you allow the fly to touch the water.

Timing and coordination are far more important in fly casting than brute strength, although some muscle is required. What you want to accomplish in fly casting is to create a bend in the rod on both the forward cast and back cast. This bend in the rod slings the fly line in the direction of the cast, almost like a bow catapults an arrow. You throw the line ahead of you in the forward cast. Watch to see and sense the line straightening. Just as the line fully extends, pull the rod back to begin the back cast. The line then extends behind you. Look back and see and feel the line reach full extension. Then, push forward to begin the forward cast. As you get accustomed to the back and forth motion, gradually release more line until you are ready to put the fly on the water.

It is during this back and forth motion of the false cast that a fly caster determines exactly where he or she wants to land the fly. Normally, it only takes a few false casts to get enough line out to make an average 30- to 40-foot cast. If you've witnessed someone false casting more often than that, you've either seen someone trying to make a longer cast or someone drying out a fly.

This matter of fly casting is really much easier done than said. Ask someone to show you or take a lesson, and you'll be on your way. Like a lot of sports, once you've actually done it and sensed how the system works, it will be much easier to keep at it. Such persistence is, for the most part, the mindset needed to master fly casting.

Now comes the fun part: determining what kind of fly to tie on the end of your leader. There are dry flies, wet flies, nymphs, streamers, and a host of variations thereof. The saying, "match the hatch," means putting on an insect that looks like the ones on which the fish are feeding. "Matching the hatch" also implies that you are watching trout grabbing insects off the surface. This is classic dry fly fishing,

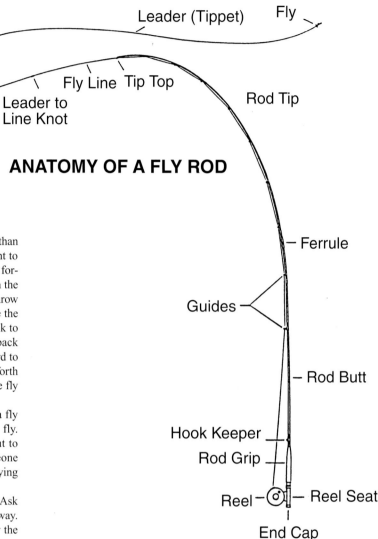

ANATOMY OF A FLY ROD

Leader (Tippet) Fly
Fly Line Tip Top
Leader to Line Knot
Rod Tip
Ferrule
Guides
Rod Butt
Hook Keeper
Rod Grip
Reel Reel Seat
End Cap

Information and illustrations courtesy of
Central Oregon Flyfishers

in which the fish come up to the surface to take your fly. A fish slashing at your fly never fails to get adrenaline pumping, as you try to react fast enough. Even if you don't hook a fish, being in an area where fish are feeding on the surface is exciting. Mayflies, caddisflies, and stoneflies represent the elite of Central Oregon's dry fly hatches, although there are dozens more.

Wet flies, appropriately, are flies fished under the surface. It's quite a hurdle for some anglers to comprehend trout eating flies underwater, but the fact is they do. Probably 90 percent of what fish eat is captured below the surface. What they are eating are immature forms of insects called nymphs.

Wet fly fishing is primarily done by feel, although watching the line at the point where it enters the water or watching a strike indicator, akin to watching a bobber, provides a lot of information as to what's happening down below. If the line or strike indicator should suddenly stop or move against the current (a dead giveaway), you can immediately suspect a fish has taken the nymph and set the hook. Often, you will see a fish flash or roll in the water near the area where you expect your nymph to be. This is another sign to set the hook.

Although fly fishing is traditionally associated with streams and rivers, it is just as effective in lakes. Trout in lakes tend to be larger than trout in streams, simply because they don't have to fight current all the time, and lakes often offer a more abundant food supply. Lake fishing typically involves nymphs and wet flies, although some surface feeding occurs, usually in early morning and late evening.

An 8.5- to 9.5-foot, 5- to 6-weight fly rod should handle most conditions you'll encounter in Central Oregon. Come prepared with a full complement of floating, sink-tip, and full-sinking lines, along with a variety of leader material, and you should be able to reach fish no matter where they're holding. On small creeks and high-altitude lakes, lighter gear may provide more sport for the pan-sized trout in those waters. By the same token, you might consider heavier rods for bigger fish, such as those in Crane Prairie Reservoir (up to 10 pounds) or to challenge steelhead in the fast-flowing, big water of the lower Deschutes River.

If you're buying fly fishing gear for the first time, take an experienced fly fisher with you or trust the professionals at your local fly shop. It's easy to spend hundreds, or even thousands, of dollars on fly fishing equipment. Good serviceable, pre-packaged fly fishing systems can be bought for under $200. Later, when you discover you like fly fishing, you'll be able to purchase a higher quality outfit with a much better idea of the type of gear you want.

If you come empty-handed when taking a class or guided trip, most instructors and guides will provide quality equipment at no additional cost. Further, you'll be getting advice on how to use the gear and how to select your own from from a seasoned professional.

MOST TROUT EAT aquatic invertebrates, some of which have complex life cycles. Mayflies, caddisflies, midges, and stoneflies have several stages of their life cycle that are available to the trout. The successful angler must try to imitate these stages with his flies.

Most aquatic insects have four stages in their life cycle: the egg, the larval or nymph stage, the pupal stage, and the adult stage. The first three stages are aquatic, while the last stage is terrestrial.

Below are two examples of such life cycles.

The Life Cycle of a Typical Mayfly
The mayfly stages that are most often imitated are the nymph, the emerging subadult, and the spent adult. Mayflies are common on both streams and lakes.

EGGS

NYMPH

ADULT

SUBADULT

The Life Cycle of a Typical Stonefly
The life cycle of the stonefly is similar to that of the mayfly; however, they do not have a subadult stage. Cold western streams, such as the Deschutes, are well-known for their stonefly (salmonfly) hatches.

EGGS

ADULT

NYMPH

Information and illustrations courtesy of Central Oregon Flyfishers

CENTRAL OREGON FLY PATTERNS

LAKE FLIES

ALL AROUND COLLECTION

MIDGE & EMERGERS

NYMPHS

Having a variety of flies from which to choose is the key to fishing the waters of Central Oregon. The season, type of water, the hatch, and species of fish will dictate what fly to use.

Photos by Brian O'Keefe

STEELHEAD FLIES

FLOAT TUBES

The last few years have seen a dramatic increase in the use of float tubes. Newer technology provides a variety of shapes and sizes, and, for the most part, better quality than earlier models, which means safety afloat.

Float tubes allow fishers to reach water that cannot otherwise be fished from shore or to approach quietly an area without spooking the fish, which may not be possible by boat. Float tubes open up a lot of water that may not be fished effectively any other way.

Most users of float tubes are flyfishers fishing for trout, but various techniques can be used for both trout and other game fish. It is a relaxing, comfortable way to fish and can be very rewarding.

Besides the float tube, one must wear chest-high waders and a Coast Guard certified life jacket (some fishing vests have flotation and have been Coast Guard certified) with swim fins over the feet. The fins are used for propelling the float tube around the lake or pond. The movement of the float tube is backwards. Fishers raise their legs almost horizontally in front of them and use a slow, flutter kick.

Another advantage of float tubes is their compact size and portability. They can easily be packed-in to a back country lake and inflated with a foot pump. On the lake, fishers can move out from shoreline trees and bushes and have plenty of space to backcast. Some of these waters are only fishable by float tube and, thus, are seldom fished. A stealth approach to fish holding snags or vegetation can result in some exciting fishing.

When purchasing a float tube, it is wise to shop with someone who is knowledgeable of them or to the clerk many questions about the pros and cons of the various models; there is a wide price range from basic model to luxury model. A basic float tube that is built around an inner tube sells for approximately $100, a Urethane or PVC float tube with an open ended u-shape averages $100 to $300 (much easier to enter and exit tube), and the pontoon style ranges from $150 to $800. Some tubes offer an extra air chamber which doubles as a backrest and is well-worth the expense. Other options include storage compartments, small batteries and small electric motors, anchors, rod holders, beverage can holders, and brackets for electronic fish-finders.

The most popular type of fins are those that slip over stocking waders. They sell from $30 to $90. Fins are also available that strap over boot waders.

A beginning float tuber should start out with an experienced

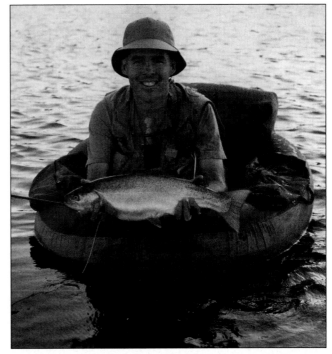

Fishing from a float tube allows anglers to reach water that cannot otherwise be fished. This float-tuber got lucky at Crane Prairie.
Photo courtesy of Sunriver Fly Shop

friend in shallow water with a gradual slope, until comfortable with the feel and maneuverability of the float tube.

There are several precautions that should be heeded. Do not use float tubes in rivers, tidal bays, or oceans and avoid large bodies of water where power boats are in use — float tubers are difficult to see, compared to other boats. It is not safe to inflate tubes at lower elevations then put in the car; they might over-inflate or burst while traveling to a higher elevation. And, do not attempt to make your own float tube — it could lead to an accident.

While float tubing on larger lakes or reservoirs, anglers should pack hiking boots in case the wind blows them across the lake. Whitecaps may give tubers a bumpy ride and mean more work with the fins, but they can usually be navigated safely.

Central Oregon offers many opportunities for float tubers. Hosmer Lake, Todd Lake, Sparks Lake, and North and South Twin lakes are popular, to name a few. Crane Prairie's shorelines, channels, and dead snag areas are also frequented by float tube fishers, with good results. And not to be over-looked are back country lakes.

ABOVE: This fisherman lands a big rainbow with the help of a well-equipped pontoon style float tube, complete with electronic fish-finder.

RIGHT: Some anglers opt for the luxury of "rowing oars" on their pontoon style boat/float tubes.
Photos courtesy of The Fly Box

TROLLING

Trolling is an excellent technique for fishing Central Oregon's lakes and reservoirs. Trolling allows you to cover a large area in a short time, pinpointing actively feeding fish. Once you catch a fish, turn around and troll repeatedly through that same area. If you've stumbled across a good concentration of fish, you may consider casting or still-fishing. And if you don't catch fish, trolling is a fine excuse for a leisurely boat ride through some wonderful scenery.

Depending on the season, trolling can be done on or near the surface (0 to10 feet), medium deep (10 to 30 feet), or really deep (40 feet plus.) In all instances, you should troll slowly but not steadily. Vary trolling speed by speeding up or slowing down the boat, by turning in a series of "S" curves, or by occasionally pulling the rod forward several feet then letting it fall back. Almost always, fish will strike when they think the lure is acting erratically or trying to get away from them.

Surface trolling is great, because it doesn't require any specialized equipment, and anyone can do it. Using either a small trolling lure, fly, or bait, strip off 50 or more feet of line and troll slowly behind whatever boat to which you have access.

Many anglers prefer a small rowboat, canoe, or kayak. The rower gets a little excercise while the means of propulsion – rowing – provides nearly perfect action to the lure. Hookups while surface trolling are great fun, because there is no weight to impede the fight of the fish. Surface trolling is best in the spring and fall when fish are near the surface and worth trying early in the morning and late in the evening throughout the summer.

In the summer when the water temperature warms, trout move deeper in search of the thermocline. This trout comfort zone can be anywhere from 20 to 80 feet deep, and if you're not fishing in it, you're wasting your time. Locate the thermocline with a depth finder or by asking other anglers who are catching fish, then fish in that depth of water. Also, plan on using gang trolls or flashers, as fish are spread out and need a reason to be attracted to your lure.

"Banana" weights ranging from .5 to 4 ounces can extend the effective trolling range of standard spinning gear down to about 40 feet. Many anglers go this route, but you can tell they struggle to feel anything with their overworked spinning rods bent double under the heavy weights. You'll feel more in control with lead-core line or a downrigger and beefier tackle.

Lead-core line is exactly that, line built around a core of lead which sinks, depending on the density of line, at a predictable rate. Lead-core line is usually colored in 20-foot increments. So when anglers talk about fishing "four-and-a-half colors," they suggest they were trolling 90 feet of line about 30 feet deep. Further, the depth is affected by the weight and drag of the rudder, flasher, and lure. Trolling with lead-core takes a little getting used to, but it works so well, and the equipment is so durable that it's usually worth the investment.

A typical lead-core trolling outfit consists of a large-capacity level wind reel and a stout 6- or 7-foot salmon-size rod and costs about $75. A recent trend toward lighter rods and smaller trolling blades has heightened the sporting aspect of lead-core gear. But there will be times when the largest blades and heaviest weights are necessary to reach and attract fish. Downriggers are state-of-the-art trolling tools, expensive, and awkward to handle. But once you understand their application, they are particularly useful for trolling. Their advantage is precise depth control. If the depth finder says fish are holding at 62 feet, a downrigger can put the lure at precisely that depth. This is a big advantage during the hottest weather when fish refuse to come up from the cool depths.

Downriggers are the way to go for mackinaw or lake trout and browns when they get in their bottom hugging mode. With a downrigger, you can physically drag the bottom of the deepest lake and literally stir the fish up. Big dodgers and flasher blades, followed by

Most lakes stratify into three layers during late spring and stay that way until late fall. The middle layer of water, the thermocline, contains both a large amount of dissolved oxygen and forage fish. Your trolling, to be most effective, should be concentrated close to or in the thermocline, which will be from 15 to 50 feet down in most lakes.
Illustrations courtesy of Luhr Jensen & Sons

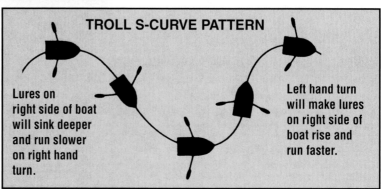

plastic squids, hoochies, and flatfish tipped with worms, will trigger these fish.

For novices, accompanying someone who knows how to use downriggers is a good way to see how they work. There are quite a few elements of their operation that are new to most casual anglers. Portable models that attach to any boat are available from $100. More expensive models include electric motors to lower and raise the weight, among other features. It's difficult to fish downriggers effectively without a good quality depth finder. Therefore, you're tied into two expensive purchases.

Leader strength and length are important considerations in trolling. If you're fishing with hard-digging flatfish, you'll need a strong leader just to withstand that kind of action, let alone land the big brown or mackinaw you're hoping to catch. Fluttering spoons require long, light leaders to work properly. Run the lure experimentally in the water where you can see it to ensure it works properly before sending it down. Trolling spoons, such as the Needlefish,

Triple-Teazer, and Dick Nite, is effective throughout Central Oregon. They are often combined with flashers and gang-trolls, such as the Beer Can, School-of-Minnows, and Ford Fender. When fishing for kokanee, it's a good idea to include a rubber snubber between the flasher and lure to absorb the strike of these soft-lipped fish, which often shake the hook.

Rudders and swivels are key to successful trolling, in that they prevent line twist and lure tangles. Nothing is worse than spending five minutes letting out enough line to reach the magic depth only to have a tangle somewhere between the reel and the lure. The time saved using rudders and swivels more than makes up for their minor cost.

Adding a kernel of white or yellow corn, a piece of worm, grub, or maggot can often make the difference between success and failure. No matter where you troll in Central Oregon, don't be afraid to consult with other anglers, especially those you see catching fish. The vast majority of people who fish in Central Oregon are more than willing to share their secrets.

SPINNING AND JIGGING

Spin fishing is a catch-all phrase for a variety of methods that can be performed with spinning tackle. Quite literally, a spinning reel spins when wound or cranked. Spinning reels are equally well-suited for casting, jigging, still-fishing, and even a modified form of fly fishing. Spinning reels are easy to learn with, affordable, and reliable, making them the single most popular type of fishing reel today.

To cast with a spinning reel, pin the line just above the reel against the rod or hold it in your hand. Open the bail. Swing the rod forward while simultaneously releasing the line. The combination of momentum, timing of release, and weight will pull the line off the reel. When the line stops flowing off the reel, turn the handle. This will automatically close the bail, readying the reel for the retrieve.

Your next action depends on the type of fishing you wish to perform. For instance, if you are casting with a lure, you will have to reel it back in order to give it action. By reeling quickly, you will cause the lure to run shallow. A slower retrieval allows the lure to sink. It's important to fish a lure at all depths until you find where the fish are holding. By fishing from top to bottom and casting to all the reachable water, you effectively cover an area. If you fail to catch a fish, move to another area.

Giving a little thought to each area before stomping or splashing through the shallows to get to deep water will bring rewards. Fish are frequently close to shore or hiding against undercut banks. Probe these shore areas first. If you are really patient, stay far back from the shore for a few minutes and see what you can see. If not disturbed, fish may reveal their location by feeding on the surface. Sometimes, when fish are really spooky, you may have to crawl on hands and knees through brush to get close enough to make a cast without scaring them away.

When river or stream fishing, always work upstream. Because fish swim against the current, their attention is focused upstream; therefore, you'll be approaching them from behind where they are least likely to see you. With a spinner, such as a Rooster Tail, cast upstream and work the lure back toward you. Reel just fast enough to keep the spinner blade turning but slow enough so that it runs near the bottom. It's okay for the lure to bounce occassionally along the bottom. The fish are looking for things drifting and tumbling in the current.

If you are fishing with bait, cast into a likely spot and let the offering – be it a worm, salmon egg, or other tempting goody – sink to the bottom. Once the bait has settled to the bottom, reel up just enough slack line so that when a fish bites, you will be able to see the rod bend or the line move. Bait fishing with a bobber means watching the bobber instead of the pole, and when it moves or goes underwater, you know the time has come to set the hook and reel in a fish.

Still-fishing is basically straight up and down fishing from a dock or boat. There's no casting involved; just open the bail and let the bait sink. Usually, it's best to fish just above the bottom then reel up in 5-foot increments until you find the depth the fish are holding. Once you catch a fish, put the bait back at the same level and chances are you'll catch some more.

Jigging involves raising and lowering your bait or lure. The technique works best with lures that flutter, such as Buzz Bombs, Crippled Herrings, and Nordics. Fish usually grab a jig while it's falling. Often, all the angler will detect is a slight bump or tap. That's the sign to set the hook. When fish are highly concentrated, such as often happens in the fall, jigging can be sensational.

To spin fish with a fly, use 4-pound test or lighter line and a clear, plastic bobber. Use whichever fly everyone says is working at the end of a 5- or 6-foot leader. Cast gently into an area where fish are feeding on flies and reel in very slowly. This is a good way to get hooked on fly fishing, which is covered on pages 158 and 159.

Illustrations courtesy of Luhr Jensen & Sons

READING WATER AND STALKING

For anglers to have much success at all, they must learn to read and fish the water effectively. Before stomping along the streamside path, or wading and splashing water along the bank, anglers should stand back and analyze the situation before approaching.

Reading and stalking includes viewing the entire area, planning a cautious approach, and having a plan for the section of water to be fished. First, it is recommended to begin with water along the bank and then progressively work the water outwards, upstream, and downstream. While doing this, anglers should pay attention to structures that provide protection from the current, such as boulders, fallen trees, vegetation, or rock shelves, and study river flows that carry the fish's food supply near these structures. Back eddies and slower, deeper water where fish might be holding are promising areas. After the area is worked systematically and fished completely, anglers can move to another section and start the procedure over again.

Fish will often seek the shade and protection offered by undercut banks, and walking along a path close to (or above) the water will send vibrations to the fish, alerting them of the presence of danger, or spooking them out in a black, shadowy flash to deeper water. It is better to stay off the path, stay low, and sneak up to a point where a carefully presented offering will be drawn under the bank to the unsuspecting fish.

When undercut banks are not present, and shallow water leads to deeper, more interesting water, patience is necessary. Checking the shallow water for feeding fish, especially water just below riffles, is a good idea. The riffles provide oxygen and carry food. Fish face upstream, so anglers are smart to approach from behind and carefully present the fly, lure, or bait. Many nice fish have been caught in the shallows through which many anglers step to get to the deep water.

Sometimes, it is good to "take five" and relax under a tree, have a snack and drink, and watch the water. If feeding fish are located, it is best to figure out on what they are feeding. Fly fishers will "match the hatch." If fish are not surfacing, they are probably feeding under the surface on nymphs, emergers, or other aquatic delicacies, such as crawfish or minnows.

"Being sneaky" when stream- or lake-side fishing is a wise approach. Fish have very keen eyesight and can detect movement, especially against the sky and along high banks. Some helpful hints include staying low to the water; wearing clothing that blends with surroundings (as opposed to brightly colored clothing); staying as still as possible; hiding behind trees; crouching in bushes or high grass; limiting casting motion; moving slowly; and fishing upstream. It is the element of surprise that catches most stream fish, and it does not take much to spook them.

Larger streams, such as the lower Deschutes River, are a little more forgiving; the deep, wide expanse of water allows anglers to make long casts to undisturbed fish, but stealth is still important.

Stalking is not often done on lakes, but it can be very helpful, especially on back country lakes. Anglers should begin by hiking to a high vantage point (while carefully concealing movements) and observing any fish activity that might be taking place. Binoculars can be helpful in scouting from a distance. Fish may or may not be rising to bug hatches, but, even if they are not, the usually clear, shallow lakes will reveal where the fish are. Often circling an entire lake will only take a few minutes, but it is probably time well-spent. Many back country lakes do not have fish populations due to winterkill. Signs of winterkill might be detected by scouting.

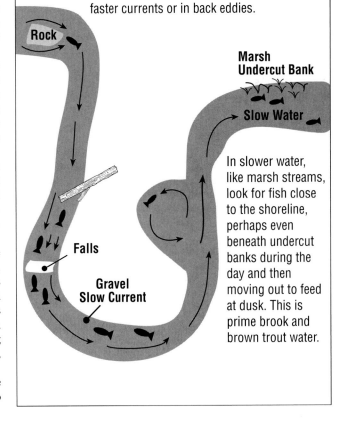

HOW TO FISH A STREAM

Trout in a stream are attracted to structure for protection from both predators and current. They can be found behind rocks and logs; above falls, where they feed on passing insects; below falls; and at the edges of faster currents or in back eddies.

Rock

Marsh Undercut Bank

Slow Water

Falls

Gravel Slow Current

In slower water, like marsh streams, look for fish close to the shoreline, perhaps even beneath undercut banks during the day and then moving out to feed at dusk. This is prime brook and brown trout water.

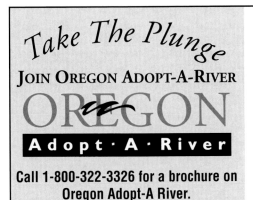

FISHING WITH BAIT

Although all kinds of bait work in Central Oregon's lakes and rivers, Velveeta cheese holds a special place in the tastebuds of trout throughout the region. The nearly indestructable cheese, which conveniently doesn't require refrigeration, milks an essence when submerged that trout love. The Kraft pasteurized product is so popular among bait fishermen that at least two good fishing holes on local lakes have been dubbed, "Velveeta Point."

You can make a cheeseball by rolling a chunk of Velveeta between your palms. Use just enough cheese to cover the hook points. Resist the urge to use more. The extra weight will cause the bait to tear off the hook during casting, not to mention the fact it will give the fish more bait to nibble on without getting near a hook. Trout tend to peck at cheese, so the smaller the cheeseball, the better.

Close behind is Berkley Power Bait. Quite simply, this is one of the most innovative products introduced in fishing in the past decade. Power Bait contains a "secret" fish-attracting formula. But unlike all other products that make such claims, it works. A majority of fish caught with Power Bait have swallowed it.

Power Bait is available in paste, allowing you to customize the size of your bait, in pre-formed nuggets that hold together longer, as salmon eggs, worms, and small grubs. To further spice the selection, all Power Bait products come in a variety of colors and flavors. At times, one color works better than another. In Central Oregon, green and yellow Power Bait seem to work best.

One advantage of Power Bait is that it floats, whereas cheese doesn't. Rig Power Bait on a treble hook and run the leader through a sliding or slip sinker. It's a simple matter of pinching on a split shot to control the amount of leader, and thus the height the bait floats above the bottom. In many fishing situations, the bait needs to float above the bottom vegetation in order to be visible. On the other hand, there are lakes and rivers with little or no weeds where the fish scour the bottom for food; thus, a bait that sinks is appropriate.

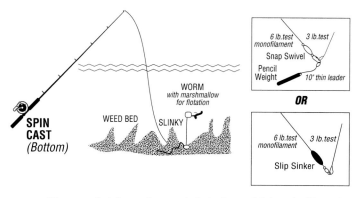

Worms and nightcrawlers catch their share of fish and will continue to do so long after the fish have learned to avoid other baits. Few things are more tempting to a trout than a wiggling, squiggling, juicy nightcrawler. For surefire action, drift worms in the eddies and pools of the Deschutes River for rainbow and brown trout.

Any bait can be floated with the addition of a marshmallow. Marshmallows, in and of themselves, are good bait. The fact that they're available in garlic and cheese flavors proves it. Marshmallows are often combined with other bait to make what local anglers euphamistically refer to as sandwiches. Such offerings might include marshmallows, salmon eggs, corn, and worms. Anglers often douse the entire works in anise oil, WD-40, or some secret sauce they've concocted.

Any conversation about bait fishing in Central Oregon wouldn't be complete without mentioning the myriad of natural baits available for free to those willing to spend a little time looking for them.

Crawdads, which, of course, can be bought at most bait stores, can also be caught in many waters. Crawdad traps, much like crab and lobster pots, baited with nearly anything and left overnight will usually be full of freshwater crustaceans come morning.

Another method of catching crawdads in a stream is to wade in shallow areas, turning rocks over until you locate one. With sleeves rolled up, you slip your arm in the water and slowly reach from behind the crawdad. When within three or four inches, you can make a quick grab for it, "pinching" its main body with your thumb and forefinger, just behind the crawdad's pincers. Their grasping claws cannot pinch you from that angle. Keep in mind that crawdads scoot backwards …very quickly. It may take a couple of tries to catch one, but your efforts won't be for naught: the tail, with the

Reach behind the crawdad's pincers. Photo by Brian O'Keefe

shell peeled off, or the entire body is an excellent bait. Furthermore, unlike most baits which aren't fit for human consumption, a hard boil in salted water and a dip in melted butter transform crawdads into a tasty treat.

Crawdads are good for duping large brown trout. Try drifting crawdad tails into deep holes of the upper Deschutes River for a shot at lunker browns. (Check current OSFR before fishing.) The best time is dusk and dawn. Just remember not to fish too early or late, as fishing is closed in Oregon until one hour before sunrise and one hour after sunset.

Periwinkles are easy to collect and make great bait. The larval form of caddisflies, periwinkles are essentially tiny grubs that build little cocoons around themselves of whatever material is most available. In some places, they'll look like little pin cushions, utilizing pine needles and sticks. In other waters, they may cover themselves with tiny pebbles. Simply peel the shell off to reveal the larva inside. Fish one or more of them on a small hook. Periwinkles are good for trout and kokanee.

Be sure to try fishing with the live damselfly and dragon fly nymphs when they make their annual appearance in late May, early June. These bugs will literally crawl onto your boat where you can grab them, skewer them on a hook beneath a bobber, and toss them back into the water to meet their fate in the jaws of a ravenous rainbow.

There's an abundance of bait to be found on dry land, as well. In the evening after any rainstorm, look for nightcrawlers above ground in landscaped areas. Approach quietly and grab firmly, otherwise, they'll zip back down their holes with astonishing speed. Usually, you can dig for worms anytime. Also look for grubs in the bark of decaying trees. Just peel back the bark of downed logs. Almost everything there, including ants, makes good bait. Late summer is a good time for grasshoppers. A grasshopper drifted along a grassy bank is too tempting for many trout to pass up.

Even though bait fishing is widely practiced, it has come under fire as being very harmful and, in some cases, fatal for fish. The rap on bait fishing is that too many anglers allow the fish to swallow the bait (hook) and, therefore, kill the fish while removing it. To avoid this malady, strike early when you first detect the nibble or bite, when chances are you'll hook the fish only in the lip. If the fish does swallow the hook, and you want to release it, just cut the line as close to the hook as possible, handling the fish with care. *(See Catch & Release on pages 170 and 171.)* The hook will rust apart in a short time, relieving the fish of it, and it will only take you a minute to tie another hook on your line.

When performed carefully, bait fishing is not bad. Instead, it can be safe for fish and a very relaxing way to spend a few hours enjoying the sights and sounds of the outdoors. Traditionally, bait fishing is how most anglers get started, especially small children.

BASS TECHNIQUES

Bass fishing is gaining popularity in Central Oregon as more and more anglers discover the pleasures of these mean, green fish. Opposed to the delicate takes of trout, bass literally mug their prey by swallowing whole in one vicious gulp, then charge back to their hideouts. Breathtaking jumps, vigorous headshakes and powerful runs follow explosive strikes after they feel the sting of a hook. With a basic understanding of their ambush style of feeding, a handful of simple lures and a willingness to fish near snags, anyone can catch bass.

There are two species of bass in Central Oregon: largemouth and smallmouth. The difference is the size of their mouth and habitat preferences. Largemouth have round, bucket-shaped mouths with a lower jaw that extends beyond their eyes. They thrive in shallow, warm, weedy water eating a variety of foods ranging from small fish, frogs and insect larvae to turtles, mice and even birds. Smallmouth, as the name implies, have smaller mouths, prefer cooler, deeper water and are more comfortable in current. Their diet is similar to largemouth, but they key on crawdads whenever the freshwater lobsters are available. Both species stay close to structure (rocks, stumps, weeds, etc.), grabbing things that stray too close, and then retreat to their lairs. Bass are homebodies, rarely venturing more than a few hundred yards from food and shelter. Where there's one, there's usually a bunch.

Plastic worms catch more bass than any other lure. Worm, lizard, grub or crawdad shapes, plastic's subtle movements and squishy feel closely imitate natural food items. Their primary advantage is they can be rigged weedless and fished in heavy cover where bass spend most of their time. Upon detecting a strike, which feels like a slight tug as a bass inhales the lure, point the rod tip directly at the fish, reel up the slack feeling for the weight of the fish, and set the hook. Use 10- to 20-lb. test line, stiff rod and a strong reel to horse bass out of structure before the line tangles or breaks on obstructions.

Crankbaits include a variety of diving and vibrating minnow-imitating lures that are effective when bass are actively feeding. Cast beyond a suspected bass lie then "crank" through the spot, pausing occasionally to imitate the struggles of an injured fish. Or troll the edge of weed lines and underwater shelves. Strikes are obvious as bass attack from behind, pulling the rod down sharply. Commonly referred to as "Rapalas" (a popular brand) crankbaits come in a variety of shapes, colors and sizes that can be fished from the surface down to 25 feet.

Few things rival the thrill of seeing a big bass attack a top water bait. Hula Poppers, Jitter Bugs and buzz baits are the best known. Designed to splash and make noise as they move across the surface, top water baits get bit mostly in low light conditions, early morning before sunrise and late evening after sunset. Fly fishers get in on the fun with small popper style flies made of cork, balsa, and feather. In Central Oregon's clear waters, top water baits catch relatively few but larger bass compared to other methods.

Spinnerbait

Spinnerbaits don't resemble anything bass feed on. But their flashing blades and pulsing rubber skirts are an appealing combination. Cast and retrieve spinnerbaits like crankbaits, only slower through bullrushes, around trees and rocks, as they are relatively snag free. Because they sink slowly, spinnerbaits are particularly effective in shallow backwaters. Another good technique is to let them free fall down stumps and rock piles in water as deep as 20 feet, then hop them across the bottom.

Jig

Jigs are necessary when bass refuse to chase lures and the only way to get a bite is put a lure directly in front of them. Dressed with feathers, hair or rubber skirts, anglers frequently add live bait or pork attractors to create a "jig and pig" combination. The result is a heavy lure that sinks straight into a bass hideout then is bounced along the bottom. Detecting strikes is challenging, because bass normally strike a jigging lure as it sinks. Keep the line tight to feel the light tap then immediately set the hook.

Bass are fools for live bait. Large nightcrawlers, frogs, waterdogs (immature salamanders) crawdads, leeches and minnows are all very effective. Presentation can be as simple as a nightcrawler below a bobber fished near structure, to casting and retrieving the live bait as if it were a lure, albeit gently. The use of live minnows as bait is not legal in Central Oregon but fresh dead, dehydrated and frozen minnows are available.

Minnow-imitating crankbaits

HIRING A GUIDE

One's fishing trip begins not when one steps on the boat, casts a line, or brings in the first fish, but the day a call is made to reserve a trip. Reservations are a fact of life during the busy summer months. They can be had as little as 24 hours in advance, but it is safer to make a request a week or more ahead of the intended fishing day. Customers should note that guides listed under professional organizations are licensed and fully trained and are recommended for a safe and enjoyable trip. While arranging the guided trip, the customer should be told in detail exactly what to bring. Most likely, one will need a license, food, and a range of clothing suitable for cold to hot weather. A lot of people also bring along a camera, sunscreen, sunglasses, and hat. At the least, the guide will provide tackle, bait, boat and the expertise necessary to catch fish.

On many of Central Oregon's Cascade lakes trips, guides often will not pick up a customer until 8:00 a.m. the day of the trip. Trout keep bankers' hours in the cold waters of the high lakes. As most of the lakes are spring fed and very cold, the food chain needs to be energized by the sun for a couple of hours before the fishing really gets good. The stereotype of being on the water before dawn is soon dispelled. Fishers likely return home long before dark, as well.

Also, customers can expect a lot more comfort; the days of sitting on a wooden plank in a small dingy are over. Guides today use larger boats, featuring everything from swivel chairs to couches. Collapsible tops provide shade from blistering sun or a dry spot in the rain. Pontoon or deck boats are becoming increasingly popular,

Pontoon boats are spacious and comfortable.
Photo courtesy of Garrison's Guide Service

because of their large, stable surface area and wheelchair accessibility.

Lake fishing tactics in these parts include still fishing, trolling, casting, and fly fishing. Where the guide plans the trip and what expectations the client has dictate what techniques are employed. But whatever the method, anglers must be prepared to stick with it.

As mentioned before, the trout in the high Cascade lakes are mid-day biters. As for exactly when in the middle of the day they'll bite, no one can say for sure. Trusting one's guide to go to the right spot with the right fly, lure, or bait is the key, because when the fish bite, they're likely to be caught. While waiting, anglers can enjoy the scenery, ask questions, and let the clean mountain air and peaceful surroundings recharge the soul.

This unhurried approach lends itself to the low-key attitude fishers will want to take when it comes to minding one's line, lure, or bait. Most people, when they hire guides, assume the fish will come fast and furious. Likely at some point in the day that will happen, but probably not from the get-go. It's good to come prepared with an open mind and listen to the guide's instructions about what to do and when to do it.

In areas where fish are to be released, the guide will either remove the hook with a specialized tool or cut the line if the hook is deeply imbedded. The fish's digestive acids and rusting action of water will corrode the hook in a few days, giving the fish a very good chance of surviving.

On most of the high Cascade lakes, the limit is 5 trout per person, of which only one may be over 20 inches. A 20-inch trout weighs in the neighborhood of 4 pounds, enough to feed four or more adults. Ethical guides will quiz their customers extensively about how much one really needs to take home. While Central Oregon waters have a lot of trout, there is not an endless supply.

Planning a guided fishing trip on a river might require a little more preparation Most river guides are dedicated to fly fishing only and practice catch-and-release. Usually, fly fishers bring their own equipment: rod, reels, vest with tackle and hackle, waders, etc. Guides establish a meeting place, provide the river boat and a fishing guide, lunch, snacks, and the shuttle ride back to the meeting place.

Extended trips, up to three or four days, are available on the lower Deschutes and John Day rivers. Guides generally provide meals and utensils, snacks, beverages, and tents. Anglers will most likely be informed of what personal gear and clothing to bring along.

After a successful day on the water, anglers can be thinking about next year; guides accept reservations up to a year in advance. This way, fishers are assured of getting the guide they want for the trip they want during their next visit to Central Oregon.

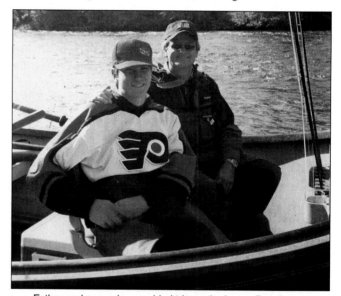

Father and son enjoy a guided trip on the Lower Deschutes.
Photo courtesy of The Fly Box

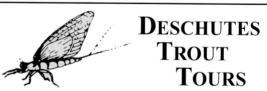

CARE OF FRESH-CAUGHT FISH

Unlike red meat, fish does not improve with age – the fresher the catch, the better the flavor. Fish flesh is extremely perishable; heat and humidity are its ruin. Keep your catch out of direct sunlight and heat. Fresh-caught fish have been known to spoil in the boat before the angler could get them home. The sooner the fish is cleaned and cooled, the better it will taste when cooked. This means that fresh-caught fish should be properly cared for within minutes of being caught.

When cleaning your catch, it is important to remove the guts, gills, and any blood, veins, or organs adhering to the backbone. To avoid improper disposal, boat anglers should carry a container for the storage of internal organs and blood. Wipe the fish dry inside and out and keep each fish dry in its own plastic bag. On cool days, some anglers allow large, cleaned fish to hang in the cool air until a pellicle, or sticky film, forms on the meat, sealing in flavor and moisture. However, the best method of preservation after cleaning, drying, and bagging is to keep the fish in an ice chest full of ice. It is important to prevent the meat's direct contact with ice by placing ice on the bottom of the cooler, followed by some sort of divider on which the fish is laid. This keeps the fish dry and cold, not wet and cold. Usually, one pound of ice for each two pounds of fish – with more ice used for longer trips home – will adequately cool the fish. Further, crushed ice, versus cubed, will not cut into the soft flesh, preventing tiny cuts in which spoilage bacteria can settle.

Keeping dead fish in the water to keep them cool is not effective. Unlike the cool water depths in which fish swim, surface water can reach temperatures of 70°F in the summer. Anything above 42°F (refrigerator temperature), will cause the fish to spoil. In fact, if warm enough, the surface water will start to cook the fish. Additionally, pollutants, such as oil and boat fuel, debris, and bacteria may be prevalent on the surface water, creating an undesirable place to store fish. A living fish kept tied to a boat's hull can thrash about, bruising itself. Finally, in the winter, wind can dry the flesh of the fish if not protected.

The finest flavor will come from fresh fish rather than from thawed frozen fish. But if your intention is to freeze your catch for later consumption, remember that air causes spoilage. Make sure you squeeze all the air possible out of packaging. Whole fish with gills and guts removed or fillets can be frozen. Anglers should be sure to wash the catch in fresh water before storing. The meat should be covered with several layers of protective wrap before freezing: a plastic wrap first, followed by heavy aluminum foil or heavy freezer paper. Fish should be good for 4 to 12 months in the freezer, where harmful bacteria will not grow. Fatter fish, such as salmonids, have the shortest freezer life. Thawing and refreezing will result in a tasteless offering when finally consumed. Thawed frozen fish should be cooked when still slightly frozen for the freshest flavor.

For refrigeration of fresh-caught fish, store the meat at 42°F for no longer than 3.5 days. Portable vacuum packers are becoming increasingly popular and allow the angler to seal fresh-caught fish immediately after cleaning, saving time and effort in storage preparation at home.

For more information on freezing, canning, drying, and pickling fish, anglers can contact Oregon Extension Service offices that offer descriptive pamphlets.

"Limit your kill, don't kill your limit."

FAVORITE RECIPES

GEOFF'S HI-HO FRIED TROUT

There's nothing like a good fish fry once in awhile, especially when you're camping out. I like pan-sized trout sprinkled inside and out with Hi-Ho® Cracker crumbs. Here's how to prepare:

Place a few Hi-Ho® (or Ritz®) crackers on a sheet of aluminum foil and crunch up with a rolling pin or, if out camping, with the base of a coffee mug. Mix 1 egg with a little milk in a bowl for an "egg wash," dip the fish in the egg wash, then roll it in the cracker crumbs on both sides, sprinkling some crackers in the cavity. You may add spices as you choose.

Place fish in a pre-heated, greased skillet and cook on each side until golden brown. The cracker-covered skin becomes my favorite part of the meal. I also believe in leaving the fish's head attached while cooking to retain flavor.

To go with a fish breakfast, I will usually bake a few potatoes the night before while sitting around the campfire. I wipe the spuds with butter (to keep from burning the skin), double wrap in foil, and place in hot coals for about 45 minutes, turning periodically with tongs. Store the cooked potatoes in a cooler overnight and, in the morning, slice them into a frying pan, add some chopped green peppers and/or onions, and fry them.

Fresh trout, fried potatoes, with a couple of eggs, make a delicious, hearty breakfast to start your day.

CAMPFIRE TROUT

1 large (2- to 3-lb) trout (or salmon or steelhead)
Apples
Sweet onions
Mayonnaise
Seasonings

Clean the fish well and coat the entire body, including inside the cavity, with mayonnaise. Stuff the body cavity with chunks of apple and sweet onion. Add preferred seasonings.

Double wrap the fish in heavy foil and seal. Place in the coal bed of a campfire for about 45 minutes (45 to 60 minutes in an oven at 350°F). Makes 4 servings.

–From Bob Penington, ODFW (retired), Bend

TROUT WITH ALMONDS

1 cup coarsely chopped blanched almonds
1/4 cup plus 2 tablespoons butter, melted
1 1/2 tablespoons fresh lemon juice
1 cup all-purpose flour
1 teaspoon salt
8 (8 to 10 oz each) trout fillets
3/4 cup butter, divided

Saute almonds in 1/4 cup plus 2 tablespoons butter in a large skillet over medium heat until golden brown. Stir in lemon juice. Remove from heat and set aside.

Combine flour and salt; dredge fillets in flour mixture. Melt 1/4 cup plus 2 tablespoons butter in a large skillet over medium-high heat. Add half of the fillets: cook 5 minutes on each side or until fish flakes easily when tested with fork.

Remove to a serving platter and keep warm. Repeat procedure with remaining 1/4 cup plus 2 tablespoons butter and fillets.

Sprinkle with reserved almond mixture. Garnish, if desired. Makes 8 servings.

–From "America's Best Recipes"

CATCH-AND-RELEASE

To release fish is to allow them to be enjoyed more than once and to produce more of their kind, especially important with wild fish. Unlike hatchery fish that are protected in a hatchery pond until adulthood, wild fish are faced from birth with the challenges of wild water and predators. Returning wild fish to their stream insures the maintenance of strong, wild fish populations, since the fish we catch are the survivors, the best of their species. When too many people take too many fish from a body of water, the quality of our angling declines. Since the largest fish are the ones usually killed first, over-harvesting leaves no large fish and eventually no spawning fish. Therefore, the fittest fish are unable to pass their survival skills on to offspring, stunting the growth of healthy and cunning populations of wild species. The phrase, "Limit your kill, don't kill your limit," is becoming more and more common. We can measure fishing pleasure by the angling difficulty involved in successfully hooking and landing the fish rather than in the heft of a stringer. Catch-and-release fishing can be practiced by anglers using all methods.

There are exceptions to the concept of catch-and-release. For instance, releasing your catch in a pond of stunted fish will not improve the angling. The ideal is to have healthy, self-sustaining fish populations with good age distribution in every body of water. Catch-and-release works only if fish recover after release to rejoin the fishery. Gentle handling and time out of the water are the most important factors in fish survival.

HANDLING YOUR CATCH

If you must handle a fish:

- Use a wet glove or rag to hold it; or, at least, wet your hands.
- Turn a fish on its back or cover eyes with a wet towel to calm it.
- Don't put your fingers in the eyes, mouth, or gills of your catch
- Avoid removing mucous or scales
- Get the fish back in the water as quickly as possible.

Information and illustrations courtesy of ODFW

WILD FISH

All fins are straight, branced fin rays and the adipose fin is intact.

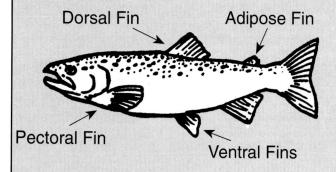

Dorsal Fin
Adipose Fin
Pectoral Fin
Ventral Fins

HATCHERY FISH

Hatchery fish have had adipose, ventral, or pectoral fins clipped off at the hatchery. To confirm hatchery origin, look for the healed fin clip.

Information and illustrations courtesy of ODFW

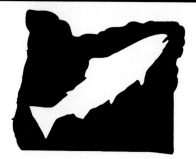

TIPS FOR CATCH-AND-RELEASE:

- Use barbless hooks; it's the law on some waters.
- Use hooks that biodegrade quickly.
- Use hooks smaller than size 2 on lures fished for steelhead and salmon so that trout caught by accident will not be injured. Set the hook immediately and try to prevent a fish from swallowing the bait.
- Play fish briefly, land them quickly. Don't play the fish to exhaustion. This is especially important during spawning season and as water temperatures increase.
- Use appropriate size tackle. Gear that is too light can force you to play a fish long enough to kill it from exhaustion.
- Wet your hands before touching a fish and if possible try not to touch the fish at all. If you must handle a fish, wear a wet glove or rag to hold it.
- Keep release tools handy.
- Release a fish as soon as it is landed.
- Keep the fish in the water if at all possible. Every second out of the water decreases its chance for survival.
- Remove the hook gently.
- Avoid squeezing the fish.
- Turn a fish on its back or cover its eyes with a wet towel to calm it.
- Keep your fingers out of the fish's mouth, eyes, and gills.
- Do not remove mucous or scales (a fish's outer body protection).
- Don't let it thrash around on rocks.
- If the fish is hooked too deeply to safely remove the hook, cut your leader quickly. The hook will work its way out of the fish in a short time.
- If possible, don't use a net. Otherwise, use a cotton net and wet it before touching the fish. Do not use a nylon net.
- Revive the fish carefully before releasing. Grasp the fish in front of the tail, support it underneath, and point it into a slow moving current, holding it gently until it is strong enough to swim off under its own power. Make sure the gills are working before letting it go.
- To resuscitate an exhausted fish, move it back and forth in the water or tow it gently alongside the boat to force water into its gills.
- If the fish does not swim away, recover it and try again.
- Get the fish back in the water as soon as possible.
- A fish handled carefully and released properly has a great chance of survival.

THE BIOLOGY OF FISH

The fish's eye is much like our own, except that the pupils cannot adjust to the brightness of light. Fish cannot see surface food in bright sun as well as they can in the shade and may seek deeper, darker areas during bright daylight. Fish have a field of view of about 330°. The 30° directly behind the fish is its only blind spot. Consequently, stealth is required in the angler's approach.

190°
190°

Top view of fish showing wide angle of vision

Objects above water and farther than 30 feet away are unclear to a fish, but at 15 feet, it can see any part of your body more than 2.5 feet above the surface of the water. At times you will need to stay lower and farther away than preferred in order not to be seen. Fish are seldom frightened by the sight of still, quiet objects in the water, such as your lower body. On the bank, keep vegetation between you and the fish or directly behind you as you approach the fish and move slowly. In rough water, the fish's "window" of vision comes and goes with the chop of the waves, and it is much easier to approach without being seen.

Normally, a fish can see insects on the surface quite clearly. A trout will follow what it thinks may be food downstream, whether on the surface or sub-surface, inspecting it before taking it. Bass lie in wait for prey to pass within reach. Recent research indicates that fish see mostly form and size but no detail, while contrast and perception of motion are heightened. They definitely see color. Fish are color blind at night but, nonetheless, can see well in the dark.

The fish's hearing is much more sensitive than ours, but they hear only low-frequency noises, such as the crunch of gravel under wading boots, the vibration of a lure hitting the water, or the sounds of noisy anglers in a boat. The sound of moving water in a riffle hides many of our noisy approaches, which are audible in calm water. The clump of boots along a bank carries into the water to alert the fish.

Equipped with nostrils and a very sensitive sense of smell, fish are able to distinguish between species and even recognize individual fish. A frightened fish releases an alarm odor that others can smell. Salmonids are repelled by the smell of human skin, so many anglers use masking scents on flies and lures.

Fish also have a good sense of taste. Taste buds on their "lips" allow them to investigate your offering without taking it into their mouth. They hate the taste of gas, oil, and insect repellent.

As wild species, fish have senses that are accordingly acute. Keeping this fact in mind is one key to angling success.

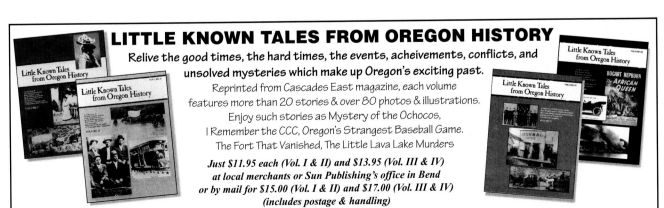

OFFICIAL OREGON COLD WATER GAME FISH RECORDS

Compiled By The Oregon Department of Fish and Wildlife.

Species	Weight Lbs./Ozs.	Caught Where	Date	Angler
Trout, Brook	9 6	Deschutes River (below Little Lava Lake)	6/21/80	Burt Westbrook
	6 12	Hosmer Lake	7/13/77	Tad Walker
Trout, Brown	35 8*	Paulina Lake	7/3/65	Ike & Darrell Fox
	27 12	Paulina Lake	5/21/93	Guy Carl
Trout, Bull	23 2	Lake Billy Chinook (Metolius Arm)	3/25/89	Don Yow
	20 7	Lake Billy Chinook	3/19/88	William E. Reid
Trout, Coastal Cutthroat	6 4	Siltcoos Lake	8/20/84	Kay Schmidt
Trout, Lahontan	9 8	Malheur River	1986	Phillip Grove
Trout, Golden	7 10	Eagle Cap Wilderness	1987	Douglas White
Trout, Mackinaw or Lake	40 8	Odell Lake	6/11/84	Kenneth Erickson
	36 8	Odell Lake	6/76	H.V. Hannon
Trout, Rainbow	28 0	Rogue River	5/19/82	Mike McGonagle
	24 2.25	Lake Simtustus	6/74	Jerry Fifield
Trout, Steelhead	35 8	Columbia River	9/9/70	Berdell Todd
	31 4	Cascade Locks	9/63	Gus Hesgard
Salmon, Chinook	83 0	Umpqua River	1910	Ernie St. Claire
	62 (dressed)	Nestucca River	10/70	Craig Hansen
Salmon, Chum (species now catch & release only)	23 0	Kilchis River	1990	Roger Nelson
Salmon, Coho	25 5.25	Siltcoos Lake	11/5/66	Ed Martin
	23	Tillamook Bay	10/63	Chuck Walters
Salmon, Atlantic	No entries — catch-and-keep only legal at Davis Lake & East Lake			
Salmon, Kokanee	5 5	Wallowa Lake	5/00	Larry Campbell
	4 2	Paulina Lake	6/17/90	Howard Morgan
Striped Bass	64 8**	Umpqua River	1973	Beryl Bliss
Shad	5 13	Columbia River	5/31/94	Patricia Ann Young
Whitefish	4 14 ***	Crane Prairie Reservoir	7/21/94	Roger A. Massey
	4 0	McKenzie River	1974	Todd Fisher

*Caught with net – not a legal catch.
** World record for fly rod
*** Not "officially" recorded

See the information on the opposite page for entry instructions and how to obtain official entry forms for the Oregon State Record Fish.

The world's third largest brown trout (35 lbs., 8 oz.) came from Paulina Lake. The mounted fish is now back home at Paulina Lodge restaurant.
Photo by Diane Kulpinski

STATE OF OREGON WARM WATER GAME FISH RECORDS

Compiled By The Oregon Bass And Panfish Club Inc. Revised January, 2001

Species	Weight Lbs./Ozs.		Length	Girth	Date	Caught Where	Angler
Bass, Hybrid White	18	8	29"	24.75"	2/21/96	Ana Reservoir	John Saunders
Bass, Largemouth	11	9.6	25.5"	21.25"	4/15/94	Farm pond near Butte Falls*	Randy T. Spaur
Bass, Smallmouth	7	14	—	—	10/8/00	Henry Hagg Lake	Kevin Silver
Bluegill	2	5.5	11.75"	14"	5/12/81	Farm pond near Prineville*	Wayne Elmore
Catfish, Bullhead	3	6	20"	11.88"	6/10/86	Brownlee Reservoir	Loretta Fitzgerald
Catfish, Channel	36	8	38"	22"	9/17/80	McKay Reservoir	Boone Haddock
Catfish, Flathead	42	0	40.5"		6/27/94	Snake River near Farewell Bend	Joshua Kralicek
Catfish, White	15	0	30.25"	—	4/22/89	Tualatin River	Wayne Welch
Crappie, Black	4	6.1	18.5"	16.88"	6/29/95	Private pond, Corvallis*	John E. Doss
Crappie, White	4	12	18.5"	17.75"	5/22/67	Gerber Reservoir	Jim Duckett
Perch, Yellow	2	2	—	—	6/5/71	Brownsmead Slough	Ernie Affolter III
Perch, Sacramento	0	11.2	—	—	1998	Lost River	Jonathan Cogley
Sturgeon: There is no state record information for sturgeon in Oregon because the maximum size limit is 60". It is unlawful to remove an oversized sturgeon from the water because the bouyancy of water can cause internal organ damage and death.							
Sunfish, Green	0	11	10"	9.25"	4/25/91	Umpqua River near Tyee	John L. Baker
Sunfish, Redear	1	15.5	13"	12.75"	8/1/92	Reynolds Pond near Redmond	Terrence C. Bice
Sunfish, Pumpkinseed	0	7.68	—	—	1996	Lake Oswego	Linda Mar
Walleye	19	15.3	37"	21.5"	2/20/90	Columbia River up from John Day Dam	Arnold R. Berg
Warmouth	1	14.2	11"	12.75"	12/27/75	Columbia Slough	Jess Newell

*Effective January 1, 1996, fish from private waters will no longer be accepted for state records. Records will be from public waters only.

Instructions for Entering Oregon State Record Fish*

1. Submit all entries within one month to:

COLD WATER ENTRIES:
Oregon Dept. of Fish and Wildlife, Information & Education
2501 SW First Ave., P.O. Box 59; Portland, OR 97207

WARM WATER ENTRIES:
Oregon Bass & Panfish Club
P.O. Box 1021; Portland, OR 97202

2. The fish must be caught with a hook and line, and the weight of the fish is what will qualify it as a record catch.

3. A photo showing a recognizable side view of the fish must accompany the application for positive identification.

4. Please fill out application completely along with having the signatures of two witnesses, one being the person weighing the fish.

5. All catches must be weighed on certified scales.

* NOTE: Official entry forms may be obtained from the addresses above.

OREGON RECORD FISH ENTRY FORM

Kind of Fish _____
Location Caught _____ Date Caught _____

Additional Fish Entry Information:

Weight _____ lbs. _____ oz. Length _____ in. Girth _____ in.
(Must Be Weighed on a State Inspected Scale)
Location of Scale _____ Date Weighed _____

Angler Information:

Name _____
Address _____
City _____ State _____ Zip _____

Witness Information:

Signature _____ Date _____
Affiliation _____ Title _____
Address _____
City _____ State _____ Zip _____
Phone _____

Signature _____ Date _____
Affiliation _____ Title _____
Address _____
City _____ State _____ Zip _____
Phone number _____

Contestant's Signature _____ Date _____

SEE REVERSE SIDE FOR ENTRY INSTRUCTIONS AND MAILING ADDRESS.

OREGON
Fish & Wildlife

GLOSSARY OF FISHING TERMS

Adipose fin - The small fin behind the dorsal fin and in front of the tail fin, found only on salmonids.

Anadromous - Fish which migrate from salt water to spawn and rear in fresh water.

Atlantic salmon - An anadromous species of salmon native to the East Coast, which survives well in landlocked lakes in Central Oregon.

Bait - Any item used to attract fish which is not an artificial fly or lure (ODFW).

Baitfish - A small fish of any species resembling a minnow, regularly eaten by larger fish of numerous species.

Banana weights - Lake trolling weights with swivels attached at each end. Shaped similar to a banana.

Barbless hook - A hook manufactured without a barb or a hook with the barb removed or bent down flush with the shank.

BLM - Bureau of Land Management

Bobber - A floating device attached to the fishing line to float bait or flies at a chosen level beneath the surface of the water.

Brood trout - Fish that are used by ODFW for breeding purposes, either in hatcheries or in their natural environment.

Brook trout - A long-lived species of char native to the East Coast, which does very well in western streams and lakes. Prefers cold water.

Brown trout (German brown trout) - A species of trout native to Europe, now broadly distributed throughout the Western United States. These trout are known for their pisciverous, nocturnal habits, and ability to grow to trophy size.

Bucktail - The long hair of a deer's tail, used to tie streamer-style flies which imitate baitfish.

Bullhead, brown - The most common species of catfish in Central Oregon, not native to this area.

Bull trout - A native inland char known for its trophy size; a state-sensitive species in Oregon; it is now on the federal threatened list in most Oregon waters.

Caddis - A very abundant insect in Central Oregon savored by trout. Over 1,200 species in North America, caddis are recognized by their "periwinkle" cases on river bottoms and, as adults, by tent-shaped wings lying over their backs. A popular and effective fly pattern.

Caddis larva - The "worm" stage of the caddis' life during which most species form a case composed of small pebbles, twigs, or other vegetation. A popular trout food and fly imitation.

Char - A group of fish in the salmonid family which includes brook trout, bull trout, and mackinaw (lake trout). Char technically are not trout.

Chinook salmon - The largest of the native anadromous salmon species in Oregon.

Chub - A rough fish found all too often in Central Oregon reservoirs, prone to overpopulate and out-compete game fish.

Coho salmon - A native anadromous salmon species in Oregon, hatchery raised coho are sometimes stocked in Central Oregon lakes and adapt well to landlocked situations.

Coyote Camp - A primitive campsite created by use by the public.

Crappie - A species of sunfish not very common in Central Oregon but good eating and fun to catch.

Crayfish - Also known as crawdads and crawfish, these little crustaceans are abundant in healthy Central Oregon waters. Excellent eating and for bait, they can be found up to 4 inches long.

CTWS - Confederated Tribes of Warm Springs

Cutthroat trout - A native Oregon trout species identified by the orange "slashes" under the jaw.

Damselfly - An abundant insect on most Central Oregon lakes and reservoirs, the adults are blue, delicate dragonfly-like creatures.

Damselfly nymph - The aquatic, swimming stage of the damselfly, a very popular food item for resident fish.

Depth finder - A battery powered electronic device with many variations but usually showing the depth and location of fish.

Dodger - A large trolling attractor blade.

Downrigger - A fishing system involving a pulley in place of a rod, used to troll heavily weighted lines at great depths.

Dragonfly larva - A commonly used bait on Central Oregon lakes, these big, ugly insects can be found under and around rocks and logs at the edges of lakes.

Drifting (wind drifting) - Letting your boat and/or bait drift at the same speed of the water or wind.

Dry flies - Fly imitations which float on the surface of the water and usually imitate adult insects.

Emergers - The insect as it changes from larva to adult on or just under the surface of the water.

False cast - A cast in which the fly does not touch the water. Used to dry flies, lengthen line, and change direction of the cast.

Fin-clipped - Hatcheries mark their fish by clipping adipose fins or a combination of other fins.

Fingerlings - Fish between 2 and 5 inches in length and less than 1 year old.

Fish finder - See *Depth finder.*

Flashers - A string of blades attached to a steel leader in front of a lure or bait. Used to attract fish by imitating a school of small fish.

Floating fly line - A waterproof fly line that stays on top of the water, used with dry flies but also sometimes with wet flies.

Fly (artificial) - A weighted or unweighted hook dressed with conventional fly-tying materials.

Fly angling only - Angling with an artificial fly, fly line, and fly rod.

Game fish - All trout; steelhead; Atlantic salmon; whitefish; grayling; coho, chinook, chum, pink and sockeye salmon; largemouth and smallmouth bass; catfish; crappie; sunfish; yellow perch; mullet; shad; striped bass; sturgeon; walleye; and bullfrogs. Game species are determined by Oregon statute and are subject to state fishing regulations (ODFW).

Gang troll - A string of attractor blades on a trolling rig.

Green Drake - An unusually large mayfly up to a size 6 that lives in flowing water and hatches in late spring to early summer.

Hackles - The feathers and/or materials used in artificial flies.

Hatchery trout - Fish that are raised and released directly from hatcheries at fingerling size or "legal" size, often finclipped.

Ice-out - When the ice on lakes first begins to melt in the spring, usually pulling away from the edges first. This is a great time to fish.

Jig - A type of lure and an action imparted to a lure by pulling it up in the water and letting it fall back down repeatedly to attract fish.

Kokanee - A landlocked variety of sockeye salmon, native to Oregon.

Largemouth bass - A popular species of game fish known for powerful fights and excellent eating. Prefers warmer water.

Lead core line - A very heavy trolling line with a lead core used to troll at great depths, usually for mackinaw.

Leader - Fine monofilament at the terminal end of the line and the part the fish are going to see (or not see). A large variety of "tests" or diameters is available.

Leech - A common worm-like organism in Central Oregon lakes and streams, they come in a variety of colors and lengths. Leech imitations are popular and effective.

Lunker - A trophy fish of any species.

Lure - An artificial device with hooks used to attract fish but is without molded, soft plastic, rubber bait imitations, or artificial flies.

Mackinaw (lake trout) - A char of deep, cold lakes that can grow to trophy size and is excellent eating.

Marabou - A fly tying material with excellent action used to imitate long, slender insects, baitfish, and leeches.

March Brown - A size 14 to 16 mayfly that hatches in late winter to early spring on flowing water, a popular hatch with fly fishers.

Marshmallows - The small, colored variety is used to float bait off the bottom. Some fish will even take the marshmallow.

Match the hatch - A fly fishing method by which the fly on the line resembles the insects on which the fish are feeding. Also implies that the angler is watching trout taking insects off the surface.

Mayfly - A common insect that is a favorite fish food, identified by delicate, upright wings resembling sails on a slender body.

Midge - A tiny insect that makes up a substantial portion of any self-respecting trout's diet, in the same family as mosquitoes. They come in a variety of sizes and colors, and both the adult and the "worm" stage are consumed by fish.

Minnow - Technically a small fish of a specific species, but the term is often used for any very small baitfish.

Native - Fish that are indigenous to the region. Different from a "wild" fish.

Non-game fish - Includes the minnow family, chubs, suckers, and pikeminnow. These species are not subject to state fishing regulations, but some are protected by law under the threatened and endangered species list (ODFW).

Nymph - The aquatic stage of an insect and a major portion of a trout's diet.

ODFW - Oregon Department of Fish and Wildlife.

OSFR - Oregon Sports Fishing Regulations.

Periwinkle - A caddis nymph that builds a case of tiny pebbles or grains of sand.

Pisciverous - Something which habitually eats fish; fish-eating fish.

Pikeminnow *(formerly squawfish)* - A native non-game fish species and voracious, pisciverous predator present in both flowing and still water.

Planted fish - see *Hatchery.*

Plug - Deep-bodied plastic or wood lures often used to catch larger pisciverous fish.

Power Bait® **(Berkley)** - A popular, scented, and flavored manufactured floating bait.

Rainbow trout - A trout species native to Oregon and capable of growing to trophy size in Central Oregon.

Redd - A fish nest dug in the gravel of a stream.

Redside - A strain of rainbow trout for which the lower Deschutes River is renowned, identified by their broad, deep red stripes and gill covers.

Riffle - Shallower water in a river that flows rapidly over rocks or gravel.

Roach - A rough fish found in some Central Oregon lakes. They can become a big problem when overpopulation creates competition with game fish in the same water.

Rubber snubber - A length of surgical tubing with a swivel attached at both ends. Absorbs shock of initial strike. Necessary for soft-mouthed species such as kokanee.

Rudder - An essential piece of trolling equipment to keep lake troll blades tracking straight without line twist.

Salmonfly - A huge stonefly up to 3 inches in length, an insect for which the lower Deschutes River is well-known. It hatches in late May to early June.

Salmonids - A family of fish which includes salmon, trout, char, whitefish, and grayling.

Sculpin - A small, native, bottom-hugging fish of flowing water and a favorite snack of larger fish.

Setting the hook - The action of sweeping the rod up and back to cause the hook to penetrate the fish's mouth.

Sink-tip fly line - A floating fly line with a variable number of feet at the tip which sinks. Often used in trolling lakes; heavier ones sometimes used in fishing big rivers.

Slip sinker - A weight with a hole through the center allowing the main fishing line to slip through it to attach to a swivel. Allows fish to take line without feeling the weight.

Smallmouth bass - Not too common in Central Oregon but excellent fighters like their cousins, the largemouth bass.

Spawners - Fish in reproductive condition, often showing changes in color and jaw deformations. Salmon in this condition are not good eating. Trout in this condition can be lousy fighters and easily exhausted.

Spin fishing - Fishing with a spinning rod and spinning reel.

Spinnerbaits - A popular bass lure with a rubber skirt covering the hook and a spinner blade just above or below the hook.

Split shot - Small lead pieces of various sizes and weight that clamp onto the line above the hook.

Steelhead - Native and hatchery sea-run rainbow trout, sizes of adults vary according to the rivers to which they are native.

Stickleback, three-spine - A small, non-game species native to the Oregon coast, illegally introduced into the Deschutes River above the town of Bend.

Still-fishing - Fishing with bait in one spot usually with a marshmallow or bobber.

Strike indicator - A colorful material attached to fly line leader a few feet above the fly to help track it and detect strikes.

Stocked - see *Hatchery.*

Stonefly - A very common insect in Central Oregon. Many species are present from tiny flies that hatch in the winter to the huge salmonfly on the Deschutes. Fish eat both the nymphs and adults voraciously.

Structure, in-stream - Any item in a stream or lake that provides cover for fish and habitat for insects. Includes rocks, dead vegetation, and manmade objects.

Streamer - A long, flowing fly tied to imitate baitfish, leeches, and long slender insects.

Tailout - The increasingly shallow, downstream end of a calm section of a stream where the water begins to pick up speed as it enters a riffle or rapid.

Thermocline - A layer of water, usually in a lake, which is cooler than the layer above or below.

Tributary - A stream or river flowing into a larger stream or river.

Trolling - Dragging a lure or fly behind a moving boat or other floating device.

Turning over - When wind and/or large differences in water temperature cause the bottom layers of water in a lake to come to the surface. Important in nutrient cycling.

Whitefish - An abundant native species of the salmonid family, often good fighters and definitely good eating; however, they don't get much respect.

Wild fish - A wild fish has been spawned and reared in the wild, not in a hatchery. Not all wild fish are necessarily native fish; they can be natural reproduction of hatchery fish.

Wind drift - See *Drifting.*

Winterkill - An occurrence in the high lakes whereby deep snow levels deprive fish of the oxygen necessary to live.

INDEX OF ADVERTISERS

Publisher Geoff Hill Gets His Grandkids Started Early

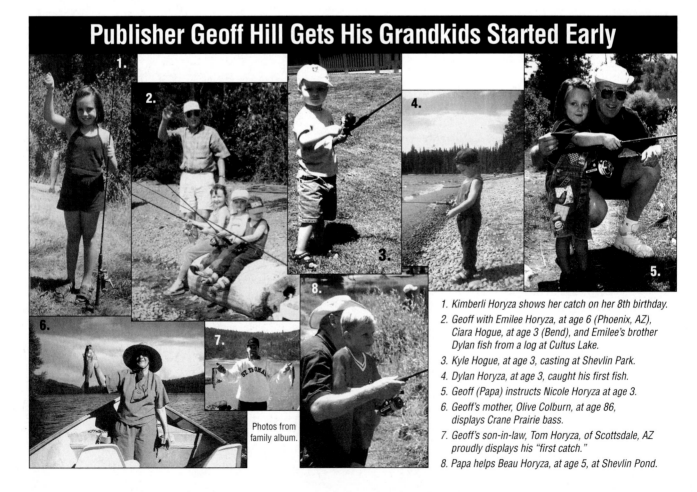

Photos from family album.

1. Kimberli Horyza shows her catch on her 8th birthday.
2. Geoff with Emilee Horyza, at age 6 (Phoenix, AZ), Ciara Hogue, at age 3 (Bend), and Emilee's brother Dylan fish from a log at Cultus Lake.
3. Kyle Hogue, at age 3, casting at Shevlin Park.
4. Dylan Horyza, at age 3, caught his first fish.
5. Geoff (Papa) instructs Nicole Horyza at age 3.
6. Geoff's mother, Olive Colburn, at age 86, displays Crane Prairie bass.
7. Geoff's son-in-law, Tom Horyza, of Scottsdale, AZ proudly displays his "first catch."
8. Papa helps Beau Horyza, at age 5, at Shevlin Pond.